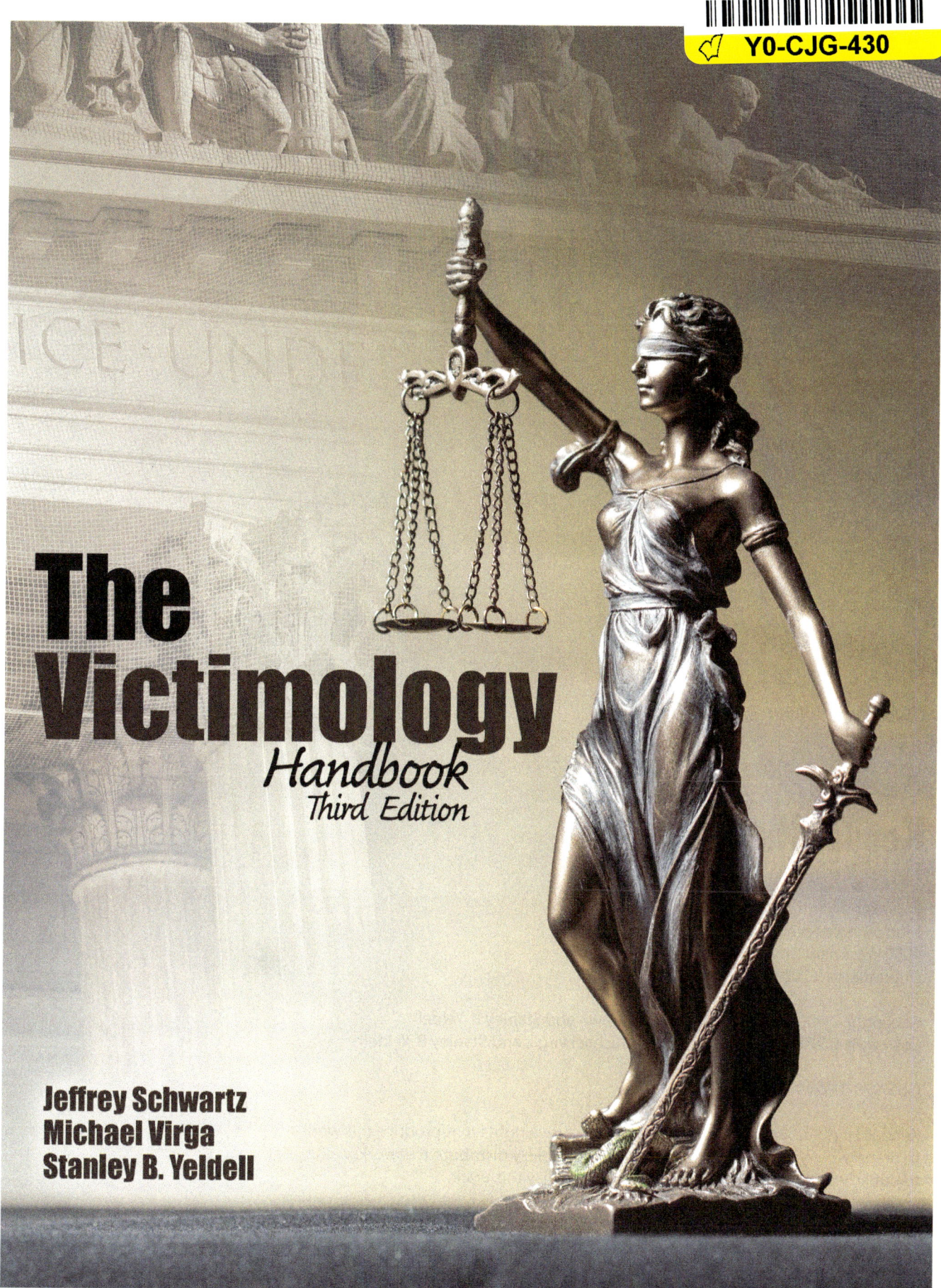

Cover Image © Shutterstock.com

www.kendallhunt.com
Send all inquiries to:
4050 Westmark Drive
Dubuque, IA 52004-1840

Copyright © 2002, 2013 by Margaret L. Brown and Stanley B. Yeldell
Copyright © 2017 by Jeffrey Schwartz, Michael Virga, and Stanley B. Yeldell

ISBN 978-1-5249-0617-7

Kendall Hunt Publishing Company has the exclusive rights to reproduce this work,
to prepare derivative works from this work, to publicly distribute this work,
to publicly perform this work and to publicly display this work.

All rights reserved. No part of this publication may be reproduced,
stored in a retrieval system, or transmitted, in any form or by any
means, electronic, mechanical, photocopying, recording, or otherwise,
without the prior written permission of the copyright owner.

Published in the United States of America

Contents

Acknowlegments ....
About the Authors ....

CHAPTER ONE   **Introduction** 1

CHAPTER TWO   **Educational Requirements** 3

    Introduction 3
    Victimology Syllabus 5
    Course Description 5
    Course Objectives 6
    Required Textbook 6
    General Education Goals 6
    Content Outline 6
    Required Learning Resources 8
    Course Requirements 8
    Basis and Methods for Grading 8
    Instructor Grading Rubric for Written Assignments 9
    Student Accommodation 10
    Academic Integrity 10
    Misc. Policies/Rowan Student Handbook 10
    Mobile Electronic Device Policy 10
    Emergency Closings 11
    Faculty Mailbox 11

CHAPTER THREE   **History of Victim Rights** 13

    Learning Objectives 13
    Key Terms 13
    I. Right of Due Process, Fairness, Dignity, Respect, and Privacy .. 15
    II. Right to Notice 16
    III. Right to Be Present 16

IV. Right to Be Heard 17
V. Right to Reasonable Protection. 18
VI. Right to Restitution 18
VII. Right to Information and Referral 19
VIII. Right to Apply for Victim Compensation. 20
IX. Right to Proceedings Free from Unreasonable Delay 20
X. Right to Confer. 20
XI. Right to a Copy of the Presentence Report and Transcripts . . . 21
XII. Right to Standing and Remedies 21
New Jersey Specific Information 25
Discussion Questions. 27
Chapter Assignment 29

CHAPTER FOUR **Current Victim Assistance Programs. 31**

Learning Objectives. 31
Key Terms 31
Introduction 32
Victim-Witness Advocacy Units 32
Criminal Justice Orientation and Information 33
Victim Information and Impact Form 33
Counseling and Support Services 34
Case Status Notification 34
Court Accompaniment and Transportation Services. 35
Child Care to Attend Meetings and Court Proceedings 35
HIV Testing of Defendants and HIV Information and Referrals
    for Victims. 35
Assistance in Obtaining Restitution 35
Employer and Creditor Intercession 35
Assistance with Property Return. 36
Victim-Witness Waiting Rooms 36
Parole Eligibility and Release Notification 36
Victim Notification Systems: VNS and VINE 36
Telephone Registration. 40
Web Registration. 41
Conclusion 42
Discussion Questions. 43
References 43

CHAPTER FIVE — Victims of Domestic Abuse (Intimate Partner Violence) ... 47

- Learning Objectives ... 47
- Key Terms ... 47
- Introduction ... 47
- What Is Safety Planning? ... 49
- Types of Safety Planning ... 49
- What Is a Healthy Relationship? ... 58
- Setting Boundaries ... 60
- What Does an Abusive Relationship Look Like? ... 61
- Warning Signs and Red Flags ... 62
- What Is Abuse? ... 62
- Types of Abuse ... 63
- Why Do People Abuse? ... 66
- Who Can Be in an Abusive Relationship? ... 66
- Why Do People Stay in Abusive Relationships? ... 67
- LGBTQ Relationship Violence ... 68
- Domestic Violence ... 71
- Conclusion ... 79
- Discussion Questions ... 80
- Chapter Assignment ... 81

CHAPTER SIX — Children Victims of Crime ... 83

- Learning Objectives ... 83
- Key Terms ... 83
- Introduction ... 84
- Kidnapping ... 84
- Short-Term Abductions ... 85
- Long-Term Abductions ... 85
- The Reduction of Parental Abduction Risks ... 86
- Stranger Abductions—Reducing the Risks ... 86
- Amber Alerts ... 87
- CART (Child Abduction Response Team) ... 88
- Summary ... 88
- Victims of Child Abuse ... 89
- Definition of Concepts ... 89

Signs and Symptoms of Child Abuse. 89
Child Interviews and Investigation 90
Prevention Strategies 92
Conclusion 93
Discussion Questions. 94
Chapter Assignment 97

CHAPTER SEVEN   **Victims of Bullying, Cyber-Bullying, and Hazing. . . . 99**

Learning Objectives. 99
Key Terms 99
Introduction 100
Effects of Bullying 102
Status of Current Research 103
The Relationship between Youth Aggression
    and Partner Violence. 106
Other Risk Factors for Partner Violence. 107
Sex-Based Harassment 108
Discussion Questions. 113
Chapter Assignment 115

CHAPTER EIGHT   **Victims of Crime Perpetrated by Juvenile—Rights and the Juvenile Justice Process. 117**

Learning Objectives. 117
Key Terms 117
Federal Juvenile Delinquency Prosecution—Introduction 118
Referral to State Authorities. 119
Juvenile Delinquency Proceedings—Certification. 119
Hearing to Determine Delinquency 120
Adjudication as a Juvenile Delinquent 121
Disposition Hearing. 121
New Jersey Juvenile Justice System—
    Comparison with the Federal System 122
After a Youth is Taken into Custody 126
If Your Case Goes to Adjudication and Disposition. 127
AFter Disposition 127
Discussion Questions. 130
Chapter Assignment 131

CHAPTER NINE Victims of Drunk/Drugged Drivers 133

Learning Objectives.. 133
Key Terms 133
Introduction.. 134
Blood Alcohol Concentration [G/DL] 138
Drug Recognition Experts.................................. 140
DUI: Driving Under the Influence........................... 142
Parents and Guardians 143
Consequences of Underage Drinking and Driving............. 145
Impaired Driving 146
Discussion Questions...................................... 149
Chapter Assignment 151

CHAPTER TEN Victims of Sexual Assault 153

Learning Objectives....................................... 153
Key Terms 153
Introduction... 154
Historical Development 154
Evolution of the Definition of Sexual Assault and Rape 154
The Measurement of Rape—Sexual Assault 155
Sexual Assaults 155
Facts about Date Rape 155
Rape Trauma Syndrome 156
Myths about Rape.. 156
Preventing Date Rape 156
Rape Prevention in Your Home 157
Rape Prevention in Your Automobile 157
Megan's Law 157
Sex Offender Notification for Neighborhoods
    and Communities (Megan's Law) 158
Guidelines... 159
Sexual Assault Protocols.................................. 159
A Coordinated Sexual Assault Response.................... 160
Role of the Advocate 161
Sexual Assault Nurse Examiner (SANE)..................... 162
Sexual Assault Examination Kits 162

Safety Plans for Victims of Sexual Assault 163
Evaluation and Follow-Up 164
Conclusion 165
Discussion Questions. 165
Chapter Assignment 167

CHAPTER ELEVEN **Victims of Hate Crimes 169**

Learning Objectives. 169
Key Terms 169
Introduction. 170
Defining A Hate Crime 172
The FBI's Role 172
Uneven Data Collection Makes Estimating Prevalence Difficult . 173
Reporting Under the Hate Crime Statistic Act 174
Victimization Survey Reports Higher Numbers 174
Immigrants as Victims 174
What Motivates Hate Offenders?. 174
Other National Hate Crime Resources. 175
Hate Crimes Timeline 181
Discussion Questions. 186
Chapter Assignment 187

CHAPTER TWELVE **Victims of Stalking. 189**

Learning Objectives. 189
Key Terms 189
Interstate Stalking. 190
Stalking Safety Planning 193
Discussion Questions. 199
Chapter Assignment 201

CHAPTER THIRTEEN **Elder Victims of Crime. 203**

Learning Objectives. 203
Key Terms 203
Introduction. 204
Definition of Concepts. 204
Who Are the Victims of Elder Abuse? 204
Who Are the Abusers?. 205

Why Does Elder Abuse Happen? 205
Why Does The Problem Continue? 205
Prevention 206
Conclusion 209
References 210
Discussion Questions 210
Chapter Assignment 211

CHAPTER FOURTEEN **Victims of Human Trafficking** 213

Learning Objectives 213
Key Terms 213
Introduction 214
Strategic Action Plan Objectives 214
ACF Regional Programs 216
Human Trafficking 220
Domestic Victims 221
Foreign Nationals 221
Federal Assistance 222
Human Trafficking Information 228
Human Trafficking Enactments 2005–2011 229
Discussion Questions 252
Chapter Assignment 253

APPENDIX A **General Websites** 255

APPENDIX B **Various Victim Resources** 261

APPENDIX C **Federal Agencies Websites** 295

APPENDIX D **State Victim Compensation Websites** 299

APPENDIX E **Resource Phone Numbers** 303

Acknowledgments

To my soulmate, Shirl, the person who gives light to each day and solace to every evening. Although the ebb and flow of life brings ups and downs, the center we have found is a true love that always prevails. Our special connection is indeed unique. Thank you for your support, thank you for your understanding; most of all, I am thankful we have each other.

—Jeff

To my family, for their continued love and support, you inspire me daily. Especially my father, Andrew Virga Jr., who is no longer with us in this world. You are so very missed everyday.

—Mike

This text is dedicated to my beautiful and resourceful wife, Doris Yeldell, who understood the need to update and revise the existing textbook. She provided a critical analysis of the chapters so they could be easily comprehended. She urged me to extrapolate the confusing concepts so students and criminal justice personnel could appreciate the clarity of the manuscript.

—Stan

To all of the people who struggle everyday as a result of their victimization. Know there is help, healing, and hope.

A special recognition to William Gratton, a highly skilled teaching assistant, researcher, lawyer, and now a graduate student at Rowan University, in pursuit of another career. William has helped immensely with this project.

Thank you to Richard Toto, intern at Rowan University who has helped on research for this project.

About the Authors

Jeffrey L. Schwartz, Assistant Professor Rowan University Law and Justice Studies Department. Professor Schwartz, besides possessing advanced educational degrees, has numerous certifications and ongoing practical experience in the law enforcement field. He is a retired police officer, an approved instructor with numerous agencies, a licensed private detective, and an instructor trainer in many facets of policing. Further, Professor Schwartz is a subject matter expert in terrorism, use of force, supervision, and tactical training. He has instructed at various police academies, security training academies, consulted with public and private schools, as well as, consulted with numerous private businesses.

Professor Schwartz has published articles in professional journals, authored chapters in textbooks, author of *The Criminal Justice Internship Manual* (2015), author of *The Invariable Evolution: Police Use of Force in America* (2017), developed curriculum for several universities, conducted major research for a level one trauma center in New Jersey, collaborated in research and policy with numerous police agencies, is co-advisor for internships at Rowan University, and continues to mentor students on a daily basis. Professor Schwartz is the faculty advisor for the Criminal Justice Preparation Club, of which he is the founder at Rowan University. Professor Schwartz has lectured across the country as a use of force expert. He was a lecturer for the Federal Law Enforcement Training Center and conducted seminars on use of force in various venues. He consulted on anti-terrorism and other related issues for the Department of Defense with several federal defense contractors. Professor Schwartz continues to be a resource for many agencies in policy, diversity, recruiting, and training. Further, he continues research and publications.

Michael Virga is an active police officer with the Township of Hamilton Police Department, in Mays Landing, NJ. He has worked as a patrolman, police detective, and now works as a front-line supervisor in the role of a patrol sergeant. He is also a professor at Rowan University in the Law and Justice Studies Department in Glassboro, NJ. He received his PhD in Criminal Justice from Nova Southeastern University, in Fort Lauderdale, FL. His dissertation focused on the perceptions of stress by law enforcement officers. He is interested in research affecting policing and other current criminal justice issues. He is extensively trained in criminal investigations, such as interview and interrogation, child forensic interviews, fingerprint classification and comparison, among others. He served as a detective for significant portion of his police career, leading and participating in many criminal investigations throughout southern New Jersey. In addition to lecturing at Rowan University, he is a member of the instructional staff for the

New Jersey State Association of Chiefs of Police Command and Leadership Academy, where students in police command and supervisory positions learn to hone their skills to effectively lead and manage police personnel using select leadership theories and best practices. He recently co-authored a book about contemporary issues regarding police use of force in America.

Stanley B. Yeldell is an Associate Professor of the Law/Justice Studies of Rowan University. He received his B.A. Degree from Bowie State University and his J.D. from the Howard University School of Law. He has more than forty-three years of experience in Law/Justice Studies with specific emphasis in the field of Victimology and as the internship coordinator. In 2012, Stanley received an award from the New Jersey College & University Public Safety Association in recognition of the Student Patrol Program at Rowan University; the first time that a college professor received this award out of forty state colleges and universities within the State of New Jersey. Stanley has been the recipient of seven Hall of Fame Awards for outstanding teaching and advisement at Rowan University. Stanley has been awarded the Prestigious Gary Hunter Mentoring Award by Rowan University (2015) and the Gloucester County NAACP Educational Changer Award (2015). Professor Yeldell is the faculty advisor for Gamma Chi- National Criminal Justice Student Organization and the Victim Awareness Organization at Rowan.

His publications are: *The Bilingual Court Interpreter Handbook of New Jersey* (1974), *The Court Interpreter Guide for Judicial Officers and Related in New Jersey* (1974), *Criminal Law* text (1999), and the revised edition of the *Criminal Justice Internship Manual* (2016), and *The Victim Assistance Handbook* (2002).

Stanley is a Subject Specialist for the American Council on Education (ACE) and the Thomas Edison College Corporate Higher Education and Distance Educational Programs. He was appointed by the Chief Justice of the Supreme Court of New Jersey to be the Chairman of the Gloucester County Advisory Probation Board (1991-2001), and he serves on the Glassboro Awareness Advisory Scholarship Committee. He is an Affiliate Member of the New Jersey Crime Victims Bar Association. He is an Advisory Board member of The International Journal of Criminal Justice Sciences and the South Asian Society of Criminology and Victimology of India.

Chapter One

INTRODUCTION

The Victimology Handbook provides the student with innovative changes within the field of Victimology. This Handbook will continue to serve as an invaluable resource text for students. The victim concepts coupled with the numerous victim assistance programs will enable the student to navigate through the complex world of victimology.

Each chapter will share some understanding of the obstacles that victims face in a few unique categories. The literature presented will enable the students to foster empathy for the victims' relationship with the criminal justice system.

Although, less than exhaustive in its examination of the broad issues, the Handbook has addressed the complex crime victim problems, which will enhance the reader's understanding of the prevailing trends in Victimology.

The Handbook consists of fourteen chapters which discuss some categories of victim concepts within the field of Victimology.

    Chapter One—Introduction
    Chapter Two—Educational Requirements
    Chapter Three—Victim Rights
    Chapter Four—Current Victim Assistance Programs
    Chapter Five—Victims of Domestic and Intimate Partner Violence
    Chapter Six—Children Victims of Crime
    Chapter Seven—Victims of Bullying, Cyberbullying, and Hazing
    Chapter Eight—Victims of Juvenile Offenders
    Chapter Nine—Victims of Drunk/Drugged Drivers
    Chapter Ten—Victims of Sexual Assault
    Chapter Eleven—Victims of Hate Crimes
    Chapter Twelve—Victims of Stalking
    Chapter Thirteen—-Elder Victims of Crime
    Chapter Fourteen—Victims of Human Trafficking

Appendix A—General Websites
Appendix B—Various Victim Organizations
Appendix C—Federal Agencies
Appendix D—State Victim Compensation
Appendix E—Resource Phone Numbers

The substantive text chapters include learning objectives, key terms, discussion questions, and an essay that is on a distinctly colored perforated page (original to be turned in as an assignment). If used as an eBook, these pages come as a supplement or download feature.

Chapter Two
EDUCATIONAL REQUIREMENTS

Individuals who are vulnerable and/or in crisis, may indeed constitute the common linkage of Victimology with other relevant disciplines and provide a focus for intervention.

© Rashad Ashurov/Shutterstock.com

INTRODUCTION

It is only recently that researchers have turned their attention to victims of crime. In fact, the word victim did not appear in the English language until 1497. Derived from the Latin word victima, the word originally did not refer to crime victims but to a living creature killed and offered as a sacrifice to a deity or supernatural power (*Oxford Dictionary,* 1983)

© Solomnikov/Shutterstock.com

We can still find traces of this original meaning of the word victim in modern languages, such as, Dutch and German. In Dutch the word for victim is slachtofffer. The word, slachtofffer, consists of two parts: slacht, refers to slaughter and offer, refers to offering. Similarly, in German the word for victim is opfer; which represents a person or thing that is offered in sacrifice.

It was not until 1660 that the word victim was first used in the sense of a person who is hurt, tortured, or killed by another. So, it would seem, the concept of a victim of crime did not exist until well into the seventeenth century. Why were victims ignored for so long?

The first academic journal dedicated to victimology was *Victimology: An International Journal*, which appeared in 1976 and was edited by Emilio Viano. In 1988, the *International Review of Victimology* was founded by John Freeman and continues today to be a key resource for victimologists. (Wemmers, 2003).

3

Since its early beginnings, victimology has struggled with delineating its boundaries. Sparked by Mendelsohn's plea for a separate science of victimology, one of the first debates in the area was whether or not victimology was a branch of criminology or a separate science.[1]

Victimology can be defined as *the scientific study of victims and victimizations attributable to the violation of human rights, including crimes and the reaction to crime and to the victimization* (Kirchhoff, 1994).

Victimology has changed the way we look at crime. Fifty years after Mendelsohn first introduced the word "victimology," it is impossible to think of crimes without including the consequences for victims. Victimologists have successfully drawn attention to the plight of victims.

The awareness of victimology in America arrived mostly from Europe with the early writings of Benjamin Mendelsohn (1937) from Rumania, Hans von Hentig (1948) from Germany, Willem Nagel (1949) from the Netherlands, and Henri Ellenberger (1954) from Switzerland. They all wrote mostly from a traditional European *criminological* perspective. However, it was Mendelsohn, who, although he started from the perspective of a criminal attorney, went on to not only coin the term victimology but also to develop victimology beyond the bounds of crime. Mendelsohn is credited with the concept of General Victimology, which also included victims of traffic accidents, disasters, and genocide.

Yet, the evolution of victimology, especially in America, mostly occurred within the confines of penal victimology with the major American works from such criminologists as Marvin Wolfgang (1958), Walter Reckless (1967), and Stephan Schafer (1968).

Two important victim events drew much official attention. One was the enactment of California's Victim Compensation program in 1965; the other was the institutionalization of the national victimization surveys in 1966. These two activities supported each other. The surveys provided new hard data as to the "dark figure" of victims that had never been measured; the compensation programs used these data to justify their implementation in other states; and, these new programs validated the growing need for better victim statistics. We will further examine all these concepts and much more in the coming chapters.

This chapter is designed to introduce the students to the essential course requirements:

1. Victimology Syllabus
2. Course Background
3. Course Objectives
4. Required Textbook
5. Evaluations
6. Requirements and Grading
7. Required Readings

VICTIMOLOGY SYLLABUS

The Victimology syllabus serves as an example or working model that can be utilized by colleges and universities.

1. LAWJ 05220

COURSE DESCRIPTION

The course gives students insight into those "forgotten" in a crime, the victim. The student will examine victims' rights with specific focus on the following: the social, economic, and emotional impacts of crime on victims; victim interaction with law enforcement and the judicial system; victim compensation and resources available.

COURSE OBJECTIVES

1. Explain the development of Victimology;
2. List the fundamental victim rights;
3. Discuss policy developments in victim programs;
4. Examine victim rights legislation;
5. Discuss various victim assistance programs;
6. Describe the historical development of victim's rights;
7. Outline several victim categories and several resources available to those victims.

REQUIRED TEXTBOOK

The Victimology Handbook
Schwartz, Vigra and Yeldell, Stanley B. Kendall Hunt Publishing Company
ISBN: 978-1-5249-0617-7

GENERAL EDUCATION GOALS

In addition to the above objectives, the more general goals of this course are to provide the student with the following tools to help develop his or her potential:

1. Development of the student's analytical thinking capabilities through comparison and contrast in the application of theories and concepts to social problems
2. Enhancement of the student's literacy skills through assigned readings, discussions, examinations, and other requirements
3. Utilization of the historical perspective which helps with student understanding of evolutionary developments over time
4. Understanding of the scientific method through research requirements and in-depth case studies
5. Improvement in social interaction skills and understanding human behavior through consideration of the impact legal and social systems have on individuals
6. Increased student awareness of cultural and multi-cultural issues through study of how social problems and social movements are related to, and affect, minority groups
7. Preparation for more advanced study in criminal justice/homeland security

CONTENT OUTLINE

Chapter reading will be assigned.

Reading and Assignment Outline (SUBJECT TO CHANGE BY THE INSTRUCTOR):

Blackboard—You will find it beneficial to utilize this resource. Access Bb via www.rowan.edu and "Quick links." If you need assistance, contact the Rowan Helpdesk.

Follow login instructions.

There will be two exams (each exam is worth 30 points): 60 out of the 100 point total. Mid Term and Final Exam.

There will be one final paper worth 25 points: 25 out of the 100 point total.

There will be in-class assignments each class—i.e., quiz, position paper, writing assignment, in class essay, etc. worth a total of 15 points. The number of assignments divided into 15 will determine the weight of each assignment. Assignments are only counted for credit if turned in or completed in class. Exigent circumstances will be the only mitigating factor when determining credit. Therefore, unexcused absences will detract from your in-class assignment grade. If you miss class, you cannot make up an in-class assignment, unless it is a university excused absence. In this case, you will be allowed to make up the in-class assignment or complete an alternative assignment for the same point value. It is incumbent upon the student to provide adequate reasoning for an excused absence (see student handbook link provided on following page).

Late Assignments

Assignments and papers that are turned in late will be downgraded 10 points for every day that the assignment is late from the original due date. Late assignments will only be accepted if arrangements are made with the instructor.

Tentative Reading and Assignment Outline

Reading from the required text (*The Victimology Handbook*—Schwartz/Virga/Yeldell, Kendall Hunt) and other resources will be assigned in accordance with topic sections, along with other materials and class discussion/lecture will follow along.

The chapters from the assigned text are listed below. Chapter reading will be assigned. There are associated discussion questions (within the chapter) and assignments (perforated pages *to be removed from text* **completed and turned in when given due date—in class or as assigned)**

1. Chapter One — Introduction
2. Chapter Two — Educational Requirements
3. Chapter Three — Victim Rights
4. Chapter Four — Current Victim Assistance Programs
5. Chapter Five — Victims of Domestic and Intimate Partner Violence
6. Chapter Six — Children Victims of Crime
7. Chapter Seven — Victims of Bullying, Cyberbullying, and Hazing
8. Chapter Eight — Victims of Juvenile Offenders
9. Chapter Nine — Victims of Drunk/Drugged Drivers
10. Chapter Ten — Victims of Sexual Assault
11. Chapter Eleven — Victims of Hate Crimes
12. Chapter Twelve — Victims of Stalking
13. Chapter Thirteen — Elder Victims of Crime
14. Chapter Fourteen — Victims of Human Trafficking

CHAPTER 2 Educational Requirements

REQUIRED LEARNING RESOURCES

Main Textbook/Required Textbook:

The Victimology Handbook
Schwartz, Virga and Yeldell, Stanley B. Publisher: Kendall Hunt Publishing Company
ISBN: 978-1-5249-0617-7

COURSE REQUIREMENTS

Students are expected to read assigned text chapters, to read assigned Lecture Notes, and to seek and read additional suggested resources as provided by the textbook and Instructor. In addition, students are expected to be alert and attentive with note taking in class and have a demonstrated desire to participate in any discussion. Exams are to be completed within the deadlines given by the Instructor, and any special instructions for the paper assignment and/or writing assignment(s) are to be followed precisely. All guidelines from the University will be followed–discipline, honesty, attendance, etc.

Please refer to the student handbook and course catalogs—See links below

(http://www.rowan.edu/studentaffairs/communitystandards/handbook.html.)

A more inclusive link for students can be retrieved at www.rowan.edu/studentlife

BASIS AND METHODS FOR GRADING

15% Assignments—TBD based upon actual number assigned. Based upon class discussion, current events or other such topics assigned.

60% Exams—30 points each (2). Exams cover the chapters we discuss in class and the materials assigned.

25% Research Paper—25 points.

Grading Scale:		
A 93–100	A– 90–92	
B+ 87–89	B 84–86	B– 80–83
C+ 77–79	C 76–74	C– 70–73
D+ 69–72	D 64–66	D– 60–63
F 59 and below		

INSTRUCTOR GRADING RUBRIC FOR WRITTEN ASSIGNMENTS

Note: These are only guidelines—exceptional work can earn a larger percentage while work below level may earn less.

   A. **Grammar/Spelling: 10 points**

      Proper use of grammar and punctuation Proper spelling

   B. **Style: 15 points**

      Sentences are complete in thought

      Sentences are concise, eliminating unnecessary words or phrases

      Sentences vary in structure

      Sentence transitions are present

      Words used are precise, unambiguous and used properly

      There is an appropriate tone for the assignment

   C. **Organization: 15 points**

      There is clear structure to the paper

      There is a central theme or thesis

      It is written for the appropriate audience

      Logical flow of ideas

      Appropriate introduction to the paper or topics being covered

      Logical conclusion that results from the thesis

   D. **Research/Format/Analysis of topic: 15 points**

      Orderly presentation of materials, thoughtful discussion, following general format requirements (margins, header, footer, font size, general amount of work)

      Proper citations and references to resources, following APA or Blue Book format.

      Use of headings, italics, and other aids (e.g., appendices, tables of contents, when appropriate), to improve the flow of the paper

   E. **Content: 45 points**

      Purpose of the paper is clear

      All questions/requirements of the assignment are answered in a substantive manner. Major topics/theories are stated clearly and are supported by details and analysis. Content is comprehensive, accurate, and/or persuasive integration of theory and practice. Research is adequate and up-to-date.

Blackboard—You will find it beneficial to utilize this resource. Go to **https://rowan.blackboard.com** for login instructions.

Regular attendance in class is required. If you miss two or more classes, whether excused or unexcused, you may be asked to withdraw from the class. Excused absences will be handled per the university attendance policy found at: **http://www.rowan.edu/provost/policies/documents/AttendancePolicy-FacultyStudentsResponsibilities5-31-12_001.pdf**

Missing more than one class unexcused will result in a full unit downgrade in your final grade.

The grading policy of the university will be used.

STUDENT ACCOMMODATION

"Your academic success is important. If you have a documented disability that may have an impact upon your work in this class, please contact me. Students must provide documentation of their disability to the Academic Success Center in order to receive official University services and accommodations. The Academic Success Center can be reached at 856-256-4234. The Center is located on the third floor of Savitz Hall. The staff is available to answer questions regarding accommodations or assist you in your pursuit of accommodations. We all look forward to working with you to meet your learning goals."

ACADEMIC INTEGRITY

Academic Integrity: Each student is responsible for Rowan's policy on academic integrity. See: **http://www.rowan.edu/provost/policies/documents/academic_integrity_policy_04-12.pdf**

MISC. POLICIES/ROWAN STUDENT HANDBOOK

You may want to refer students to the *Rowan University's Student Handbook* for information on university policies on attendance, academic integrity, accommodation for special needs, grade grievances, classroom behavior, and other matters. *Rowan University's Student Handbook* can be found at the following link: **http://www.rowan.edu/studentaffairs/communitystandards/documents/RowanUniversityStudentHandbook2014-2015.pdf**

MOBILE ELECTRONIC DEVICE POLICY

The use of laptop or notebook microcomputers and other mobile electronic devices for classroom activities is allowed at the discretion of the instructor or in the case of a documented disability. The use of such electronic devices should not be a distraction to other students or the instructor. Students are expected to use electronic devices only as part of ongoing class activities. If an instructor believes the use of electronic devices is detrimental to the learning environment or gives any student an unfair advantage, then the instructor may prohibit their use at any time. Also, the use of any device for purposes of audio or video recording may occur only with the prior approval of the instructor.

Rowan Success Network powered by Starfish® is designed to make it easier for you to connect with the resources you need to be successful at Rowan. Throughout the term, you may receive email from the Rowan Success Network team (Starfish®) regarding your academic performance. Please pay attention to these emails and consider taking the recommended actions. Utilize the scheduling tools to make appointments at your convenience including tutoring. Additional information about RSN may be found at **www.rowan.edu/rsn**

EMERGENCY CLOSINGS

Emergency closings and delayed opening information are available through Banner's Emergency Alert system at **http://www.rowan.edu/emergency/weather/weather.cfm**

FACULTY MAILBOX

If you place any correspondence in my faculty mailbox located in the Law and Justice Studies 5th floor office complex in the Campbell Library, you must notify me in writing via e-mail so I can retrieve it in a timely manner. Additionally, if you place any correspondence under my door into my office; you must notify me via e-mail.

Chapter Three

HISTORY OF VICTIM RIGHTS

LEARNING OBJECTIVES

After exploring Chapter Three (3), the student will be able to:

1. Identify several modern crime victim rights that are now guaranteed in the United States.
2. List major legislative changes to the victim rights movement in the United States in the past thirty years.
3. Describe the impact of the Victim and Witness Protection Act.
4. Explain the Federal Crime Rights Victims Act.

KEY TERMS

Federal Crime Rights Victims Act, Victim and Witness Protection Act, Notice, Compensation, Due Process, Remedies, Mandatory Victim Restitution Act, National Victims Center, Standing, Victim

At common law, victims played a central role in the criminal justice process. The practice of private prosecution, whereby the crime victim initiated and controlled criminal prosecutions, dates back to the Middle Ages. Although notions of prosecuting on behalf of the crown began in the eleventh and twelfth centuries, even at that time most crime was viewed as a wrong against the individual victim rather than against the king or society as a whole. A crime victim's right to initiate and conduct criminal proceedings remained the norm in England well into the nineteenth century. The rationale for this

© Zerbor/Shutterstock.com

victim-centered approach to criminal justice was the view that crime was a harm inflicted primarily against the individual. Gradually, this view shifted and crime was seen as a harm against the individual and the state.

As with English common law, the concept of private prosecution became part of early American jurisprudence, and the American criminal justice process began as one in which crime victims controlled the investigation and prosecution of the crimes against them. This system of victim as private police and prosecutor existed as the norm in the United States through the nineteenth century. The United States Supreme Court has acknowledged this private prosecution model as the foundation of our criminal justice system.

© 3D_creation/Shutterstock.com

By the early twentieth century, however, the American system had evolved to one in which crime victims were no longer central players in most jurisdictions, and a public prosecution system became the norm. The victims' role progressively reduced until they essentially had no formal legal status beyond that of witness or piece of evidence. At one point, the United States Supreme Court observed in dicta that "in American jurisprudence at least, a private citizen lacks a judicially cognizable interest in the prosecution or non-prosecution of another."

Starting in the late 1970s, a strong victims' rights movement developed, and changes began to be made to state constitutions, statutes, and rules, as well as; federal statutes and rules, to define and afford explicit legal status to crime victims. More than thirty states have amended their constitutions to afford victims' rights, and all fifty states, along with the District Columbia and the federal government have enacted statutory and rule-based protections for victims. The scope of these protections varies considerably from jurisdiction-to-jurisdiction, but all are aimed at re-integrating the victim into the criminal and juvenile justice systems in a manner more closely aligned with the more victim centric approach.

The Modern Crime Victims' Rights Movement began more than thirty years ago and aspired to improve the treatment of crime victims in the justice system.

The legal impetus for the Modern Crime Victims' Rights Movement was, in part, the 1973 United States Supreme Court decision in *Linda R.S. v. Richard D.*, 410 U.S. 614 (1972).

In Linda R.S., the Supreme Court considered whether an unmarried woman could seek to enjoin the prosecutors' office from discriminately applying a statute criminalizing the non-payment of child support by refusing to prosecute fathers of children born to unmarried women.

© artboySHF/Shutterstock.com

The Court's holding was the victim could not demonstrate a nexus between the prosecutor's alleged discriminatory enforcement of the child support statute and the woman's failure to secure child support payments, and as such, the victim did not have standing to seek the relief she requested.

In dicta, the Court acknowledged the then-prevailing view that a crime victim cannot compel a criminal prosecution because "a private citizen lacks a judicially cognizable interest in the prosecution or non-prosecution of another."

The Court went on to provide a foundation for remedying the above-described situation when it stated that Congress could "enact statutes creating legal rights, the invasion of which creates standing, even though no injury would exist without the statute."

In the federal system, Congress passed the first of several pieces of crime victims' rights legislation in 1982, the Victim and Witness Protection Act, and subsequently passed a series of laws, successively giving greater legislative recognition to the rights of crime victims. The following are better known as the twelve basic rights of victims:

I. Right to Due Process, Fairness, Dignity, Respect, and Privacy
II. Right to Notice
III. Right to be Present
IV. Right to be Heard
V. Right to Reasonable Protection
VI. Right to Restitution
VII. Right to Information and Referral
VIII. Right to Apply for Victim Compensation
IX. Right to Proceedings Free from Unreasonable Delay
X. Right to Confer
XI. Right to a Copy of the Presentence Report and Transcripts
XII. Right to Standing and Remedies

I. RIGHT TO DUE PROCESS, FAIRNESS, DIGNITY, RESPECT, AND PRIVACY

A majority of states provide victims with the right to be treated with fairness, dignity, and respect. In addition, while there is an implicit right to privacy in the United States Constitution, a handful of states explicitly provide victims with a constitutional right to privacy, and other states provide for victim privacy through numerous statutory or rule provisions, such as: rape shield laws; counseling and other privileges; protection of victim contact information; and the right to refuse a defense request for an interview. One of the most recent codifications of these rights is found in the federal Crime Victims' Rights Act (CVRA), which provides that victims have the right to be treated with fairness and with respect for the victim's dignity and privacy.

II. RIGHT TO NOTICE

The right to notice is the right to advisement of the existence of crime victims' rights and the right to advisement of specific events during the criminal justice process. The right to notice is distinct from the right to information, which refers to a crime victim's right to be generally informed about criminal proceedings and about available resources. The language of the right to notice varies by jurisdiction.

At the state level, there are substantial variations regarding whether a victim must enter a request to trigger the right to notice. The requirement that a victim "request" notice takes numerous forms: some states explicitly require written request, while others do not include a writing requirement; at least one state requires "registration" with the prosecutor; and at least one state requires the victim maintain a land line through which the victim can be reached.

On the federal level, subsection of the CVRA provides that a crime victim has the "right to reasonable, accurate, and timely notice of any public court proceeding, or any parole proceeding, involving the crime or of any release or escape of the accused."

The right to notice is at the heart of victims' participatory status because, if a victim is unaware of his or her rights or proceedings in which those rights are implicated, the victim cannot participate in the system.

III. RIGHT TO BE PRESENT

The right to be present refers to the victim's right to physically attend the criminal trial and other criminal justice proceedings related to the investigation, prosecution, and incarceration of his or her offender. Historically, in-person victim attendance was well-accepted. A shift happened in 1975, however, when, with the adoption of Federal Rule of Evidence 615 (the rule of sequestration), exclusion of victims from criminal proceedings became routine. The Rule of Sequestration required automatic exclusion of witnesses if requested by either the prosecutor or defendant. Most states adopted a rule similar to the federal rule, and as a result, crime victims were routinely identified as potential witnesses, resulting in their systematic exclusion from trial. Importantly, however, beginning in the early 1980's, an overwhelming majority of jurisdictions passed constitutional or statutory provisions guaranteeing a crime victim the right to be present.

Eleven states give victims the right to be present at trial subject to exclusion for interference with the defendant's constitutional rights, including the rights to due process and a fair trial. At least sixteen states provide crime victims with an unqualified right to be present at trial. Ten additional states provide victims with the right to be present at trial, subject to other qualifications: five give victims the right to be present unless their testimony is affected; two give victims the right to be present if practicable; two give victims the right to be present subject to the discretion of the court; and one gives victims the right to be present after testifying.

The CVRA sets forth an expansive right to be present at criminal justice proceedings. Subsection (a)(3) provides a crime victim with the right "not to be excluded from any such public court proceeding, unless the court, after receiving clear and convincing evidence, determines that testimony by the victim would be materially altered if the victim heard other testimony at that proceeding." This places a heavy burden on the party opposing the victim's presence. As the Ninth Circuit Court of Appeals explained: [A] district court must find by clear and convincing evidence that it is highly likely, not merely possible, that the victim-witness will alter his or her testimony.

Further, under the CVRA, the court must "make every effort to permit the fullest attendance possible by the victim and shall consider reasonable alternatives to the exclusion of the victim from the criminal proceeding." Which, allows crime victims in the vast majority of cases to attend the hearings and trial of the case involving their victimization. This is so important because crime victims share an interest with the government in seeing that justice is done in a criminal case and this interest supports the idea that victims should not be excluded from public criminal proceedings, whether these are pretrial, trial, or post-trial proceedings.

Notably, an overwhelming majority of courts have concluded that mere victim presence does not violate a defendant's federal constitutional rights. Instead, a defendant's federal constitutional rights are implicated only where a crime victim affirmatively engages in disruptive or other prejudicial behavior. Further, in most jurisdictions, passage of constitutional and statutory rights to be present effectively abrogated the court rule of sequestration as it applied to crime victims.

IV. RIGHT TO BE HEARD

The right to be heard refers to the right to make an oral and/or written statement to the court at a criminal justice proceeding. Most statutory and constitutional rights to be heard are drafted in mandatory terms, leaving judges no discretion whether to allow crime victims to make a statement at sentencing. Even in the absence of an explicit law providing a victim with the right to be heard, such as where a person does not meet the legal definition of victim, a sentencing court retains discretion to hear relevant information from any person. A few states explicitly provide for how a victim may exercise the right to be heard. Unless the right is specifically limited by constitution, statute, or rule, the victim may elect the method by which he or she wishes to be heard at sentencing. A few jurisdictions have codified this choice of method.

Depending upon jurisdiction, victims have the right to be heard at release, plea, sentencing, and parole. Focusing on the critical stages of plea and sentence, at least twelve states provide for the right to be heard by the court prior to the acceptance of any proposed plea agreement; and thirty-three states provide for the right to be heard by the prosecutor prior to the presentation of the plea agreement to the court. A handful of states provide for the victim to be heard both by the prosecutor and the court prior to acceptance of a plea agreement. At least thirty-nine states provide crime victims with a constitutional or statutory right to be heard at sentencing. These laws provide generally that a victim has the right to be heard at sentencing or, more specifically, that a victim has the right to make a statement to the court at sentencing. An additional four states provide that crime victims have the right to make a verbal statement subject to the court's discretion or to submit a written impact statement that the sentencing court must consider prior to sentencing the defendant. A few states require that the victim make a request to be heard prior to exercising that right.

On the federal level, subsection (a)(4) of the CVRA provides a crime victim with "the right to be reasonably heard at any public proceeding in the district court involving release, plea, sentencing, or any parole proceeding."

V. RIGHT TO REASONABLE PROTECTION

The right to reasonable protection relates to the victim's right to safety from the accused. It is generally reflected in constitutional and statutory provisions that address issues of the victim's physical safety and mental and emotional health.

At least nine states provide victims with a broad constitutional right to protection. In several other states, victims have constitutional and statutory rights to be free from intimidation, harassment, or abuse. In addition to these broad rights to protection, many states afford protection by providing crime victims with sufficient information and/or notice to allow them take steps to ensure their own protection. For instance, state statutes include the right to notice of the offender's: release on bail (thirty-five states); pretrial release (thirty-one states); conditional or temporary release from prison (thirty-nine states); commutation (fourteen states); parole (forty-six states); final release (forty states); and release from a mental health institution (twenty-two states). Most state statutory schemes also provide victims with notice of offender escape (forty-one states) and, in some cases, recapture (sixteen states). Protection rights are also provided through a myriad of other laws, including those providing for: no contact orders as a condition of release; the availability of civil orders of protection; the right to be heard at bail and other release proceedings regarding the dangerousness of the offender; the right to not disclose personal or contact information during testimony; and the right to a separate victim waiting area in the courthouse.

On the federal level, subsection (a)(1) of the CVRA provides crime victims with "the right to be reasonably protected from the accused." In addition to the CVRA, the Victims' Rights and Restitution Act of 1990, provides that "at the earliest opportunity after the detection of a crime at which it may be done without interfering with an investigation, a responsible official shall inform the victims of their right to receive, on request, the services described in subsection (c) of this section," which includes the right to "reasonable protection from a suspected offender and persons acting in concert with or at the behest of the suspected offender."

VI. RIGHT TO RESTITUTION

Restitution is money paid from the offender to the victim for losses that the victim suffered as a result of the offender's crime. Depending upon the jurisdiction's statutory or constitutional provision, the right to restitution can be mandatory or discretionary, and can entitle the victim to full or partial restitution.

Every state has a statutory provision providing some right to restitution, and at least eighteen states have enshrined the right in their constitutions. A number of states make restitution mandatory in virtually all cases. Several states mandate restitution or require a court to state on the record their reasons for failing to order restitution. In other states, restitution orders are made at the discretion of the court.

On the federal level, Mandatory Victim Restitution Act (MVRA), requires the court to order restitution in certain cases for each victim in the full amount of the victim's out-of-pocket losses. The MVRA defines "victim" as:

> [A] person directly and proximately harmed as a result of the commission of an offense for which restitution may be ordered including, in the case of an offense that involves as an element a scheme, conspiracy, or pattern of criminal activity, any person directly harmed by the defendant's criminal conduct in the course of the scheme, conspiracy or pattern.

When interpreting the predecessor to the MVRA, the Victim and Witness Protection Act, the United States Supreme Court authorized an award of restitution only for the loss caused by the specific conduct that is the basis for the offense of conviction. After the enactment of the MVRA, courts have concluded that a "direct victim" must suffer losses by criminal conduct underlying a defendant's convictions. This is illustrated in *United States v. Menza* (137 F. 3d 533, 1998), where the court remanded the issue of restitution to the trial court to determine whether losses incurred by the DEA in cleaning up defendant's methamphetamine laboratories directly related to the criminal conduct involved in defendant's underlying convictions for possession of chemicals with the intent to manufacture a controlled substance.

The CVRA also provides for restitution. In subsection (a)(6), the CVRA provides crime victims with "the right to full and timely restitution as provided in law." Further, to follow the definition of restitution given by Judge *Cassell in U.S. v. Bedonie* (317 F.Supp.2d 1285 ,2004) and *U.S. v. Serawop* (303 F.Supp.2d 1259 ,2004) ," in which the Federal District Court for the District of Utah afforded future lost earnings to a crime victim.

VII. RIGHT TO INFORMATION AND REFERRAL

The right to information is the right to be informed about criminal proceedings and available resources. Victims' rights statutes and constitutional provisions generally entitle victims to be provided information related to three broad categories: victim services; the criminal justice process itself; and the specific criminal justice proceeding or case involving the person accused of the crime committed against the victim.

An overwhelming number of states require that crime victims be provided with information about victim services. This includes information about governmental agencies that provide victim services; information or referrals to private organizations that provide victim services—often including medical services, social services, and crisis or emergency services; and compensation benefits. Several states require the provision of victim services, but do not require that the victim receive information about those services. In most states, either law enforcement personnel or the prosecutor is the government entity required to provide information about such services to the victim. Turning to the second category, at least twenty states require that victims be provided general information about the criminal justice process, sometimes including information about their role in that process. Regarding the third category, it is difficult to quantify the number of states that require that victims be provided information about the case involving the crime committed against them. Some states require that victims be provided information, upon request, about the status of their case, while other states require that crime victims be provided such information only at specific points during the proceedings. Several states that do not explicitly provide the right to information, provide victims with the right to confer with the prosecutor, which necessarily includes the right to information about the victim's case. In addition, other victim's rights, such as the right to notice, when properly afforded, require that information about a victim's case be provided on an ongoing basis.

On the federal level, the Victims' Rights and Restitution Act of 1990, provides that "at the earliest opportunity after the detection of a crime at which it may be done without interfering with an investigation, a responsible official shall inform the victims of their right to receive, on request, the services described in subsection (c) of this section." The services mentioned in this provision also fall into the three categories identified above.

VIII. RIGHT TO APPLY FOR VICTIM COMPENSATION

Compensation is money paid from the government to a crime victim to reimburse the victim for certain losses incurred as a result of a crime. While victims do not have the right to automatically receive compensation, victims in every state have the right to apply for compensation, since all states receive funds under the Victims of Crime Act that support some form of compensation or reparations program. Recovery of monies from state compensation programs is typically limited: only certain types of losses are compensated; states generally "cap" the amount of compensation available; and victims are required to reimburse the compensation fund from monies received from other sources, such as insurance, civil settlements, or restitution. In general, victims of crime do not have a right to or expectation of full recovery from their state's compensation fund for the full amount of losses suffered as a result of the crime committed against them. Detailed information about compensation programs nationwide can be found on the National Association of Crime Victim Compensation Boards' website, **http://www.nacvcb.org/**. More later in Chapter Four.

IX. RIGHT TO PROCEEDINGS FREE FROM UNREASONABLE DELAY

The right to proceedings free from unreasonable delay is not the right to proceedings free from any delay, but from unreasonable delay. "Unreasonableness" is often fact-specific.

At least twenty-five states provide victims with some version of a right to prompt disposition of a criminal proceeding. In addition to a general right for crime victims to have proceedings free from unreasonable delay, some jurisdictions afford child victims and other vulnerable populations with a specific right to a "speedy trial" in certain situations.

Federally, subsection (a)(7) of the CVRA provides crime victims with "the right to proceedings free from unreasonable delay." While this right to proceedings free from unreasonable delay does not give a crime victim control of the criminal justice process, it does help ensure crime victim presence and independent participation throughout the process and helps avoid the secondary victimization caused by delay.

X. RIGHT TO CONFER

The right to confer is a right for the victim to both gather and provide information about the crime and the process to the prosecutor. The right to confer it is not a right to control the prosecution. The timing of affording the right to confer is critical; so many criminal cases are resolved by a plea. For the right to have any meaning it must mean a victim has the right to confer prior to the government reaching a binding plea agreement.

Constitutions and statutes in a number of states give victims a right to confer with the prosecution concerning charging or disposition.

Federally, subsection (a)(5) of the CVRA provides crime victims with "the reasonable right to confer with the attorney for the Government in the case."

Courts have recognized that failing to afford the right to confer prior to reaching a plea agreement or a final disposition violates the right.

XI. RIGHT TO A COPY OF THE PRESENTENCE REPORT AND TRANSCRIPTS

The right to access a copy of the presentence report and transcripts of court proceedings is critical to a victim's ability to actively and meaningfully participate in the proceedings.

A number of states explicitly provide victims the right to a copy of these materials.

At the federal level, the law allowing appointment of a guardian ad litem for juvenile victims allows access to these materials, by providing that, upon appointment, a guardian ad litem "may have access to all reports, evaluations and records, except attorney's work product, necessary to effectively advocate for the child." The CVRA does not, however, contain an explicit provision affording a similar right. Even where the right to access these materials is not explicit, arguments can be made that, in order for a victim to meaningfully exercise his or her other rights, including the rights to be treated with fairness, to be heard at sentencing and to restitution, a victim must have access to all relevant portions of a presentence report and to transcripts of proceedings.

XII. RIGHT TO STANDING AND REMEDIES

Legal standing refers to a crime victim's ability to independently assert and enforce his or her constitutional and statutory rights at both the trial level and, when appropriate, in appellate courts. Meaningful enforcement of rights requires victims to have both trial level standing to assert crime victims' rights and a mechanism for appellate review of a rights violation.

© Steven Frame/Shutterstock.com

The United States Supreme Court has explained that the question of standing is whether the party seeking relief has such a personal stake in the outcome of the controversy. For federal courts, the Supreme Court has set forth a three-part test to determine whether a litigant has standing:

1. the litigant must have suffered an "injury in fact";
2. there must be a nexus between the injury and the conduct complained of; and
3. the injury must be redressable by a favorable decision.

Historically, party-status has not been a prerequisite to standing to assert constitutional and statutory rights.

In general, state constitutional and statutory crime victims' rights legislation have no explicit provisions addressing trial level standing. Instead, states have generally established state-specific standing analyses that must be undertaken in each case. Generally, if a person meets the federal three-prong standing test, he or she will meet a state's standing requirements. Similarly, very few states explicitly provide for appellate review of decisions affecting crime victims' rights. The lack of an explicit provision for appellate review, though, does not preclude a victim from seeking review of a rights violation through a petition for writ of mandamus, prohibition, or certiorari.

On the federal level, the CVRA explicitly provides trial level standing to crime victims to assert their rights and sets forth a specific, expedited mechanism for appellate review of any denial of such rights. With regard to trial level standing, subsection (d)(1) of the CVRA provides: "The crime victim or the crime victim's lawful representative, and the attorney for the Government may assert the rights." This statement indicates that crime victims have standing in federal trial court to assert their CVRA rights.

© Rob Wilson/Shutterstock.com

A victim's trial level standing is bolstered by subsection (d)(3) of the CVRA, which provides the method of assertion: "The rights described in subsection (a) shall be asserted in the district court in which a defendant is being prosecuted for the crime or, if no prosecution is underway, in the district court in the district in which the crime occurred. The district court shall take up and decide any motion asserting a victim's right forthwith."

Standing to seek appellate review is also explicit in the CVRA. If the district court denies the relief sought by a crime victim for a rights violation, the CVRA sets forth a clear, expedited appellate review process. Specifically, subsection (d)(3) provides that a crime victim may petition for a writ of mandamus and that the court of appeals must take up and decide the issue within seventy-two hours. Generally, under federal mandamus law, review is discretionary; in contrast, the CVRA "contemplates active review of orders denying crime victims' rights claims even in routine cases." The CVRA "creates a unique regime that does, in fact, contemplate routine interlocutory review of district court decisions denying rights asserted under the statute."*

The President's Task Force held six hearings across the Nation and produced a "Final Report" with sixty-eight recommendations to improve assistance to victims of crime.

The Task Force's Report launched four critical initiatives. First, it recommended federal legislation to fund state victim compensation programs and local victim assistance programs. That pair of recommendations was the precipitating force for the enactment of VOCA. The Act established the Crime Victims Fund, made up of federal criminal fines, penalties, forfeitures, and special assessments, as the resource for the two programs.

During this time in the academic field, the first Victim Services Certificate Program was offered through California

© nazlisart/Shutterstock.com

---

*National Crime Victim Law Institute Law Bulletin November 2011

State University, Fresno. Now in addition to the Certificate, students can also earn a Bachelor of Science in Criminology degree with a major in Victimology.

Victim-oriented justice gained international recognition with the adoption of the United Nations Declaration of Basic Principles of Justice for Victims of Crime and Abuse of Power in 1985. This document helped spur other nations to start or expand victim rights and services.

The development of the OVC/NOVA Model Victim Assistance Program Brief in 1986-1988 served as a management tool for programs. It articulated eight basic services that programs should provide: crisis intervention, counseling and advocacy, support during criminal investigations, support during prosecution, support after case disposition, crime prevention, public education, and training of allied professions.

States were also moving rapidly to institutionalize victim assistance through funding legislation and the development of program networks. Bills of rights were adopted in every state by 1990; at present, thirty-two states have adopted constitutional amendments, and there are more than 32,000 statutes that define and protect victims' rights nationwide. By the end of the 1980s, more than 8,000 victim service programs were in operation.

The 1980s brought new contributors to the crime victims' movement.

- The National Victim Center (now the National Center for Victims of Crime) was founded in 1985 in honor of Sunny von Bulow, and generated increased emphasis on media and public awareness of victims' rights and concerns; research on the impact of crime on victims; civil litigation on behalf of victims; and training about victim assistance organizational development and crime victims' legislative rights.
- The Victims' Assistance Legal Organization (VALOR) became prominent as its founder, Frank Carrington, helped to develop and promote civil litigation on behalf of crime victims.
- The National Center for Missing and Exploited Children was established in 1984 to help find missing children and provide support to their families.
- The International Association of Chiefs of Police established a Victims Committee and announced a "law enforcement bill of rights for victims."
- The American Correctional Association Victims Committee issued sixteen recommendations to improve victims' rights and services in the post-sentencing phases of criminal cases.
- The American Probation and Parole Association established a Victim Issues Committee and developed sample policies and procedures, as well as, extensive training curricula, relevant to victims' rights and needs when their offenders are sentenced to community supervision or released on parole.
- The Spiritual Dimension in Victim Services became a source of education and training for clergy on victim issues.
- Neighbors Who Care was initiated by Justice Fellowship to develop victim assistance within religious communities.

- The International Society of Traumatic Stress Studies and the International Association of Trauma Counselors were established to serve as research and education resources for individuals working in the field of trauma.

The growth of the understanding of trauma was particularly important during the 1980s. Drawing on the experiences of seasoned crisis intervenors, NOVA initiated a practical model for community crisis intervention in the aftermath of tragedy that affects large groups of people. Its first crisis response team was fielded in 1986 after the mass murders committed in the Edmond, Oklahoma, Post Office. The success of that effort engendered the National Crisis Response Project, which made trained volunteer crisis intervenors available to address the emotional impact of crime and other disasters. It also influenced the growth of new local and state networks of crisis response teams.

The 1990s also saw the expansion of programs offering crisis intervention to groups of people affected by the same disaster. There emerged a number of different approaches for providing "group crisis interventions" or "debriefings" and while researchers continue to raise questions about the effectiveness of some of these approaches in some circumstances, proponents of "crisis response teams" remain committed to properly adapting the crisis intervention services, which are offered to many thousands of victims every day, to victims too numerous to reach on just an individual basis.

A variant of this service is now used in "family assistance centers" where disaster managers provide one-stop applications for a host of services available to victims of natural disasters or man-made catastrophes, such as the attacks of September 11, 2001.

In 1995, OVC first supported the National Victim Assistance Academy (NVAA) sponsored by the Victims' Assistance Legal Organization. The NVAA includes a research-based forty-hour curriculum on victimology, victims' rights, and myriad other topics; as of 2003, 2,000 students from every state and territory, as well as, from seven other nations, have graduated from the NVAA. In 1998, OVC co-funded the first State Victim Assistance Academy in Michigan. Subsequently, OVC has funded an additional eighteen State Academies. In 1999, Colorado, Connecticut, Pennsylvania, Texas, and Utah received first-year funding. In 2002, Arizona, Maine, Maryland, Missouri, and Oregon received first-year funding. In 2003, Georgia, Illinois, and New York received first-year funding. In 2004, California, Minnesota, South Carolina, and Tennessee received first-year funding.

To its credit, the victims' movement has always been fast to recognize patterns of predation that had been overlooked by society, and has tried to respond as quickly to its victims. In the 1990s, the movement began to put technology in service to its ideals.

- The National Victim Center, with support from OVC, sponsored the first national conference on technologies that benefit crime victims in 1998.
- The National Domestic Violence Hotline, established by Congress with strong support from the movement, received more than a million calls from its February 1996 inception though August 2003.
- "Victim Information and Notification Everyday" (VINE) is a proprietary system that, by 2003, provided thirty-six states and twenty of the Nation's largest metropolitan areas a method by which victims can call a toll-free number to obtain timely information about criminal cases and the status of their incarcerated offenders, and receive advance notice of those inmates' change of status, including a scheduled release from custody, by telephone or via the web.

- OVC's Victim Services 2000 projects have proven that, with the cooperation of all agencies and aid from innovative technologies, a system can be created that offers a "seamless web" of services where "there are no wrong doors" for victims to enter into a responsive network of help.
- The Violence Intervention Program, located at the Los Angeles County and USC Medical Center, implemented the first telemedicine project to guarantee that remote areas within the United States and around the world have access to expert evaluations and quality case assessments to protect the rights of victims.

NEW JERSEY SPECIFIC INFORMATION

Crime Victims Constitutional Amendment

(N.J. Constitution, article 1, section 22.)

A victim of a crime shall be treated with fairness, compassion and respect by the criminal justice system. A victim of a crime shall not be denied the right to be present at public judicial proceedings except when, prior to completing testimony as a witness, the victim is properly sequestered in accordance with law of the Rules Governing the Courts of the State of New Jersey. A victim of a crime shall be entitled to those rights and remedies as may be provided by the Legislature. For the purposes of this paragraph, "victim of a crime" means: a) a person who has suffered physical or psychological injury or has incurred loss or damage to personal or real property as a result of a crime or an incident involving another person operating a motor vehicle while under the influence of drugs or alcohol, and b) the spouse, parent, legal guardian, grandparent, child or sibling of the decedent in the case of a criminal homicide.

© Filip Bjorkman/Shutterstock.com

Rights of Crime Victims and Witnesses (N.J.S.A. § 52:4B-36)

The Legislature finds and declares that crime victims and witnesses are entitled to the following rights:

a. To be treated with dignity and compassion by the criminal justice system;
b. To be informed about the criminal justice process;
c. To be free from intimidation, harassment or abuse by any person including the defendant or any other person acting in support of or on behalf of the defendant, due to the involvement of the victim or witness in the criminal justice process;
d. To have inconveniences associated with participation in the criminal justice process minimized to the fullest extent possible;
e. To make at least one telephone call provided the call is reasonable in both length and location called;
f. To medical assistance reasonably related to the incident in accordance with the provisions of the "Criminal Injuries Compensation Act of 1971," P.L. 1971, c. 317 (N.J.S.A. § 52:4B-1 et seq.);
g. To be notified in a timely manner, if practicable, if presence in court is not needed or if any scheduled court proceeding has been adjourned or cancelled;

h. To be informed about available remedies, financial assistance and social services;
i. To be compensated for loss sustained by the victim whenever possible;
j. To be provided a secure, but not necessarily separate, waiting area during court proceedings;
k. To be advised of case progress and final disposition and to confer with the prosecutor's representative so that the victim may be kept adequately informed;
l. To the prompt return of property when no longer needed as evidence;
m. To submit a written statement, within a reasonable amount of time, about the impact of the crime to a representative of the prosecuting agency which shall be considered prior to the prosecutor's final decision concerning whether formal criminal charges will be filed, whether the prosecutor will consent to a request by the defendant to enter into a pre-trial program, and whether the prosecutor will make or agree to a negotiated plea;
n. To make, prior to sentencing, an in-person statement directly to the sentencing court concerning the impact of the crime. This statement is to be made in addition to the statement permitted for inclusion in the presentence report by N.J.S.A. §2C:44-6;
o. To have the opportunity to consult with the prosecuting authority prior to the conclusion of any plea negotiations, and to have the prosecutor advise the court of the consultation and the victim's position regarding the plea agreement, provided however that nothing herein shall be construed to alter or limit the authority or discretion of the prosecutor to enter into any plea agreement which the prosecutor deems appropriate;
p. To be present at any judicial proceeding involving a crime or any juvenile proceeding involving a criminal offense, except as otherwise provided by Article I, paragraph 22 of the New Jersey Constitution;
q. To be notified of any release or escape of the defendant; and
r. To appear in any court before which a proceeding implicating the rights of the victim is being held, with standing to file a motion or present argument on a motion filed to enforce any right conferred herein or by Article I, paragraph 22 of the New Jersey Constitution, and to receive an adjudicative decision by the court on any such motion.

Crime Victims are NOT Required to Pay Certain Costs (N.J.S.A. § 52:4B-36-2)

a. A crime victim shall not be required to pay the maintenance, support, rehabilitation, or other costs arising from the imprisonment or commitment of a victimizer as a result of the crime; and
b. A crime victim shall not be charged any fee otherwise prescribed by law or regulation to obtain copies of the victim's own records to which the victim is entitled to access as provided in section 1 of P.L.1995, c. 23 (N.J.S.A. § 47:1A-1.1) including, but not limited to, any law enforcement agency report, domestic violence offense report, and temporary or permanent restraining order.

Rights of the Survivors of Homicide Victims (N.J.S.A. § 52:4B-36-1)

a. A victim's survivor may, at the time of making the in-person statement to the sentencing court authorized by subsection n. of section 3 of P.L.1985, c. 249 (N.J.S.A. § 52:4B-36), display directly to the sentencing court a photograph of the victim taken before the homicide including, but not limited to, a still photograph, a computer-generated presentation, or a video presentation of the victim. The time, length, and content of such presentation shall be within the sound discretion of the sentencing judge; and
b. A victim's survivor may, during any judicial proceeding involving the defendant, wear a button not exceeding four inches in diameter that contains a picture of the victim, if the court

determines that the wearing of such button will not deprive the defendant of his right to a fair trial under the Sixth Amendment of the United States Constitution and Article I of the New Jersey Constitution. Other spectators at such judicial proceedings may also wear similar buttons if the court so determines. If the victim's survivor seeks to wear the button at trial, the victim's survivor shall give notice to the defendant and to the court no less than thirty days prior to the final trial date.

DISCUSSION QUESTIONS

1. What major legislation created the first change in victim's rights in the United States?

2. What are three modern rights a victim has?

3. Name three agencies that assist victims in the United States.

Name: _____   Date _____

You must use this form and turn in the original to the instructor. No other form will be accepted.

CHAPTER ASSIGNMENT

The text identifies twelve basic, fundamental victim rights. Why do you think these rights were written into legislation? Next, of the twelve identified rights, which one is the most important and why?

_____
_____
_____
_____
_____
_____
_____
_____
_____
_____
_____
_____
_____
_____
_____
_____
_____
_____
_____
_____

Chapter Four

CURRENT VICTIM ASSISTANCE PROGRAMS

LEARNING OBJECTIVES

After exploring Chapter Four (4), the student will be able to:

1. Discuss the relevance and function of Victim-Witness Advocacy Units.
2. Describe the services available to victims and witnesses involved in crime throughout the criminal justice system.
3. Identify the law mandating victims are aware of court proceeding and institutional movement of the defendant.
4. Discuss the components of Victim Notification Systems (VNS) and VINELink.

KEY TERMS

Victim-witness advocates, Victim-witness impact statements, Second victimization, Victim Notification System (VNS), VINELink

INTRODUCTION

Victims need assistance in the aftermath of the crimes committed against them. When a victim experiences the initial effects of crime, the period unfolding afterwards often causes additional stress and even a "second victimization." It is important to educate victims about the criminal justice process, provide services to ease the difficulties of the path towards convictions/sentencing, and deliver services that may be unique to a particular crime victim.

This chapter reveals the services provided by Victim-Witness Advocates and the separate victim notification systems provided by the federal government and the individual states themselves.

VICTIM-WITNESS ADVOCACY UNITS

A Victim Witness Advocacy unit within the District Attorney's or Prosecutor's Office are formed to extend certain social services and advocacy to the victims of a variety of crimes. These divisions are trained victim counseling and court procedures. Victim-witness advocate practitioners support victims and witnesses with the difficulties that arise from their status of victim or witness. Additionally, these units help to guide these people affected by crime through the criminal justice process

Victim-witness advocates notify victims of everything they are entitled to during the process of the criminal justice system. In addition to providing these rights, advocates are tasked with continually updating the victims and witnesses as the court case moves forward with separate legal proceedings afforded to the accused through due process.

The advocates provide assistance during all of the criminal justice procedures that may arise. These circumstances may vary as criminal justice proceedings often are unique to the case at hand and may require more or less legal hearings and steps then others. These units assist victims to arrange their impact statements to be read formally in court. Victim impact statements are critical to the process and used by prosecutors and other criminal justice system practitioners in particular levels of the legal process (plea negotiations, sentencing).

© Pressmaster/Shutterstock.com

One primary function of a Victim-Witness Advocate Office is to update the victim or witness with case information. Often, this information is dispersed in letterform, apprising the users of the service with general status information from initial indictments, suppression hearings, trial dates, and sentencing. As an extension of services, these practitioners inform victims and witnesses concerning parole hearings and notifications regarding jail and prison release.

Transportation to court proceedings and childcare are just some of the additional services the victim-witness advocates can deliver to those who require them during the criminal justice system process.

Victim-Witness Advocates are staffed with counselors, however, they are to identify counselors by referral, if exclusively trained mental health providers are not part of the general staff of the unit. The general counselors (ones employed within the unit) are generally qualified to provide crisis intervention counseling. Overall, the objective is to transfer these services to full-time therapists for specific individual need who represent skills in a variety of disciplines.

Advocate offices link with local mental health and social service providers to provide victims of crime an extensive support system. Victim-Witness advocates assist victims to apply for funds for medical and other charges associated with their victimization through the Victims of Crime Compensation Board. Victim counselors assist victims with their applications, and advocate on their behalf with the Board to facilitate payment. The office can coordinate free care and recovery for child abuse and domestic violence victims (Atlantic County Prosecutors Office, 2017).

The New Jersey State Office of Victim Witness Advocacy supports the county offices and encourages them to provide the following services:

CRIMINAL JUSTICE ORIENTATION AND INFORMATION

This portion invites the victim or witness to ask questions about the flow and timeline of the criminal justice system. The counselors can give a valid forecast based upon their experience about the steps in the process. Additionally, victims and witnesses can be brought into the actual courtroom and be shown the actual environment of court. This can help to quell anxiety about the process.

VICTIM INFORMATION AND IMPACT FORM

During this process, it is encouraged that the prosecutor and the victims have contact to relay how the crime has affected their lives since the occurrence of the crime. Victim impact statements and victim information is provided to be used in court proceedings. Victim-Witness Advocate units aid victims with preparing these statements in both written and verbal forms.

COUNSELING AND SUPPORT SERVICES

Members of the Victim-Witness Advocacy Office receive training to help victims cope with the preliminary emotional effects of victimization. When victims require additional services, advocacy personnel help to find mental health services to fit their specific need. In terms of support, assistance can be acquired in obtaining food, shelter, and clothing for victims in need.

CASE STATUS NOTIFICATION

This is an important part of the process because victims and witnesses often feel jaded by the criminal justice system and experience a second victimization intensifying the victim's anguish (Wemmers, 2013). This can be caused by indifferent responses to the victim throughout their victimization by different components (police, courts, prosecutors, defense, judicial staff, etc.) of the criminal justice system. Initial contacts in case status general inform the victim their case has been reviewed by the prosecutor's office and identifies the services available through the Victim-Witness Advocate Office. As the case moves forward the victim/witness may be notified any of the following:

- Pre-grand jury remand
- Administrative dismissal
- Grand jury remand
- Grand jury dismissal (no bill)
- Indictment returned (true bill)
- Acceptance into Pre-Trial Intervention Program (PTI)
- Termination from or completion of PTI
- Negotiated plea on all charges
- Release on bail/conditions of bail
- Fugitive status
- Court dismissal
- Sentencing date
- Sentence imposed on the defendant by the court
- Defendant's filing of an appeal and subsequent status changes
- Disposition on all charges
- Mistrial/retrial
- Post-conviction release

As you can see there are a variety of ways the court can proceed depending on the uniqueness of the case. When notified of a specific proceeding, contact information is provided to contact the office to get clarification in regard to the status of the case.

© Rawpixel.com/Shutterstock.com

COURT ACCOMPANIMENT AND TRANSPORTATION SERVICES

When the victim's case is scheduled for a trial data, personnel will go to trial with them for support and to provide details about the course of the trial. In addition to providing an empathetic and helpful presence, the office will compensate the victim for travel costs (taxi or bus fares), even if the victim is not required to appear and wants to observe the court proceedings.

CHILD CARE TO ATTEND MEETINGS AND COURT PROCEEDINGS

Victim-Witness Advocacy units provide childcare for victims when they are showing up at court hearings or meetings at county court offices. Although the office recommends leaving children with friends or family (someone familiar to the children), they will make arrangements to care for children so the victim can attend legal appointments and court dates.

HIV TESTING OF DEFENDANTS AND HIV INFORMATION AND REFERRALS FOR VICTIMS

When a victim exchanges some type of bodily fluid with an attacker (blood, saliva, semen, etc.), it can be requested to court order the defendant to be tested for blood borne diseases, such as HIV or AIDS. Essentially, the victim can request for information about these diseases and receive free personal private testing for these illnesses.

ASSISTANCE IN OBTAINING RESTITUTION

When victims sustain some type of monetary loss from crime, restitution (money) is ordered by the court to be paid by the defendant. Judges, prosecutors, and probationers decide how much financial responsibility the defendant has to the victim as a result of the crime. This is established by the victim information form, which will report any losses incurred by the victim. Additionally, the victim impact statement is reviewed to discovered any other costs to be attributed to the defendant.

EMPLOYER AND CREDITOR INTERCESSION

This service involves Victim-Witness Advocate workers intervening on behalf of the victim with employers and creditors for time or money loss suffered as a result of the victimization. The loss of time or money can occur from forfeiting time at work and being unable to pay bills as a result. Personnel can mediate on behalf of the victim to mitigate the costs that accrue from loss time working, creating difficult conditions to make bill payments.

ASSISTANCE WITH PROPERTY RETURN

Defendants must be prosecuted with evidence. Many times the evidence used to indict and accuse a defendant is recovered personal property of the victim. This property can be recovered from defendant with legal methods (search warrant, plain view, etc.) by police and the prosecution and making a winnable case for the victim. However, it must remain as evidence for trial maintaining its integrity. This means it will remain in the state's possession until the case has been disposed. Victim-Witness Advocacy Office's assist with this process after the defendant is sentenced for the crime.

VICTIM-WITNESS WAITING ROOMS

Waiting rooms are provided for victims and witnesses who are waiting to speak with detectives, prosecutors, or for court/trial proceedings to commence.

PAROLE ELIGIBILITY AND RELEASE NOTIFICATION

Victims are notified when defendants are released from prison or eligible for parole by Victim-Witness Advocacy Offices (State of New Jersey–Office of Victim-Witness Advocacy).

(Retrieved from State of New Jersey–Office of Victim-Witness Advocacy at http://www.state.nj.us/lps/dcj/victimwitness/services.htm).

VICTIM NOTIFICATION SYSTEMS: VNS AND VINE

The Victim Notification System (VNS)

The Victim and Witness Protection Act of 1982, the Crime Control Act of 1990, the Violent Crime Control and Law Enforcement Act of 1994, as well as the Attorney General's Guidelines for Victim and Witness Assistance set forth procedures to meet the needs of crime victims and witnesses. A major component of each of these directives is to ensure victims/witnesses are advised of the significant stages in the criminal justice process. This Program Statement establishes Federal Bureau of Prisons procedures for responding to a request from a victim or witness who wishes to be notified regarding a specific inmate's release or release-related activities.

a. Victims who are on record to receive information will be notified, within established time frames, of an inmate's admission to, or release from, an institution or contract facility.

© Rawpixel.com/Shutterstock.com

From Vinelink.com by Appriss. Copyright © 2017 by Appriss. Reprinted by permission.

b. Victims who are on record to receive information will be notified, within established time frames, of opportunities to appear in person at an inmate's parole hearing or submit written comments for consideration.

The following is the Federal Bureau of Prisons procedure for notifying victims and witnesses about the steps within the criminal justice process:

(1) **Initial Notification.** VNS will create a pending initial notification (initial designation) once the inmate's sentence computation has been completed. Unit staff will complete the initial notification to the victim(s) within thirty calendar days of the date the notification was posted on VNS. All initial notifications (initial designation) can be made using the "Contact Preferences" option, which allows the preferred notification method of the victim to be used when processing this type of notification.

If the victim's preferred method of notification is a letter, the victim will also be provided a copy of the Department of Justice Victim Notification System Pamphlet, which contains a brief description of VNS procedures and instructions for accessing the Victim Notification Call Center. If Central Office staff or the Victim Witness Centers (VNC) enters a victim into VNS, an initial notification will be generated in VNS. In this type of notification, staff cannot use the "Contact Preferences" option for providing notification. Unit staff will complete an initial notification letter and mail it with the Department of Justice Victim Notification System Pamphlet, to the victim(s) within thirty calendar days of the date the notification was posted on VNS.

If the "Contact Preferences" option is utilized for initial designation notifications, unit staff will retrieve from VNS and review a Call Tracing Report and a Notification Report by the next work day to ensure each victim received notification. If the victim's preferred method of contact was unsuccessful, staff must follow-up with an initial notification letter to the victim. The Call Tracing Report and the Notification Report used for verification of the completed contact will be maintained in the Privacy Folder, Section I of the Inmate Central File.

(2) **Parole Hearings.** Pending parole notifications will be created by VNS sixty calendar days in advance of the date of the anticipated parole hearing. Unit staff must mail the notification letter(s) to the victim(s) 30 calendar days in advance of the parole hearing.

VNS uses the parole hearing date entered in the SENTRY Parole Hearing Update transaction to create the parole hearing notification. Therefore, it is essential that unit staff update the parole hearing date in SENTRY in order to receive notifications from VNS.

© Joe Prachatree/Shutterstock.com

VNS does not automatically create pending notifications for record review hearings, therefore, unit staff are required to manually create the pending notification(s) utilizing the forms (BP-323 forms) within VNS. Notification to the victim(s) will ordinarily occur nine months prior to the Presumptive Parole date, which coincides with when the record review Progress Report is mailed to the U.S. Parole Commission.

Additionally, unit staff must prepare a memorandum to the U.S. Parole Commission indicating a victim (not to be specifically identified) may wish to submit written comments or attend the hearing. This memorandum must be included in the review material provided to the Parole Examiners before the hearing.

(3) **Escapes.** Unit staff must notify each victim by telephone as soon as possible after the escape is discovered and confirmed (normally the same day), and provide the date and time of a Victim/Witness Program (VWP) inmate's escape. If there are multiple victims in the case, unit staff may contact the VNS Call Center via fax using the Escape/Immediate Release/Call Cancellation form to initiate the telephonic notification system. If telephonic contact is not possible, unit staff will complete the notification process by forwarding a specific form to the victim by the next workday via certified mail, return receipt requested. If telephonic contact is made, unit staff will complete the notification process by forwarding the same form to the victim within seven calendar days via certified mail, return receipt requested.

When the VNS Call Center is utilized to process the notification(s), unit staff will review a Call Tracing Report retrieved from VNS for that case by the next workday to ensure each victim received notification. The Call Tracing Report will be maintained in the Privacy Folder, Section I of the Inmate Central File. If the system is unable to contact the victim(s), unit staff will follow-up with Directory Assistance and/or alternate contacts, to obtain the correct telephone number and contact the victim immediately. The sending institution is responsible for notification(s) for escapes, which occur during an unescorted transfer. If an escape occurs while a VWP inmate is housed in a Community Corrections Center (CCC) or a state contractual facility, the Community Corrections Management (CCM) is responsible for notifying the victim(s) as soon as the escape is confirmed (normally the same day).

Once the CCM or Unit Manager receives information that the inmate has been apprehended, the victims/witnesses will be notified of the apprehension. The CCM or Unit Manager are responsible for ensuring a form is mailed as soon as possible, but no later than thirty calendar days after receiving notification of apprehension. The date the inmate was apprehended and current location or designation, if known, will be indicated on the form. The CCM will forward copies of the form to the parent institution to be included in the Privacy Folder, Section I of the Inmate Central File.

(4) **Furloughs/Unescorted Transfers.** VNS does not automatically create pending notifications for furloughs or unescorted transfers; therefore, unit staff is required to manually create the pending notification(s) within VNS. Completion of the form for unescorted transfers will include the institution's name and address, and the date of the transfer. Completion of the form for an inmate approved for a furlough will only include the city and state, and the dates the furlough will take place. If circumstances do not permit advance written notification, unit staff will furnish the information to the victim(s) by telephone. If telephonic notification is not possible, unit staff must document all efforts made to contact the victim on the Victim Notification Record (Attachment B).

© Georgios Tsichlis/Shutterstock.com

(5) **Inmate Death.** VNS will notify unit staff within twenty-four hours of SENTRY being updated to reflect the inmate is deceased. Unit staff will forward a form to the victim within thirty calendar days.

(6) **Transfer to a Community Corrections Center.** VNS will automatically forward notification to unit staff once a CCC acceptance date has been entered by community corrections staff.

Unit staff will complete a specific form. This form is considered final notification and will be forwarded to the victim(s) via regular mail. When written notification to the victim will not likely arrive in advance of the CCC transfer, telephonic contact with each victim will be made.

Ordinarily, the notification of CCC placement is the final notification to the victim/witness; however, if an event (escape, death, immediate release) in the CCC occurs, the CCM will send additional notifications to the victim/witness. CCM's are prohibited from forwarding victim/witness information to CCC staff, therefore, CCM staff will notify the victim/witness when the VWP inmate is released on furlough while at the CCC, using the same notification procedures outlined in Section 12.c.(4) of this Program Statement.

(7) **Release to the Street.** VNS will create a final release notification within sixty calendar days of the inmate's projected release date. Within thirty calendar days of receipt of this notification, unit staff will forward a completed form to the victim via regular mail. Telephonic contact must be made when the inmate's release is unexpected and/or immediate (i.e., court-ordered release, etc.). Unit staff may contact the VNS Call Center via fax using the Escape/Immediate Release/Call Cancellation form to initiate the telephone notification system. Unit staff will complete the notification process by forwarding a form to the victim/witness by the next workday via regular mail.

When the VNS Call Center is utilized to process the notification(s), unit staff will review a Call Tracing Report retrieved from VNS for that case by the next workday to ensure each victim received notification. The Call Tracing Report will be maintained in the Privacy Folder, Section I of the Inmate Central File.

If the system is unable to contact the victim(s), unit staff will follow-up with Directory Assistance and/or alternate contacts, to obtain the correct telephone number and contact the victim immediately.

A completed form must also be forwarded to the victims/witnesses for those inmates releasing to detaining authorities (INS, other state or local law enforcement detaining authorities, treaty transfer to a foreign country, etc.) via regular mail.

(8) **Compassionate Release.** VNS does not automatically create pending notifications for compassionate release consideration, therefore, unit staff are required to manually create the pending notification within VNS. During the institution's review of the inmate's request for compassionate release, the unit staff must notify the victims and solicit comments to be incorporated into the Wardens referral memorandum in accordance with the Program Statement on Compassionate Release, Procedures for Implementation of 18 U.S.C. § 3582(c)(1)(A) and 4205(g).

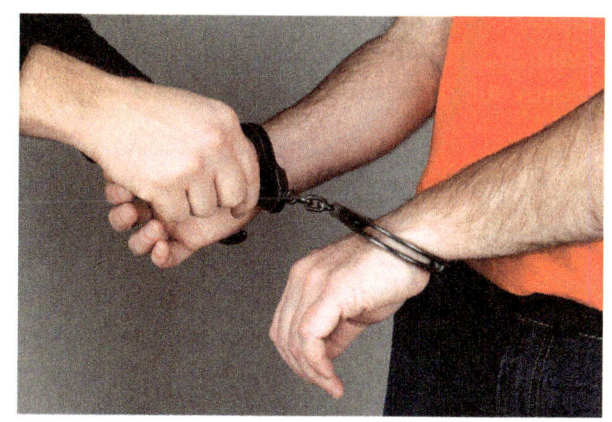

© arfo/Shutterstock.com

(9) **Writs.** Unit staff are not required to notify victims/witnesses when a VWP inmate is temporarily released on writ to other law enforcement authorities, or an escorted trip.

In the event of an escape or death of an inmate temporarily released on federal writ, unit staff from the holding institution must make the required notifications. All other writ cases will require unit staff from the parent institution to make the required notifications in accordance with Section 13.c.(3) and (5) of this Program Statement.

VINE

VINE (Victim Information and Notification Everyday) is a service through which victims of crime can use the telephone or Internet to search for information regarding their offender's custody status and register to receive telephone and e-mail notification when their offender's custody status changes. VINE is currently available in forty-eight states.

The forty-eight states participating in the VINE program allow for a variety of means to access inmate data. Registration is either done online (vinelink.com) or via phone numbers (different numbers for each state). VINE even has a mobile app for Android and Apple phones.

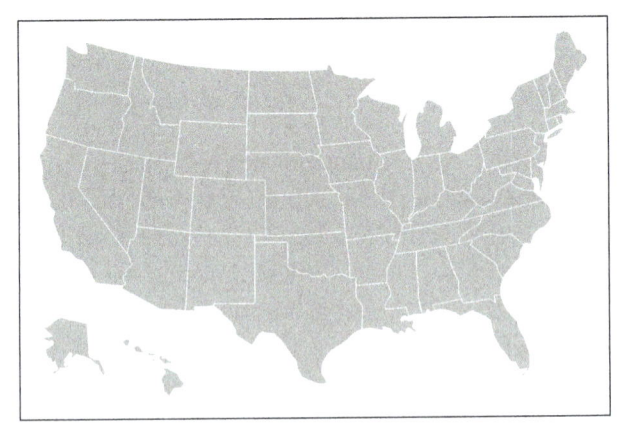

© Luchenko Yana/Shutterstock.com

The two states that do not participate are Maine and South Dakota

Maine

The victim notification law applies to victims of murder, or of a Class A, B or C crimes. A victim who wishes to receive notification MUST file a request with the office of the prosecuting attorney. A victim's request is kept confidential. The victim will be notified PRIOR to work release, furlough, or release from confinement. Forms for notification requests can be obtained on-line via the state's website and subsequently submitted electronically.

http://www.maine.gov/corrections/VictimServices/notification.htm

South Dakota

South Dakota SAVIN stands for Statewide Automated Victim Information & Notification. The South Dakota SAVIN program is a free, automated service that provides crime victims with vital information and notification twenty-four hours a day, 365 days a year. This service will allow you to obtain offender information and to register for notification of a change in offender status, such as offender release.

https://savin.sd.gov/Portal/

The following is information provided by **vinelink.com** for using their service:

TELEPHONE REGISTRATION

You can use the telephone to search for and register to receive notification about the custody status of an offender—each state/county has their own toll-free VINE phone number.

© Brian A Jackson/Shutterstock.com

WEB REGISTRATION

You can search for and register to receive notification about the custody status of an offender via VINELink at **www.vinelink.com**.

Do I Subscribe To or Pay for This Service?

VINELink is not a paid service. It is completely FREE to the public. We are aware of other services that ask you to "subscribe to" or "pay for" their information. We assure you, we are in no way affiliated with those services.

How Do I Search for an Offender and Register to Receive Notification Using VINELink?

Please note that you may register to receive notification for custody status changes only for offenders currently in custody.

To use VINELink to search for an offender in custody, please follow these steps:

1. Go to **www.vinelink.com**
2. Click on the state in which the offender is housed.
3. Choose the Search & Register tab across the top of the navigation page.
4. Select the Facility or Facilities that you would like to search, type in the Offender Identification number or the full Last Name and at least the first initial of the First Name, then click Search.
5. Verify the information for the offender that matches the person for whom you search.

To use VINELink to register to receive notification about changes in an offender's custody status, please follow these steps:

1. Complete steps 1 through 5 above.
2. Click on the magnifying glass icon under the Register/Details column next to the appropriate offender.
3. On the Offender Details screen, choose your Method of Registration, then click Continue.
4. Complete the required information for registration.
5. Click Register.

How Frequently Do You Receive Offender Information?

Our standard transaction time is every fifteen minutes for jails and twice each day for prisons. This may vary depending upon the jail activity and the resources the facility has on site to update the data. Most always, the data is current within fifteen minutes.

However, if you have reason to believe the data is out of date, you should call the jail directly for an update and invoke your personal safety plan. Do not depend solely on VINE or any other program for your safety.

Is Charge and Warrant Information Available on VINELink?

VINE does not receive charge information from all facilities and therefore it is not always available to be displayed on VINELink. We recommend that you call the facility in which you believe the offender is housed and inquire about the charges for the offender.

VINE does not track outstanding warrants. However, Appriss, provider of the VINE service, is working directly with several states to provide VINE Protective Order, a product that allows PO petitioners to receive notification when the warrant is served.

Can You Remove or Change Offender Information On Your Website?

VINE—Victim Information and Notification Everyday, is funded and provided by local and state agencies for the purpose of notifying victims upon a change in their offender's custody status.

We provide this service as a third party and do not have the ability to remove or alter offender data in the database. However, we work closely with the agencies to ensure data integrity and accuracy. If you have found incorrect data on the VINELink site, please call your local Department of Correction or jail facility to report the inaccuracy to them directly so that they might make the change in their database as appropriate.

CONCLUSION

Victims of crime are frequently shattered by the initial offense perpetrated against them. It is the responsibility of the criminal justice system (i.e. criminal justice practitioners) to comfort the victim through the process and identify the services available to them. Victims must not be subjected to insincere members of the criminal justice system. It is their duty to be empathetic to the exclusive needs of every victim. Victim-Witness Advocacy groups and notification systems provide information and a path for the victims of crime to recover. Recuperation for the victim involves participation in the criminal justice process. The progression from victimization to sentencing or release must be carefully managed by trained professionals to ensure victims are receiving the care they deserve.

DISCUSSION QUESTIONS

1. What is a "second victimization," and what steps can be taken to prevent this phenomena from occurring?

2. What service does Victim Notification Systems provide? Is there any other information that can be proved to the victim or witness of a crime?

3. Victim-Witness Advocates provide many services to the victim. What services do you think are most critical? Does it depend on the crime?

REFERENCES

Atlantic County Prosecutor's Office (2017). Victim-Witness Advocacy Office. Retrieved from http://www.acpo.org/vwitness.html

Federal Bureau of Prisons (2002). Program Statement: Victim and Witness Notification Program. Retrieved from https://www.bop.gov/policy/progstat/1490_006.pdf

State of New Jersey (2017). Office of Victim-Witness Advocacy. Retrieved from http://www.state.nj.us/lps/dcj/victimwitness/services.htm)

VineLink (2017) The National Victim Notification Network. Retrieved from https://www.vinelink.com/#/home

Wemmers, J. A. (2013). Victims' experiences in the criminal justice system and their recovery from crime. *International Review of Victimology*, *19*(3), 221–233.

Name: _____   Date _____

> **You must use this form and turn in the original to the instructor. No other form will be accepted.**

CHAPTER ASSIGNMENT

The text sketches the importance of professional victim-witness advocates. What type of characteristics do you believe someone working in this position should have? Does their formal education need to be in a specific discipline? Why is their role important to victim-assistance in general?

_____
_____
_____
_____
_____
_____
_____
_____
_____
_____
_____
_____
_____
_____
_____
_____
_____
_____
_____
_____

Chapter Five

VICTIMS OF DOMETIC ABUSE (Intimate Partner Violence)

LEARNING OBJECTIVES

After exploring Chapter Five (5), the student will be able to:

1. Define intimate partner violence.
2. Explain the power and control cycle of violence.
3. List some signs of an abusive relationship.
4. Detail some resources available to help those in need of emergency relief from a domestic abuser.
5. Explain a safety plan.
6. Define a restraining order.

KEY TERMS

Domestic Violence, IPV, Restraining order, Power and Control cycle of violence, Safety plan, Abusive relationship, Healthy relationship, Intimate Partner Violence, Violence Against Women Act

INTRODUCTION

Every day tens of thousands are the victim of domestic abuse. The type of abuse varies. Physical and emotional. Partner to partner. Partner to relative. Relative to relative. The degree of abuse varies greatly. Intimate partner violence, IPV affects too many people.

On average, twenty-four people per minute are victims of rape, physical violence or stalking by an intimate partner in the United States—more than 12 million women and men over the course of a year.

- Nearly 3 in 10 women (29 percent) and 1 in 10 men (10 percent) in the U.S. have experienced rape, physical violence and/or stalking by a partner and report a related impact on their functioning.
- Nearly, 15 percent of women (14.8 percent) and 4 percent of men have been injured as a result of IPV that included rape, physical violence and/or stalking by an intimate partner in their lifetime.
- 1 in 4 women (24.3 percent) and 1 in 7 men (13.8 percent) aged eighteen and older in the United States have been the victim of severe physical violence by an intimate partner in their lifetime.
- IPV alone affects more than 12 million people each year.
- More than 1 in 3 women (35.6 percent) and more than 1 in 4 men (28.5 percent) in the United States have experienced rape, physical violence and/or stalking by an intimate partner in their lifetime.
- Nearly half of all women and men in the United States have experienced psychological aggression by an intimate partner in their lifetime (48.4 percent and 48.8 percent, respectively).
- Females ages eighteen to twenty-four and twenty-five to thirty-four generally experienced the highest rates of intimate partner violence.
- From 1994 to 2010, about 4 in 5 victims of intimate partner violence were female.
- Most female victims of intimate partner violence were previously victimized by the same offender, including 77 percent of females ages eighteen to twenty-four, 76 percent of females ages twenty-five to thirty-four, and 81 percent of females ages thirty-five to forty-nine.

Most of the following information is written in the context of you, the reader, being a victim. Having the text written in this way and reading the information (as directed for a victim/potential victim) makes the statements truly meaningful.

One of the most dangerous situations in someone's life is being a victim of intimate partner violence. Further, when the situation escalates to the involvement of law enforcement, the dangers are extreme.

Lastly, we ask our law enforcement officials (some who are youthful, not experienced and perhaps not well trained) to mitigate and fix a volatile situation that has taken a long time to build. The situation then, becomes exacerbated by high emotions, the real possibility of arrest, loss of income, consequences, more violence, etc., and the anger/frustration can be turned against the law enforcement officer(s) at the scene. The domestic violence call is one of the most dangerous for law enforcement, as well as, those involved.

Therefore, when reading the chapter remember the very real fact that nearly 100 thousand people per day in the United States face intimate partner violence. However, there are resources and there is a way out.

WHAT IS SAFETY PLANNING?

A safety plan is a personalized, practical plan that includes ways to remain safe while in a relationship, planning to leave, or after you leave. Safety planning involves how to cope with emotions, tell friends and family about the abuse, take legal action and more.

A good safety plan will have all of the vital information you need and be tailored to your unique situation, and will help walk you through different scenarios.

Although some of the things that you outline in your safety plan may seem obvious, it's important to remember that in moments of crisis your brain doesn't function the same way as when you are calm. When adrenaline is pumping through your veins it can be hard to think clearly or make logical decisions about your safety. Having a safety plan laid out in advance can help you to protect yourself in those stressful moments.

TYPES OF SAFETY PLANNING

Safety While Living With An Abusive Partner

- Identify your partner's use and level of force so that you can assess the risk of physical danger to you and your children before it occurs.
- Identify safe areas of the house where there are no weapons and there are ways to escape. If arguments occur, try to move to those areas.
- Don't run to where the children are, as your partner may hurt them as well.
- If violence is unavoidable, make yourself a small target. Dive into a corner and curl up into a ball with your face protected and arms around each side of your head, fingers entwined.

© Rob Wilson/Shutterstock.com

- If possible, have a phone accessible at all times and know what numbers to call for help. Know where the nearest public phone is located. Know the phone number to your local shelter. If your life is in danger, call the police.
- Let trusted friends and neighbors know of your situation and develop a plan and visual signal for when you need help.
- Teach your children how to get help. Instruct them not to get involved in the violence between you and your partner. Plan a code word to signal to them that they should get help or leave the house.
- Tell your children that violence is never right, even when someone they love is being violent. Tell them that neither you, nor they, are at fault or are the cause of the violence, and that when anyone is being violent, it is important to stay safe.
- Practice how to get out safely. Practice with your children.
- Plan for what you will do if your children tells your partner of your plan or if your partner otherwise finds out about your plan.
- Keep weapons like guns and knives locked away and as inaccessible as possible.
- Make a habit of backing the car into the driveway and keeping it fueled. Keep the driver's door unlocked and others locked—for a quick escape.
- Try not to wear scarves or long jewelry that could be used to strangle you.
- Create several plausible reasons for leaving the house at different times of the day or night.

Safety Planning With Children

If you are in an abusive relationship, a safety plan should include ways that your children can stay safe when violence is happening in your home. It's key to remember that if the violence is escalating, you should avoid running to the children because your partner may hurt them as well.

Planning for Violence in the Home

- Teach your children when and how to call 911.
- Instruct them to leave the home if possible when things begin to escalate, and where they can go.
- Come up with a code word that you can say when they need to leave the home in case of an emergency—make sure that they know not to tell others what the secret word means.
- In the house: identify a room they can go to when they're afraid and something they can think about when they're scared.
- Instruct them to stay out of the kitchen, bathroom and other areas where there are items that could be used as weapons.
- Teach them that although they want to protect their parent, they should never intervene.
- Help them make a list of people that they are comfortable talking with and expressing themselves to.
- Enroll them in a counseling program. Local service providers often have children's programs.

Planning for Unsupervised Visits

If you have separated from an abusive partner and are concerned for your childrens' safety when they visit your ex, developing a safety plan for while they are visiting can be beneficial.

- ▶ Brainstorm with your children (if they are old enough) to come up with ways that they can stay safe using the same model as you would for your own home. Have them identify where they can get to a phone, how they can leave the house, and who they can go to.
- ▶ If it's safe to do, send a cell phone with the children to be used in emergency situations—this can be used to call 911, a neighbor or you if they need aid.

© MaDedee/Shutterstock.com

Planning for Safe Custody Exchanges

- ▶ Avoid exchanging custody at your home or your partner's home.
- ▶ Meet in a safe, public place such as a restaurant, a bank/other area with lots of cameras, or even near a police station. (Some police departments will work with you and actually allow you to exchange the children in the lobby of the police station.)
- ▶ Bring a friend or relative with you to the exchanges, or have them make the exchange.
- ▶ Perhaps plan to have your partner pick the children up from school at the end of the day after you drop them off in the morning—this eliminates the chances of seeing each other.
- ▶ Emotional safety plan as well—figure out something to do before the exchange to calm any nerves you're feeling, and something after to focus on yourself or the kids, such as going to a park or doing a fun activity.

How to Have These Conversations

Let your child know that what's happening is not their fault and that they didn't cause it. Let them know how much you love them and that you support them no matter what. Tell them that you want to protect them and that you want everyone to be safe, so you have to come up with a plan to use in case of emergencies. It's important to remember that when you're safety planning with a child, they might tell this information to the abusive partner, which could make the situation more dangerous (ex. "Mom said to do this if you get angry.") When talking about these plans with your child, use phrases such as "We're practicing what to do in an emergency," instead of "We're planning what you can do when dad/mom becomes violent."

Saftey Planning With Pets

Statistics show that up to 65 percent of domestic violence victims are unable to escape their abusive partners because they are concerned about what will happen to their pets when they leave. Fortunately, there are more and more resources in place to assist with this difficult situation.

If you're creating a safety plan of your own to leave an abusive relationship, safety planning for your pets is important as well. Bring extra provisions for them, copies of their medical records and important phone numbers.

© Rob Hainer/Shutterstock.com

If possible, don't leave pets alone with an abusive partner. If you are planning to leave, talk to friends, family or your veterinarian about temporary care for your pet. If that is not an option, search by state or zip code for services that assist domestic violence survivors with safekeeping for their pets. Try zip code first, and if there are no results, try a search by state. If none of the results are feasible for your situation, try contacting your local domestic violence or animal shelter directly. For help finding an animal shelter, visit the Humane Society website.

If you've had to leave your pet behind with your abusive partner, try to ask for assistance from law enforcement officials or animal control to see if they can intervene.

Take steps to prove ownership of your pet: have them vaccinated and license them with your town, ensuring that these registrations are made in your name (change them if they aren't).

If you're thinking about getting a protective order, know that some states allow pets to be a part of these.

If you've left your partner, ensure the safety of your pet by changing veterinarians and avoid leaving pets outside alone.

- ▶ The Animal Welfare Institute offers additional tips for safety planning with pets.
- ▶ Organizations like Georgia-based Ahimsa House and Littlegrass Ranch in Texas offer advice for safety planning with animals, especially with non-traditional animals like horses that are more difficult to transport.
- ▶ Red Rover offers different grant programs to enable victims to leave their abusive partners without having to leave their pets behind. The grants must be submitted by a shelter worker.

Safety Planning During Pregnancy

Pregnancy is a time of change. Pregnancy can be full of excitement but also comes with an added need for support. It's natural to need emotional support from a partner, as well as perhaps financial assistance, help to prepare for the baby and more.

If your partner is emotionally or physically abusive toward you, it can make these months of transition especially difficult. Thankfully, there are resources available to help expecting women get the support needed for a safe, healthy pregnancy.

According to the CDC, intimate partner violence affects approximately 1.5 million women each year and affects as many as 324,000 pregnant women each year. Pregnancy can be an especially dangerous time for women in abusive relationships, and abuse can often begin or escalate during the pregnancy.

How can you get help?

- If you're pregnant, there is always a heightened risk during violent situations. If you're in a home with stairs, try to stay on the first floor. Getting into the fetal position around your stomach if you're being attacked is another tactic that can be instrumental in staying safe.
- Doctor's visits can be an opportunity to discuss what is going on in your relationship.
- If your partner goes to these appointments with you, try to find a moment when they're out of the room to ask your care provider (or even the front desk receptionist) about coming up with an excuse to talk to them one-on-one.
- If you've decided to leave your relationship, a health care provider can become an active participant in your plan to leave.
- If possible, see if you can take a women-only prenatal class. This could be a comfortable atmosphere for discussing pregnancy concerns or could allow you to speak to the class instructor one-on-one.

Emotional Saftey Planning

Often, emphasis is placed on planning around physical safety, but it's important to consider your emotional safety as well. Emotional safety can look different for different people, but ultimately it's about developing a personalized plan that helps you feel accepting of your emotions and decisions when dealing with abuse. Below are some ideas for how to create and maintain an emotional safety plan that works for you.

Seek Out Supportive People: A caring presence such as a trusted friend or family member can help create a calm atmosphere to think through difficult situations and allow for you to discuss potential options.

Identify and Work Towards Achievable Goals: An achievable goal might be calling a local resource and seeing what services are available in your area.

Remember that you don't have to do anything you aren't comfortable with right now, but taking small steps can help options feel more possible when you are ready.

Create a Peaceful Space for Yourself: Designating a physical place where your mind can relax and feel safe can be good option when working through difficult emotions that can arise when dealing with abuse. This can be a room in your house, a spot under your favorite tree, a comfy chair by a window or in a room with low lights.

Remind Yourself of Your Great Value: You are important and special, and recognizing and reminding yourself of this reality is so beneficial for your emotional health. It is never your fault when someone chooses to be abusive to you, and it has no reflection on the great value you have as person.

Remember That You Deserve to Be Kind to Yourself: Taking time to practice self-care every day, even if it is only for a few minutes, really creates space for peace and emotional safety. It's healthy to give yourself emotional breaks and step back from your situation sometimes. In the end, this can help you make the decisions that are best for you.

Leaving a Relationship

Preparing to Leave

Because violence could escalate when someone tries to leave, here are some things to keep in mind before you leave:

- Keep any evidence of physical abuse, such as pictures of injuries.
- Keep a journal of all violent incidences, noting dates, events and threats made, if possible. Keep your journal in a safe place.
- Know where you can go to get help. Tell someone what is happening to you.
- If you are injured, go to a doctor or an emergency room and report what happened to you. Ask that they document your visit.
- Plan with your children and identify a safe place for them, like a room with a lock or a friend's house where they can go for help. Reassure them that their job is to stay safe, not to protect you.
- Contact your local shelter and find out about laws and other resources available to you before you have to use them during a crisis. WomensLaw.org has state by state legal information.
- Acquire job skills or take courses at a community college as you can.
- Try to set money aside or ask friends or family members to hold money for you.

© garagestock/Shutterstock.com

When You Leave

Make a plan for how and where you will escape quickly. You may request a police escort or stand-by when you leave. If you have to leave in a hurry, use the following list of items as a guide to what you need to bring with you.

1) *Identification*
   - Driver's license
   - Birth certificate and children's birth certificates
   - Social security cards
   - Financial information
   - Money and/or credit cards (in your name)
   - Checking and/or savings account books

2) *Legal Papers*
   - Protective order
   - Copies of any lease or rental agreements, or the deed to your home
   - Car registration and insurance papers
   - Health and life insurance papers
   - Medical records for you and your children
   - School records
   - Work permits/green card/visa
   - Passport
   - Divorce and custody papers
   - Marriage license

3) *Emergency Numbers*
   - Your local police and/or sheriff's department
   - Your local domestic violence program or shelter
   - Friends, relatives, and family members
   - Your local doctor's office and hospital
   - County and/or District Attorney's Office

4) *Other*
   - Medications
   - Extra set of house and car keys
   - Valuable jewelry
   - Pay-as-you-go cell phone
   - Address book
   - Pictures and sentimental items
   - Several changes of clothes for you and your children
   - Emergency money

© Sylverarts Vectors/Shutterstock.com

After You Leave

Your safety plan should include ways to ensure your continued safety after leaving an abusive relationship. Here are some safety precautions to consider:

- Change your locks and phone number.
- Call the telephone company to request caller ID. Ask that your phone number be blocked so that if you call anyone, neither your partner nor anyone else will be able to get your new, unlisted phone number.
- Change your work hours and the route you take to work.
- Change the route taken to transport children to school or consider changing your children's schools.
- Alert school authorities of the situation.
- If you have a restraining order, keep a certified copy of it with you at all times, and inform friends, neighbors, and employers that you have a restraining order in effect.
- Call law enforcement to enforce the order and give copies of the restraining order to employers, neighbors, and schools along with a picture of the offender.
- Consider renting a post office box or using the address of a friend for your mail (be aware that addresses are on restraining orders and police reports, and be careful to whom you give your new address and phone number).
- Reschedule appointments that the offender is aware of.
- Use different stores and frequent different social spots.
- Alert neighbors and request that they call the police if they feel you may be in danger.
- Replace wooden doors with steel or metal doors. Install security systems if possible.
- Install a motion sensitive lighting system.
- Tell people you work with about the situation and have your calls screened by one receptionist if possible.
- Tell people who take care of your children or drive them/pick them up from school and activities. Explain your situation to them and provide them with a copy of the restraining order.

Legal Information

Restraining Orders/ Protective Orders

There are some legal actions you can take to help keep yourself safe from your abusive partner. The Hotline does not give legal advice, but there are some great resources available to you in your community.

You can also visit WomensLaw.org and search state by state for information on laws including restraining orders and child custody information.

A protective order can help protect you immediately by legally keeping your partner from physically coming near you, harming you or harassing you, your children or your family members. This legal documentation to keep your abusive partner away from you can often contain provisions related to custody, finance and more.

While protective orders may be able to put a stop to physical abuse, psychological abuse is still possible—so a protective order should never replace a safety plan.

If you already have a protective order, it should be kept on you at all times—and copies should be given to your children and anyone they might be with—especially when you're leaving your partner.

You can get an application for a protective order at:

- Courthouses
- Women's shelters
- Volunteer legal services offices and some police stations.

Other Legal Actions

You also have the right to file a charge against your partner for things such as criminal assault, aggravated assault, harassment, stalking, or interfering with child custody. Ask a volunteer legal services organization (attorneys who provide free legal services to low-income individuals) or an advocacy group in your area about the policies in your local court.

Not a U.S. citizen?

Learn more at Casa De Esperanza about your rights as an immigrant.

According to the Violence Against Women Act (VAWA), immigrant women who are experiencing domestic violence—and are married to abusers who are US Citizens or Legal Permanent Residents—may qualify to self-petition for legal status under VAWA.

© arka38/Shutterstock.com

WHAT IS A HEALTHY RELATIONSHIP?

People define relationships in many different ways, but for a relationship to be healthy you need:

- Safe communication
- Trust
- Boundaries
- Mutual respect

Healthy

A healthy relationship means that both you and your partner are:

- *Communicating*: You talk openly about problems and listen to one another. You respect each other's opinions.
- *Respectful*: You value each other as you are.
- *Trusting*: You believe what your partner has to say. You do not feel the need to "prove" each other's trustworthiness.
- *Honest*: You are honest with each other, but can still keep some things private.
- *Equal:* You make decisions together and hold each other to the same standard.
- *Enjoying personal time*: You both enjoy spending time apart, alone or with others. You respect each other's need for time apart.
- *Making mutual sexual choices*: You talk openly about sexual and reproductive choices together. You both willingly consent to sexual activity and can safely discuss what you are and are not comfortable with.
- *Economic/financial partners*: You and your partner have equal say with regard to finances. Both partners have access to the resources they need.
- *Engaging in supportive parenting*: Both partners are able to parent in a way they feel comfortable with. You communicate together about the needs of the child(ren), as well as the needs of both parents.

Unhealthy

You may be in an unhealthy relationship if one or both partners is:

- *Not communicating:* When problems arise, you fight or you don't discuss them at all.
- *Disrespectful:* One or both partners is not considerate of the other.
- *Not trusting:* One partner doesn't believe what the other says, or feels entitled to invade their privacy.
- *Dishonest:* One or both partners tells lies.
- *Trying to take control:* One partner feels their desires and choices are more important.
- *Only spending time with your partner:* Your partner's community is the only one you socialize in.
- *Pressured by the other into sexual activity:* One partner uses pressure or guilt on the other to have sex or do anything sexual at any point.

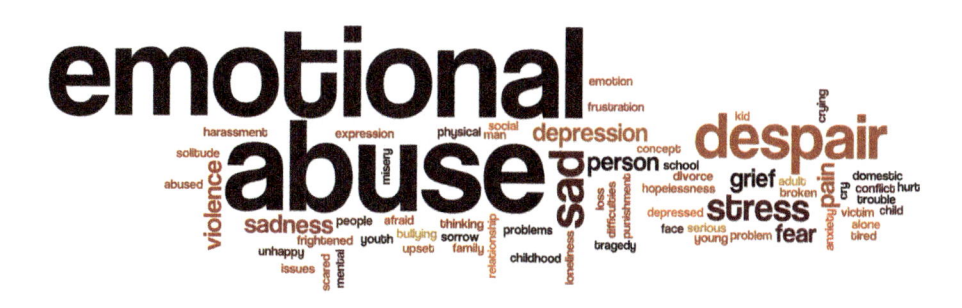

- *Ignoring a partner's boundaries:* It is assumed only one partner is responsible for making informed decisions.
- *Unequal economically:* Finances are not discussed, and/or it is assumed only one partner is in charge of finances.

Abusive Relationship

Abuse is occurring in a relationship when one partner:

- Communicates in a way that is hurtful, threatening, insulting or demeaning.
- Mistreats the other: One partner does not respect the feelings, thoughts, decisions, opinions or physical safety of the other.
- Accuses the other of cheating or having an affair when it's not true: The partner who accuses may hurt the other in a physical or verbal way as a result.
- Denies that the abusive actions are abuse: An abusive partner may try to blame the other for the harm they're doing, or makes excuses for abusive actions or minimizes the abusive behavior.
- Controls the other: There is no equality in the relationship. One partner makes all decisions for the couple without the other's input.
- Isolates the other partner: One partner controls where the other one goes and who they talk to. They may isolate their partner from family and friends.
- Forces sexual activity or pregnancy: One partner forces the other to have sex, or do anything they don't want to do sexually at any point. In relationships where pregnancy is a physical possibility, one partner may force the other to become pregnant.
- Exerts economic control: One partner controls the money and access to resources. Having an open dialogue about finances is not an option. This may include preventing a partner from earning an income or not allowing a partner access to their own income.
- Engages in manipulative parenting: One partner uses the child(ren) to gain power and control over the other partner, including telling the child(ren) lies or negative things about the other partner.

SETTING BOUNDARIES

A healthy relationship starts with mutual respect, including respect for each other's emotional, physical and digital boundaries. It's important for partners to know each other's concerns, limits, desires, and feelings, and to be prepared to respect them. Setting personal boundaries can be an ongoing process in a relationship. People and relationships evolve, and everyone has the right to change or adjust their boundaries as they see fit. Creating open conversations about boundaries in a relationship can help ensure that all partners' boundaries are respected at all times. Here are some helpful questions to ask yourself when considering boundaries in your relationship:

Does each partner get the space they need to live healthy lives as individuals?

As great as it is to want to spend time with your partner, it's important to have some time away from each other, too. It's not healthy for either partner to try to set limits or use guilt or pressure to control where their partner goes or who they spend time with. Everyone should feel free to spend time alone or with friends and family without having to get permission from their partner or check in and explain their whereabouts. If boundaries around personal space are not being respected, that may be a sign that one or both partners is having trouble with trust.

Is intimacy comfortable and consensual at all times?

Sexual consent is absolutely essential in a relationship, whether you're just starting to date or you've been married for years. Sex should never feel obligatory, and you should always feel that your partner cares about your comfort and boundaries. Everyone has different backgrounds, desires, and comfort levels when it comes to intimacy, sex, and methods of protection. It's important to feel comfortable communicating your boundaries around intimacy and to trust that your partner will always respect them.

It can help to talk with your partner about boundaries and expectations around sex before you're in the moment, as well as, talking about how you'd like to communicate with each other in the moment to make sure you are both aware of each other's boundaries throughout. While discussing boundaries beforehand can help, even in the moment you always have the right to set boundaries or change your mind. People's levels of comfort and desire change, so it should never be assumed that just because someone was okay with something in the past, they will always be okay with it. No matter how long you've been with someone or how many times you've done something, you have the right to say no at anytime for any reason.

Is there mutual respect for privacy?

Everyone has the right to privacy, and that's not something you should have to give up to be in a relationship. While it's okay to share personal information like passwords to social media, bank accounts, email, phone, etc. if you wish to, it should never feel required and it's completely reasonable to keep those private. Having access to another's personal accounts or information also doesn't give anyone the right to look through them without the owner's permission. Even if you have shared passwords with your partner, you have every right to expect them to respect your privacy and boundaries. Leaving your private accounts open is never an invitation to invade your privacy. Talking with your partner about what you do and don't wish to share can be a great way to lay some ground rules around privacy.

Do you and your partner respect each other's boundaries without getting angry or making each other feel bad?

You should always feel comfortable communicating your boundaries to your partner without being afraid of how they'll react. Personal boundaries shouldn't feel like castle walls during a siege. Once you have set boundaries, you shouldn't feel like you have to actively defend or reiterate them to have them be respected by your partner, and vice versa. In a healthy relationship, both people want their partner to feel happy, respected and comfortable and they use knowledge of each other's boundaries to help them understand how to keep the relationship happy and healthy. Using pressure, making you feel guilty, or arguing with you about whether your boundaries are reasonable is not respectful or healthy. If you don't feel comfortable or safe setting boundaries, or your boundaries are not being respected by your partner, that can be a red flag for unhealthy or abusive dynamics in the relationship.

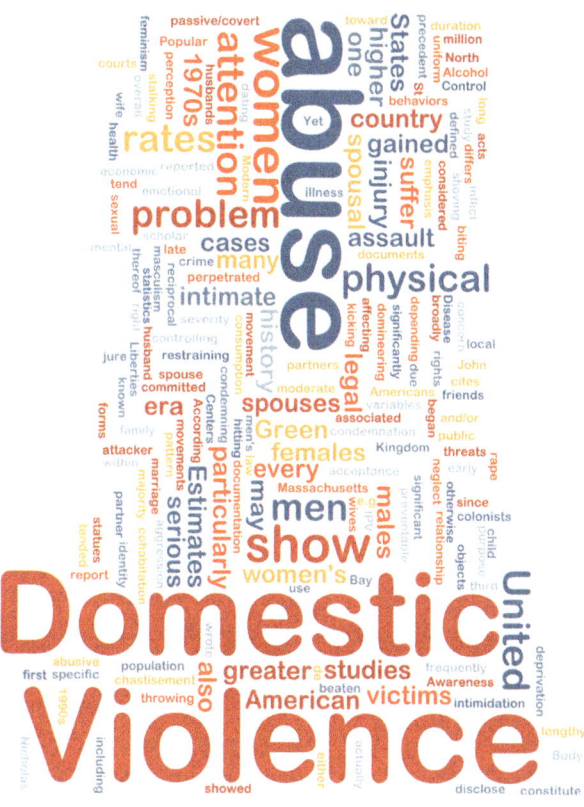

© Kheng Guan Toh/Shutterstock.com

WHAT DOES AN ABUSIVE RELATIONSHIP LOOK LIKE?

Traits of an Abusive Relationship

- Insult, demean, or embarrass you with put-downs?
- Control what you do, who you talk to, or where you go?
- Look at you or act in ways that scare you?
- Push you, slap you, choke you, or hit you?
- Stop you from seeing your friends or family members?
- Control the money in the relationship? Take your money or Social Security check, make you ask for money or refuse to give you money?
- Make all of the decisions without your input or consideration of your needs?
- Tell you that you're a bad parent or threaten to take away your children?
- Prevent you from working or attending school?
- Act like the abuse is no big deal, deny the abuse, or tell you it's your own fault?
- Destroy your property or threaten to kill your pets?
- Intimidate you with guns, knives, or other weapons?
- Attempt to force you to drop criminal charges?
- Threaten to commit suicide, or threaten to kill you?

WARNING SIGNS AND RED FLAGS

It's not always easy to tell at the beginning of a relationship if it will become abusive.

In fact, many abusive partners may seem absolutely perfect in the early stages of a relationship. Possessive and controlling behaviors don't always appear overnight, but rather emerge and intensify as the relationship grows.

Domestic violence doesn't look the same in every relationship because every relationship is different. But one thing most abusive relationships have in common is that the abusive partner does many different kinds of things to have more power and control over their partners.

If you're beginning to feel as if your partner or a loved one's partner is becoming abusive, there are a few behaviors that you can look out for. Watch out for these red flags and if you're experiencing one or more of them in your relationship.

- Telling you that you can never do anything right
- Showing jealousy of your friends and time spent away
- Keeping you or discouraging you from seeing friends or family members
- Insulting, demeaning, or shaming you with put-downs
- Controlling every penny spent in the household
- Taking your money or refusing to give you money for expenses
- Looking at you or acting in ways that scare you
- Controlling who you see, where you go, or what you do
- Preventing you from making your own decisions
- Telling you that you are a bad parent or threatening to harm or take away your children
- Preventing you from working or attending school
- Destroying your property or threatening to hurt or kill your pets
- Intimidating you with guns, knives, or other weapons
- Pressuring you to have sex when you don't want to or do things sexually you're not comfortable with
- Pressuring you to use drugs or alcohol

WHAT IS ABUSE?

Domestic violence can happen to anyone of any race, age, sexual orientation, religion or gender.

It can happen to couples who are married, living together or who are dating. Domestic violence affects people of all socioeconomic backgrounds and education levels.

Abuse is a repetitive pattern of behaviors to maintain power and control over an intimate partner. These are behaviors that physically harm, arouse fear, prevent a partner from doing what they wish or force them to behave in ways they do not want. Abuse includes the use of physical and sexual violence, threats and intimidation, emotional abuse and economic deprivation. Many of these different forms of abuse can be going on at any one time.

TYPES OF ABUSE

Physical Abuse

- You may be experiencing physical abuse if your partner has done or repeatedly does any of the following tactics of abuse:
- Pulling your hair, punching, slapping, kicking, biting, or choking you
- Forbidding you from eating or sleeping
- Hurting you with weapons
- Preventing you from calling the police or seeking medical attention
- Harming your children
- Abandoning you in unfamiliar places
- Driving recklessly or dangerously when you are in the car with them
- Forcing you to use drugs or alcohol (especially if you've had a substance abuse problem in the past)

© pockygallery/Shutterstock.com

Emotional Abuse

- Calling you names, insulting you, or continually criticizing you
- Refusing to trust you and acting jealous or possessive
- Trying to isolate you from family or friends
- Monitoring where you go, who you call, and who you spend time with
- Demanding to know where you are every minute
- Trapping you in your home or preventing you from leaving
- Using weapons to threaten to hurt you
- Punishing you by withholding affection
- Threatening to hurt you, the children, your family, or your pets
- Damaging your property when they're angry (throwing objects, punching walls, kicking doors, etc.)
- Humiliating you in any way
- Blaming you for the abuse
- Gaslighting
- Accusing you of cheating and being often jealous of your outside relationships
- Serially cheating on you and then blaming you for his or her behavior
- Cheating on you intentionally to hurt you and then threatening to cheat again
- Cheating to prove that they are more desired, worthy, etc. than you are
- Attempting to control your appearance: what you wear, how much/little makeup you wear, etc.
- Telling you that you will never find anyone better, or that you are lucky to be with a person like them

© hafakot/Shutterstock.com

Sexual Abuse and Coercion

Sexually abusive methods of retaining power and control include an abusive partner:

- Forcing you to dress in a sexual way
- Insulting you in sexual ways or calls you sexual names
- Forcing or manipulating you into to having sex or performing sexual acts
- Holding you down during sex
- Demanding sex when you're sick, tired or after hurting you
- Hurting you with weapons or objects during sex
- Involving other people in sexual activities with you against your will
- Ignoring your feelings regarding sex
- Forcing you to watch pornography
- Purposefully trying to pass on a sexually transmitted disease to you

© ibreakstock/Shutterstock.com

Sexual Coercion

Sexual coercion lies on the 'continuum' of sexually aggressive behavior. It can vary from being egged on and persuaded, to being forced to have contact. It can be verbal and emotional, in the form of statements that make you feel pressure, guilt, or shame. You can also be made to feel forced through more subtle actions. For example, an abusive partner:

- Making you feel like you owe them—ex. Because you're in a relationship, because you've had sex before, because they spent money on you or bought you a gift
- Giving you drugs and alcohol to "loosen up" your inhibitions
- Playing on the fact that you're in a relationship, saying things such as: "Sex is the way to prove your love for me," "If I don't get sex from you I'll get it somewhere else"
- Reacting negatively with sadness, anger, or resentment if you say no or don't immediately agree to something
- Continuing to pressure you after you say no
- Making you feel threatened or afraid of what might happen if you say no
- Trying to normalize their sexual expectations: ex. "I need it, I'm a man"

Even if your partner isn't forcing you to do sexual acts against your will, being made to feel obligated is coercion in itself. Dating someone, being in a relationship, or being married never means that you owe your partner intimacy of any kind.

Reproductive Coercion

Reproductive coercion is a form of power and control where one partner strips the other of the ability to control their own reproductive system. It is sometimes difficult to identify this coercion because other forms of abuse are often occurring simultaneously.

Reproductive coercion can be exerted in many ways:

- Refusing to use a condom or other type of birth control
- Breaking or removing a condom during intercourse
- Lying about their methods of birth control (ex. lying about having a vasectomy, lying about being on the pill)
- Refusing to "pull out" if that is the agreed upon method of birth control
- Forcing you to not use any birth control (ex. the pill, condom, shot, ring, etc.)
- Removing birth control methods (ex. rings, IUDs, contraceptive patches)
- Sabotaging birth control methods (ex. poking holes in condoms, tampering with pills or flushing them down the toilet)
- Withholding finances needed to purchase birth control
- Monitoring your menstrual cycles
- Forcing pregnancy and not supporting your decision about when or if you want to have a child
- Forcing you to get an abortion, or preventing you from getting one
- Threatening you or acting violent if you don't comply with their wishes to either end or continue a pregnancy
- Continually keeping you pregnant (getting you pregnant again shortly after you give birth)

Reproductive coercion can also come in the form of pressure, guilt, and shame from an abusive partner. Some examples are if your abusive partner is constantly talking about having children or making you feel guilty for not having or wanting children with them—especially if you already have kids with someone else.

Financial Abuse

Economic or financial abuse is when an abusive partner extends their power and control into the area of finances. This abuse can take different forms, including an abusive partner:

- Giving an allowance and closely watching how you spend it or demanding receipts for purchases
- Placing your paycheck in their bank account and denying you access to it
- Preventing you from viewing or having access to bank accounts
- Forbidding you to work or limiting the hours that you can work
- Maxing out credit cards in your name without permission or not paying the bills on credit cards, which could ruin your credit score
- Stealing money from you or your family and friends
- Using funds from children's savings accounts without your permission
- Living in your home but refusing to work or contribute to the household
- Making you give them your tax returns or confiscating joint tax returns
- Refusing to give you money to pay for necessities/shared expenses like food, clothing, transportation, or medical care and medicine

© Photoroyalty/Shutterstock.com

Digital Abuse

Digital abuse is the use of technologies such as texting and social networking to bully, harass, stalk or intimidate a partner. Often this behavior is a form of verbal or emotional abuse perpetrated online. You may be experiencing digital abuse if your partner:

- Tells you who you can or can't be friends with on Facebook and other sites.
- Sends you negative, insulting, or even threatening emails, Facebook messages, tweets, DMs or other messages online.
- Uses sites like Facebook, Twitter, Foursquare, and others to keep constant tabs on you.
- Puts you down in their status updates.
- Sends you unwanted, explicit pictures and demands you send some in return.
- Pressures you to send explicit video.
- Steals or insists to be given your passwords.
- Constantly texts you and makes you feel like you can't be separated from your phone for fear that you will be punished.
- Looks through your phone frequently, checks up on your pictures, texts, and outgoing calls.
- Tags you unkindly in pictures on Instagram, Tumblr, etc.

© zimmytws/Shutterstock.com

WHY DO PEOPLE ABUSE?

Domestic violence and abuse stem from a desire to gain and maintain power and control over an intimate partner. Abusive people believe they have the right to control and restrict their partners, and they may enjoy the feeling that exerting power gives them. They often believe that their own feelings and needs should be the priority in their relationships, so they use abusive tactics to dismantle equality and make their partners feel less valuable and deserving of respect in the relationship.

No matter why it happens, abuse is not okay and it's never justified.

Abuse is a learned behavior. Sometimes people see it in their own families. Other times they learn it from friends or popular culture. However, abuse is a choice, and it's not one that anyone has to make. Many people who experience or witness abuse growing up decide not to use those negative and hurtful ways of behaving in their own relationships. While outside forces such as drug or alcohol addiction can sometimes escalate abuse, it's most important to recognize that these issues do not cause abuse.

WHO CAN BE IN AN ABUSIVE RELATIONSHIP?

Anyone can be abusive and anyone can be the victim of abuse. It happens regardless of gender, age, sexual orientation, race, or economic background. While an abusive person often blames their partner to justify their behavior, abuse has nothing to do with the person it's directed at, and it's never a result of anything to do with the relationship or a particular situation. Abuse is a personal choice and a strategic behavior used to create the abusive person's desired power dynamic. Regardless of the circumstances of the relationship or the pasts of either partner, no one ever deserves to be abused.

WHY DO PEOPLE STAY IN ABUSIVE RELATIONSHIPS?

People who have never been abused often wonder why a person wouldn't just leave an abusive relationship. They don't understand that leaving can be more complicated than it seems.

Leaving is often the most dangerous time for a victim of abuse, because abuse is about power and control. When a victim leaves, they are taking control and threatening the abusive partner's power, which could cause the abusive partner to retaliate in very destructive ways.

Aside from this danger, there are many reasons why people stay in abusive relationships. Here are just a few of the common ones:

- Fear: A person may be afraid of what will happen if they decide to leave the relationship.
- Believing abuse is normal: A person may not know what a healthy relationship looks like, perhaps from growing up in an environment where abuse was common, and they may not recognize that their relationship is unhealthy.
- Fear of being outed: If someone is in an LGBTQ relationship and has not yet come out to everyone, their partner may threaten to reveal this secret.
- Embarrassment or shame: It's often difficult for someone to admit that they've been abused. They may feel they've done something wrong by becoming involved with an abusive partner. They may also worry that their friends and family will judge them.
- Low self-esteem: When an abusive partner constantly puts someone down and blames them for the abuse, it can be easy for the victim to believe those statements and think that the abuse is their fault.
- Love: So often, the victim feels love for their abusive partner. They may have children with them and want to maintain their family. Abusive people can often be charming, especially at the beginning of a relationship, and the victim may hope that their partner will go back to being that person. They may only want the violence to stop, not for the relationship to end entirely.
- Cultural/religious reasons: Traditional gender roles supported by someone's culture or religion may influence them to stay rather than end the relationship for fear of bringing shame upon their family.
- Language barriers/immigration status: If a person is undocumented, they may fear that reporting the abuse will affect their immigration status. Also, if their first language isn't English, it can be difficult to express the depth of their situation to others.
- Lack of money/resources: Financial abuse is common, and a victim may be financially dependent on their abusive partner. Without money, access to resources, or even a place to go, it can seem impossible for them to leave the relationship. This feeling of helplessness can be especially strong if the person lives with their abusive partner.
- Disability: When someone is physically dependent on their abusive partner, they can feel that their well-being is connected to the relationship. This dependency could heavily influence their decision to stay in an abusive relationship.

LGBTQ RELATIONSHIP VIOLENCE

Abusive partners in LGBTQ relationships use all the same tactics to gain power and control as abusive partners in heterosexual relationships—physical, sexual, or emotional abuse, financial control, isolation, and more.

But abusive partners in LGBTQ relationships also reinforce their tactics that maintain power and control with societal factors that compound the complexity a survivor faces in leaving or getting safe in an LGBTQ relationship.

Tactics of Power and Control for LGBTQ

"Outing" a partner's sexual orientation or gender identity. Abusive partners in LGBTQ relationships may threaten to 'out' victims to family members, employers, community members, and others.

Saying that no one will help the victim because s/he is lesbian, gay, bisexual, or transgender, or that for this reason, the partner "deserves" the abuse.

Justifying the abuse with the notion that a partner is not "really" lesbian, gay, bisexual, or transgender (i.e., the victim may once have had/may still have relationships, or express a gender identity, inconsistent with the abuser's definitions of these terms). This can be used both as a tool in verbal and emotional abuse as well as to further the isolation of a victim from the community.

Monopolizing support resources through an abusive partner's manipulation of friends and family supports and generating sympathy and trust in order to cut off these resources to the victim. This is a particular issue to members of the LGBTQ community where they may be fewer specific resources, neighborhoods, or social outlets.

Portraying the violence as mutual and even consensual, or as an expression of masculinity or some other "desirable" trait.

The Domestic Abuse Intervention Program located in Duluth, MN created the image of the Power and Control wheel. The wheel was created based off of the lived experiences from woman who participated in focus groups. It is used as a conceptual tool to help people see the patterns in behavior and their significance.

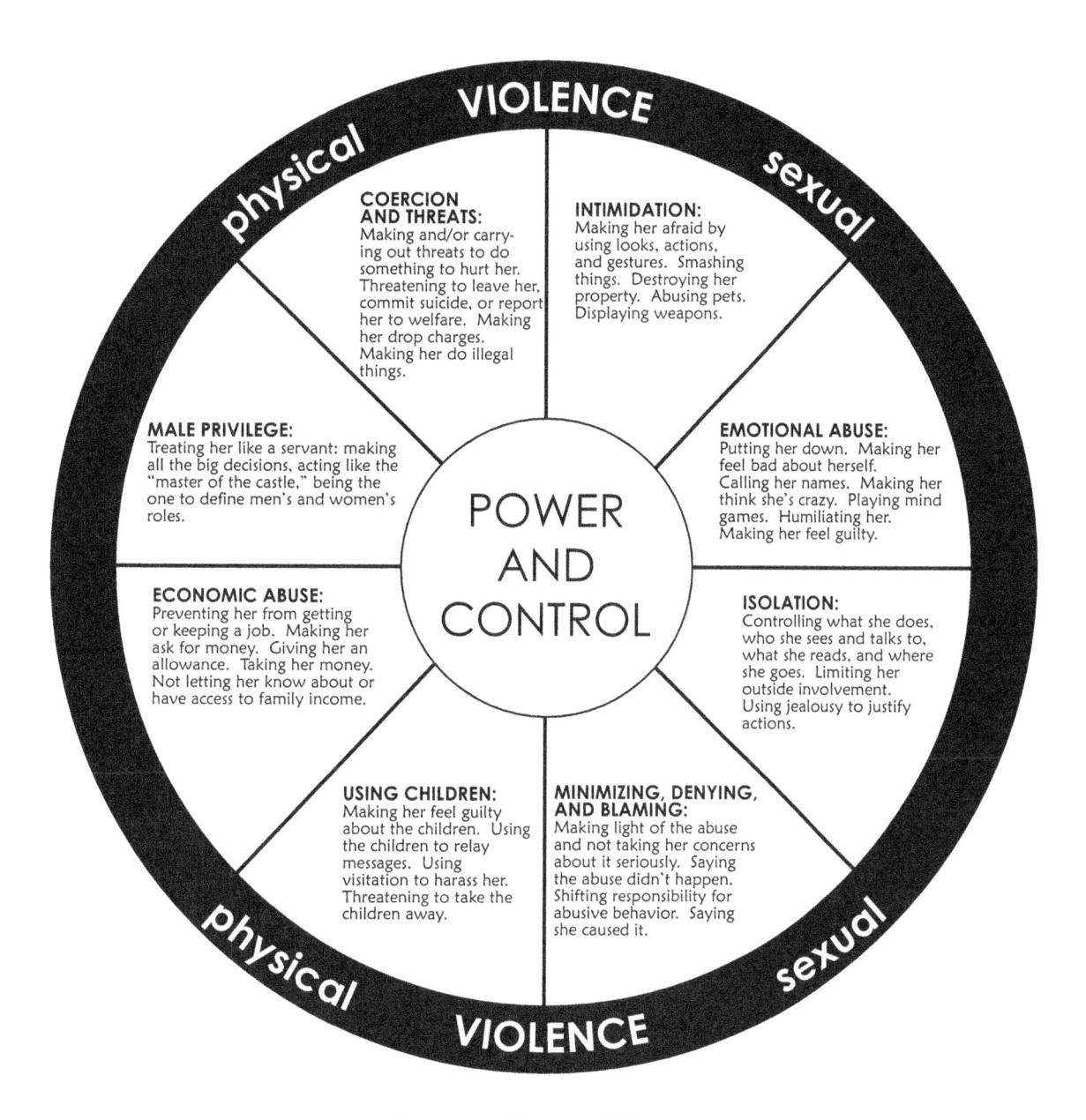

Power and Control Wheel

The wheel is surrounded by an outer ring labeled with **VIOLENCE** — physical, sexual — and is divided into eight segments around the center "POWER AND CONTROL":

- **COERCION AND THREATS:** Making and/or carrying out threats to do something to hurt her. Threatening to leave her, commit suicide, or report her to welfare. Making her drop charges. Making her do illegal things.

- **INTIMIDATION:** Making her afraid by using looks, actions, and gestures. Smashing things. Destroying her property. Abusing pets. Displaying weapons.

- **EMOTIONAL ABUSE:** Putting her down. Making her feel bad about herself. Calling her names. Making her think she's crazy. Playing mind games. Humiliating her. Making her feel guilty.

- **ISOLATION:** Controlling what she does, who she sees and talks to, what she reads, and where she goes. Limiting her outside involvement. Using jealousy to justify actions.

- **MINIMIZING, DENYING, AND BLAMING:** Making light of the abuse and not taking her concerns about it seriously. Saying the abuse didn't happen. Shifting responsibility for abusive behavior. Saying she caused it.

- **USING CHILDREN:** Making her feel guilty about the children. Using the children to relay messages. Using visitation to harass her. Threatening to take the children away.

- **ECONOMIC ABUSE:** Preventing her from getting or keeping a job. Making her ask for money. Giving her an allowance. Taking her money. Not letting her know about or have access to family income.

- **MALE PRIVILEGE:** Treating her like a servant: making all the big decisions, acting like the "master of the castle," being the one to define men's and women's roles.

© Domestic Abuse Intervention Project
202 East Superior Street
Duluth, Minnesota 55802
218-722-2781
www.duluth-model.org

CHAPTER 5 Victims of Domestic Abuse (Intimate Partner Violence)

The Domestic Abuse Intervention Program located in Duluth, MN created the image of the Power and Control wheel. The wheel was created based off of the lived experiences from woman who participated in focus groups. It is used as a conceptual tool to help people see the patterns in behavior and their significance.

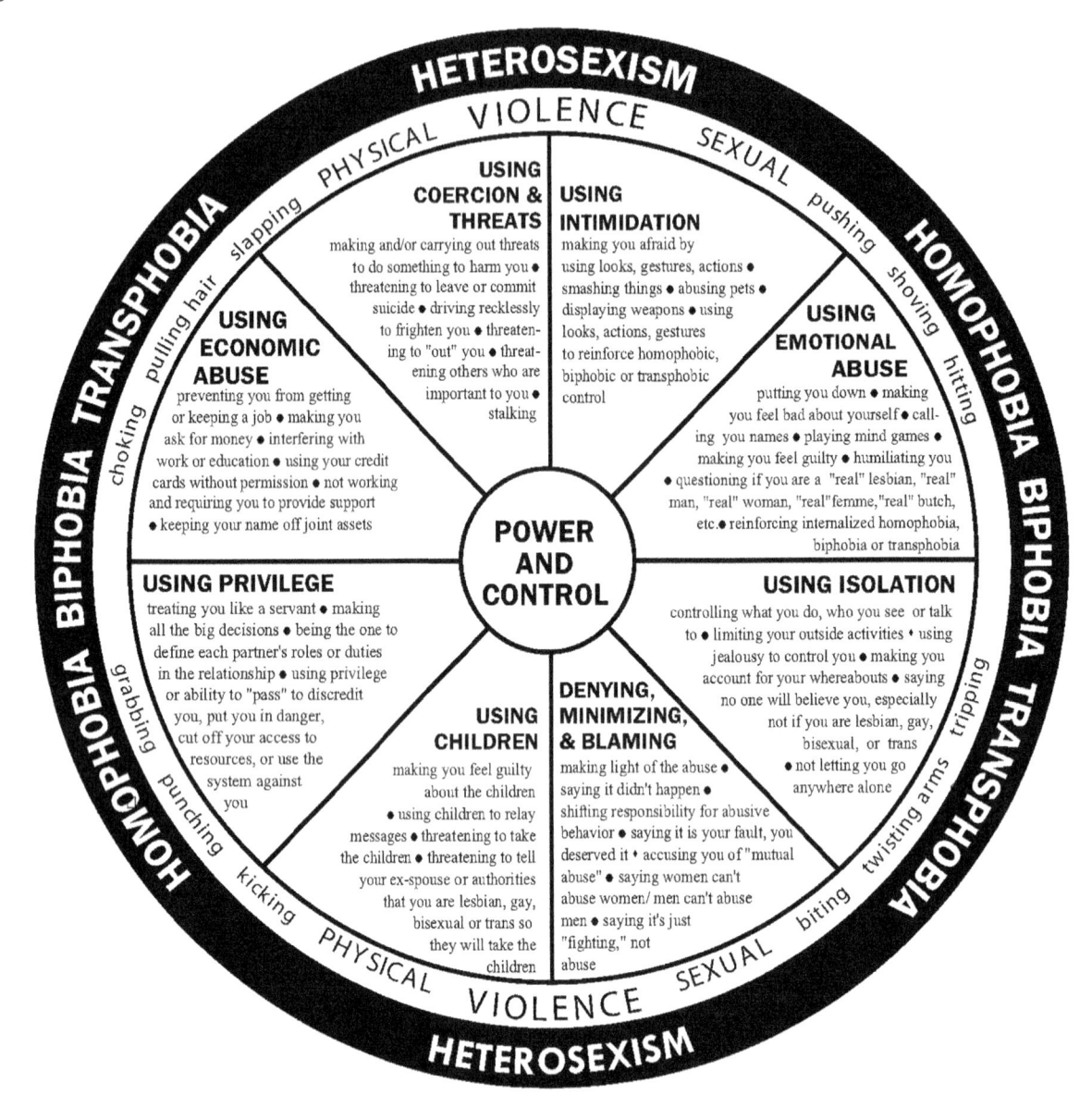

Power and Control Wheel for Lesbian, Gay, Bisexual, and Trans Relationships

© Domestic Abuse Intervention Project
202 East Superior Street
Duluth, Minnesota 55802
218-722-2781
www.duluth-model.org
Texas Council on Family Violence

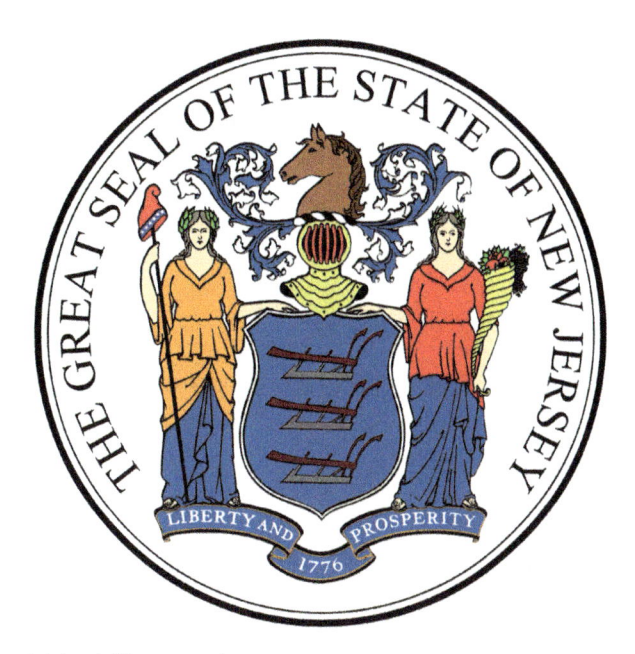

© Atlaspix/Shutterstock.com

The following is an example of how one state, New Jersey, empowers law enforcement to deal with incidents of domestic violence.

DOMESTIC VIOLENCE

Guidelines on Police Response Procedures in Domestic Violence Cases

Issued October 1991

Revised November 1994

Introduction. These general guidelines consolidate the police response procedures for domestic violence cases, including abuse and neglect of the elderly and disabled, based on state law, court rules, and the Domestic Violence Procedures Manual which was jointly prepared by the New Jersey Supreme Court and the Attorney General through the Division of Criminal Justice.

I. Definitions.

   A. Domestic violence means the occurrence of one or more of the following criminal offenses upon a person protected under the Prevention of Domestic Violence Act of 1990:
   - Homicide N.J.S.A. 2C:11-1
   - Assault N.J.S.A. 2C:12-1
   - Terroristic threats N.J.S.A. 2C:12-3
   - Kidnapping N.J.S.A. 2C:13-1
   - Criminal restraint N.J.S.A. 2C:13-2
   - False imprisonment N.J.S.A. 2C:13-3
   - Sexual assault N.J.S.A. 2C:14-2
   - Criminal sexual contact. N.J.S.A. 2C:14-3
   - Lewdness N.J.S.A. 2C:14-4
   - Criminal mischief. N.J.S.A. 2C:17-3

- Burglary N.J.S.A. 2C:18-2
- Criminal trespass N.J.S.A. 2C:18-3
- Harassment N.J.S.A. 2C:33-4
- Stalking N.J.S.A. 2C:12-10

B. Victim of Domestic Violence means a person protected by the Domestic Violence Act and includes any person:

1. who is eighteen years of age or older, or

2. who is an emancipated minor, and who has been subjected to domestic violence by:

    a. spouse

    b. former spouse

    c. any other person who is a present or former household member, OR

3. who, regardless of age, has been subjected to domestic violence by a person:

    a. with whom the victim has a child in common, or

    b. with whom the victim anticipates having a child in common, if one of the parties is pregnant, or

4. who, regardless of age, has been subjected to domestic violence by a person with whom the victim has had a dating relationship.

    a. A victim may be below the age of eighteen.

    b. The domestic violence assailant must be over the age of eighteen or emancipated at the time of the offense. See paragraph C3 below for criteria for determining whether a person is emancipated.

C. Note:

1. The Prevention of Domestic Violence Act does not define a victim of domestic violence by age, physical or psychological condition, or sex.

2. AN UNEMANCIPATED MINOR WHO COMMITS AN ACT OF DOMESTIC VIOLENCE MAY NOT BE PROSECUTED AS A DOMESTIC VIOLENCE DEFENDANT BUT CAN BE PROSECUTED UNDER THE JUVENILE DELINQUENCY LAWS. THE ENTRY OF PRE- OR POST-DISPOSITIONAL RESTRAINTS CAN ALSO BE CONSIDERED.

3. A minor is considered emancipated from his or her parents when the minor:

    a. has been married;

    b. has entered military service;

    c. has a child or is pregnant; or

    d. has been previously declared by a court or an administrative agency to be emancipated.

II. Mandatory Arrest. A police officer must arrest and take into custody a domestic violence suspect and must sign the criminal complaint against that person if:

   A. The victim exhibits signs of injury caused by an act of domestic violence. N.J.S.A. 2C:25-21a(1).

      1. The word, "exhibits," is to be liberally construed to mean any indication that a victim has suffered bodily injury, which shall include physical pain or any impairment of physical condition. Probable cause to arrest also may be established when the police officer observes manifestations of an internal injury suffered by the victim.

      2. Where the victim exhibits no visible sign of injury, but states that an injury has occurred, the officer should consider other relevant factors in determining whether there is probable cause to make an arrest.

      3. In determining which party in a domestic violence incident is the victim where both parties exhibit signs of injury, the officer should consider:

         a. the comparative extent of injuries suffered;

         b. the history of domestic violence between the parties, if any, or

         c. other relevant factors.

      4. Police shall follow standard procedures in rendering or summoning emergency treatment of the victim, if required.

   B. There is probable cause to believe that the terms of a no contact court order have been violated. If the victim does not have a copy of the court order, the officer may verify the existence of an order with the appropriate law enforcement agency.

   C. A warrant is in effect.

   D. There is probable cause to believe that a weapon as defined in N.J.S.A. 2C:39-1r has been involved in the commission of an act of domestic violence.

III. Discretionary Arrest. A police officer may arrest a person or may sign a criminal complaint against that person, or may do both, where there is probable cause to believe that an act of domestic violence has been committed but none of the conditions in Section II above applies.

IV. Seizure of Weapons.

   A. Seizure of a Weapon for Safekeeping.

      A police officer who has probable cause to believe that an act of domestic violence has been committed may:

      1. Question all persons present to determine whether there are weapons, as defined in

         N.J.S.A. 2C:39-1r, on the premises.

      2. If an officer sees or learns that a weapon is present within the premises of a domestic violence incident and reasonably believes that the weapon would expose the victim to a risk of serious bodily injury, the officer should attempt to gain possession of the weapon.

3. If the weapon is in plain view, the officer should seize the weapon.

4. If the weapon is not in plain view but is located within the premises jointly possessed by both the domestic violence assailant and the domestic violence victim, the officer should obtain the consent, preferably in writing, of the domestic violence victim to search for and to seize the weapon.

5. If the weapon is not located within the premises jointly possessed by the domestic violence victim and assailant but is located upon other premises, the officer should attempt to obtain possession of the weapon from the possessor of the weapon, either the domestic violence assailant or a third party, by a voluntary surrender of the weapon.

6. If the domestic violence assailant or the possessor of the weapon refuses to surrender the weapon or to allow the officer to enter the premises to search for the named weapon, the officer should obtain a Domestic Violence Warrant for the Search and Seizure of Weapons. [See Appendix 13.]

B. Seizure of a Weapon Pursuant to Court Order.

1. If a domestic violence victim obtains a court order directing that the domestic violence assailant surrender a named weapon, the officer should demand that the person surrender the named weapon.

2. If the domestic violence assailant or the possessor of the weapon refuses to surrender the weapon, the officer should:

    a. inform the person that the court order authorizes a search and seizure of the premises for the named weapon, and

    b. arrest the person, if the person refuses to surrender the named weapon, for failing to comply with the court order, N.J.S.A. 2C:29-9, and

    c. conduct a search of the named premises for the named weapon.

C. The officer must append an inventory of seized weapons to the domestic violence offense report.

D. Weapons seized by a police officer must be promptly delivered to the county prosecutor along with a copy of the domestic violence offense report and, where applicable, the domestic violence complaint and temporary restraining order.

V. Domestic Violence Complaint.

A. Notice. When a police officer responds to a call of a domestic violence incident, the officer must give and explain to the victim the domestic violence notice of rights which advises the victim of available court action. N.J.S.A. 2C:25-23. The victim may file:

1. A domestic violence complaint alleging the defendant committed an act of domestic violence and asking for court assistance to prevent its recurrence by asking for a temporary restraining court order (TRO) or other relief;

2. A criminal complaint alleging the defendant committed a criminal act. See Section II. Mandatory Arrest above when a police officer must sign the criminal complaint;

3. Both of the above.

B. Jurisdiction for filing domestic violence complaint by the victim.

1. During regular court hours,

    a. The victim should be transported or directed to the Family Part of the Superior Court.

    b. Where transportation of the victim to the Superior Court is not feasible, the officer should telephone the designated court for an emergent temporary restraining order in accordance with established procedure.

2. On weekends, holidays, and other times when the court is closed

    a. The victim may file the domestic violence complaint before a municipal court judge specifically assigned to accept these complaints.

3. The victim may file a domestic violence complaint:

    a. where the alleged act of domestic violence occurred.

    b. where the defendant resides, or

    c. where the victim resides or is sheltered.

C. Jurisdiction for filing criminal complaint by the victim in connection with filing domestic violence complaint.

1. A criminal complaint may be filed against the defendant in locations indicated in paragraph B3 above.

2. A criminal complaint filed pursuant to paragraph C1 above shall be investigated and prosecuted in the jurisdiction where the offense is alleged to have occurred.

3. A domestic violence complaint may be filed pursuant to the provisions of paragraph B above.

D. Jurisdiction for filing a criminal complaint but no accompanying domestic violence complaint.

1. During normal court hours, the victim may file a criminal complaint with the municipal court or police department where the alleged act occurred in accordance with departmental procedure.

2. On weekends, holidays, and other times when the court is closed, the victim may file a criminal complaint with the law enforcement agency where the alleged act occurred.

3. If the police officer believes that a no-contact order should be issued, the officer should inform the court of the circumstances justifying such request when the criminal complaint is being processed and bail is about to be set. The officer should include in the domestic violence offense report the reasons for the request and the court's disposition of the request.

E. Victim/Witness Notification Form [See Appendix 1.]

1. When either a criminal or domestic violence complaint is signed, a Victim/Witness Notification Form is to be completed by the person assisting the victim, either the police officer or a member of the court staff.

2. The victim should be informed that for the victim's protection, the prosecutor or the court must have the ability to contact the victim on short notice to inform the victim about the defendant's:

   a. impending release from custody, or

   b. application to reduce bail.

3. The victim should be provided with the telephone number of the:

   a. Victim Witness Unit of the Prosecutor's Office when a criminal complaint or domestic violence contempt complaint is signed, or

   b. Family Division Case Management Office/Domestic Violence Unit when a domestic violence complaint is signed.

4. The victim should be instructed to contact the appropriate office to provide new telephone numbers if the victim changes telephone numbers from the numbers listed on the Victim/Witness Notification Form.

F. Procedure for filing Reports.

A copy of the domestic violence offense report must be attached to all criminal complaints and to the civil domestic violence complaint when these documents are forwarded to the appropriate court.

VI. Emergent Temporary Restraining Court Orders.

A. Where a police officer determines that an immediate court order is necessary to protect the victim from further acts of domestic violence or the victim requests an immediate court order, the officer shall contact the designated judge by telephone, radio, or other means of electronic communication. The officer should:

1. Assist the victim in preparing a statement to be made to the judge.

2. Explain that the judge will place the person under oath and will ask questions about the incident.

3. If the judge issues a temporary restraining order, the police officer will be instructed to enter the judge's authorization on a prescribed form.

4. The officer also will be instructed to print the judge's name on the temporary restraining order.

5. The officer will then be instructed to serve the restraining order upon the alleged offender.

VII. Service of Temporary Restraining Order (no-contact order).

A. When the victim obtains a no-contact court order but the defendant had not been arrested by police and is present at the scene, the officer should:

1. Escort the victim to his or her home.

2. Read the conditions of the court order to the defendant if the defendant is present.

3. Order the defendant to vacate the premises.

4. Give the defendant a reasonable period of time to gather personal belongings, unless the court order includes specific limits on time or duration.

5. Arrest the defendant if required by the court order or if defendant refuses to comply with the order.

B. Where a court order had been issued but was not served upon the defendant because the defendant could not then be located but the defendant is now at the scene, police should follow paragraphs A2–5 above.

C. When a temporary or final restraining order is issued that requires service outside the issuing county,

1. The restraining order, along with the complaint and any other relevant documents (e.g., search warrant, etc.) must immediately be brought or faxed to the sheriff's department in the issuing county.

    a. The sheriff's department in the issuing county must similarly bring or fax the order and related documents to the sheriff's department in the county of the defendant's residence or business.

    b. The sheriff's department in the receiving county, pursuant to local policy, will either,

        (1) execute service on the defendant or

        (2) will immediately bring or fax the order and related documents to the police department in the municipality in which the defendant resides or works so that it can execute service accordingly.

    c. The return of service should then be faxed back to the sheriff's department in the issuing county, which in turn must immediately deliver or fax the return of service to the Family Division in the issuing county.

2. When the service of a restraining order results in the seizure of weapons,

    a. The weapons inventory should be attached to the return of service that is brought or faxed back to the issuing county.

    b. The weapons themselves, along with any licenses, I.D. cards, or other paperwork or documentation shall be secured by the prosecutor in the seizing county for storage. At such time that the seized property is needed by the prosecutor or Family Division in the issuing county, the prosecutor in the seizing county shall forward same.

3. Once service on the defendant is attempted, successfully or unsuccessfully, the return of service portion of the TRO (located on the back of the last page of the multipart TRO form) must be filled out by the police or sheriff's department and immediately returned to the Family Division prior to the scheduled final hearing date.

VIII. Court Order Violations.

A. Where a police officer determines that a party has violated an existing restraining order either by committing a new act of domestic violence or by violating the terms of a court order, the officer must:

1. Arrest and transport the defendant to the police station.

2. Sign a criminal contempt charge concerning the incident on a complaint-warrant(CDR-2).

3. The officer should sign a criminal complaint for all related criminal offenses. (The criminal charges should be listed on the same criminal complaint form that contain the contempt charge.)

4. Telephone, communicate in person, or by facsimile with the appropriate judge or bail unit and request bail be set on the contempt charge.

   a. During regular court hours, bail should be set by the emergent duty Superior Court Judge that day.

   b. On weekends, holidays, and other times when the court is closed, bail should be set by the designated emergent duty Superior Court Judge except in those counties where a municipal court judge has been authorized to set bail for non-indictable contempt charges by the assignment judge.

   c. When bail is set by a judge when the courts are closed, the officer shall arrange to have the clerk of the Family Part notified on the next working day of the new complaint, the amount of bail, the defendant's whereabouts, and all other necessary details.

   d. If a municipal court judge set the bail, the arresting officer shall notify the clerk of that municipal court of this information.

5. If the defendant is unable to post bail, take appropriate steps to have the defendant incarcerated at police headquarters or the county jail.

B. Where the officer deems there is no probable cause to arrest or sign a criminal complaint against the defendant for a violation of no contact court order, the officer must advise the victim of the procedure for completing and signing.

1. Criminal complaint alleging a violation of the court order.

   a. During regular court hours, the officer should advise the victim that the complaint must be filed with the Family Part of the Chancery Division of Superior Court.

   b. On weekends, holidays, and other hours when the court is closed,

      (1) the officer should transport or arrange for transportation to have the victim taken to headquarters to sign the complaint;

(2) the alleged offender shall be charged with contempt of a domestic violence court order, N.J.S.A. 2C:29-9. The victim must sign the complaint. A complaint-warrant (CDR-2) must be prepared;

(3) the officer in charge shall follow standard police procedure in arranging to have a court set bail.

2. Civil complaint against the defendant for violations of a court order pertaining to support or monetary compensation, custody, visitation, or counselling. The victim should be referred to the Family Division Case Management Office to pursue this civil enforcement of the court order.

IX. Criminal Offenses Against the Elderly and Disabled.

A. Where an elderly or disabled person is subjected to a criminal offense listed as an act of domestic violence, police shall follow the appropriate procedure listed above.

B. Where the actions or omissions against an elderly or disabled person do not meet the domestic violence conditions, police may file appropriate criminal charges against the offender.

C. A person may be charged with Endangering the Welfare of the Elderly or Disabled, N.J.S.A. 2C:24-8, if the person has:

1. a legal duty to care for or has assumed continuing responsibility for the care of a person who is:

   a. sixty years of age or older, or

   b. emotionally, psychologically or physically disabled, and

2. the person unreasonably neglects or fails to permit to be done any act necessary for the physical or mental health of the elderly or disabled person.

CONCLUSION

Domestic violence is a pervasive problem in the world. Within the United States, nearly one hundred thousand persons per day are a victim to some form of domestic/intimate partner violence. There are many laws, agencies, organizations, and other resources to help those victims. Early recognition and support for victims are the keys to bringing this horrible cycle of violence to an end.

DISCUSSION QUESTIONS

1. What is domestic violence? How prevalent is the problem of domestic/intimate partner violence in the United States?

2. Why is domestic/intimate partner violence under reported to law enforcement?

3. What are some power and control issues that are common in abusive relationships?

Name: _____   Date _____

You must use this form and turn in the original to the instructor. No other form will be accepted.

CHAPTER ASSIGNMENT

The text outlines some warning signs of an abusive relationship. What are some of these signs? Why do you think some people cannot identify even the most obvious signs in their relationship?

_____
_____
_____
_____
_____
_____
_____
_____
_____
_____
_____
_____
_____
_____
_____
_____
_____
_____
_____

Chapter Six

CHILDREN VICTIMS OF CRIME

LEARNING OBJECTIVES

After exploring Chapter Six (6), the student will be able to:

1. Define kidnapping.
2. Explain the difference between short-term abductions and stranger abductions.
3. Explain the process of the forensic child interview.
4. Recognize symptoms of sexual abuse.
5. Understand AMBER Alerts.
6. Discuss the importance and role of CART.

KEY TERMS

Kidnapping, AMBER Alerts, Child Abduction Response Team (CART), Child Forensic Interview

INTRODUCTION

Taking and holding a person against his or her will for some nefarious purpose was recognized many years ago as a vicious act under the English common law. Today, kidnapping is classified in state and federal statutes (Diamond, 1985). Kidnapping is essentially capturing a person against their choice, generally to facilitate another crime.

Although frequently force is employed to effectively kidnap, it is not a necessary element of the crime. The victim can be detained through trickery or manipulation to inveigle a victim. Extortion for ransom, robbery (compelling an adult to withdraw money from an automated teller machine), and sexual exploitation, are some motivators for criminals to engage in kidnapping.

Kidnapping is criminalized in both state and federal courts, often causing issues of jurisdiction in prosecutions regarding the ancillary offenses committed during the kidnapping (murder, aggravated assault, sexual assault, etc). In 1932 the United States federal government enacted the Federal Kidnapping Act, also known as the Lindbergh Law. The act was named after the famous aviator, Charles Lindbergh, whose infant son was abducted (Villanti, 2012).

On March 1, 1932 the son of Charles Lindbergh (Charles Lindbergh Jr.) was abducted from his parents New Jersey home, within a two-hour span, in East Amwell, NJ. Charles Jr. was unable to be located alive, as he was eventually found murdered with a fractured skull in Hopewell, New Jersey (Villanti, 2012).

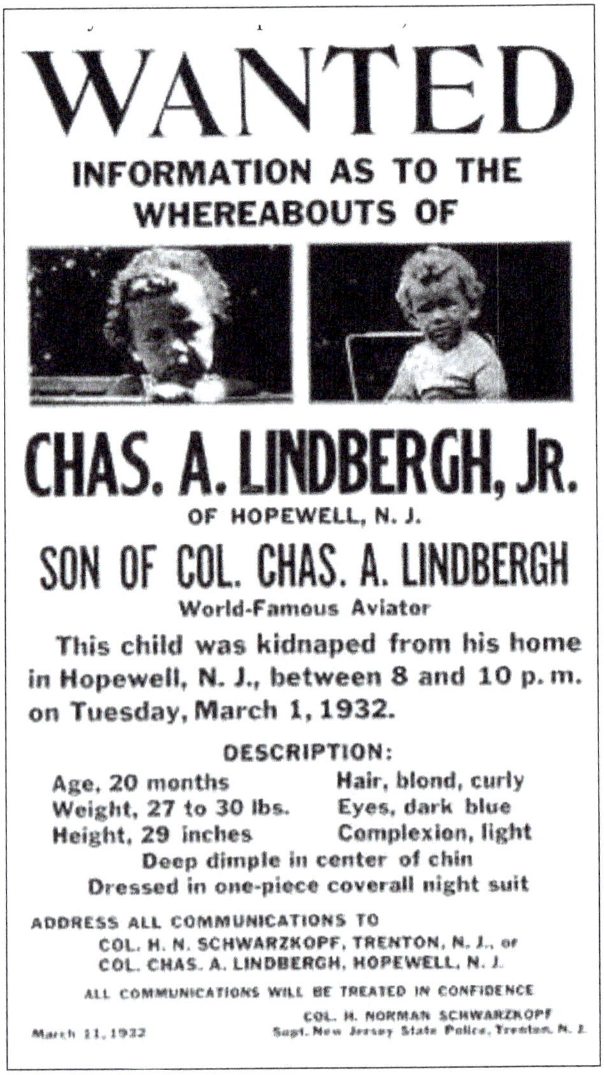

© Sasenki/Shutterstock.com

KIDNAPPING

The maximalist alarmist perspective argues that crimes against children (kidnapping, child abuse, child sexual assault) are realizing epidemic proportions and serious consequences will arise if steps are not taken to address the problem (Karmen, 2007). The maximalists believe or assume the worst case scenarios in our communities if this problem is not addressed.

Poster from the New Jersey State Police—Public Domain.

Additionally, the maximalists believed these crimes against children (specifically kidnapping or abductions) are alarmingly common. These convictions seek to stimulate the public out of complacency and assemble them to prevent these atrocities from frequent occurrence. They warned that child snatchers were everywhere, no youngster was ever completely safe, and parents could never be too careful about taking precautions and restricting their children's activities.

When a child is missing and reported to law enforcement agencies, it is required by federal law that the child's identifying information is to be entered into the Federal Bureau of Investigation's (FBI) National Crime Information Center database, known as NCIC and accessible by local, state, and federal law enforcement agencies. In 2015, the National Center for Missing and Exploited Children (NCMEC) reported there were 460,699 NCIC entries for children reported missing to police by their guardians in the U.S. NCMEC supported law enforcement with approximately 20,500 cases of reported missing children in 2016. Of these, 6 percent were family abductions and 1 percent was non-family abductions. These numbers reflect approximately 205 children were abducted by people who were unfamiliar to the family (National Center for Missing and Exploited Children, 2017 retrieved from http://www.missingkids.com/KeyFacts). The abductor intends to permanently keep the child, extort a ransom, or commit some other crime, including murder. In most of these extremely serious offenses, the kidnapper is not a complete stranger, but instead is a disgruntled former boyfriend or the child's mother or a friend of the family.

SHORT-TERM ABDUCTIONS

There are many "short-term" abductions by non-family member per year, however most cases involve family or disputes involving custody agreements (Finklehor, Hotaling & Sedlak, 1991). Although these case are identified as "short-term" they all comprise of all of the legal elements sate and federal codified laws for kidnapping: a crime by an acquaintance or by a complete stranger who takes the child by force or by deceit into buildings, vehicles, or some other place, and, or detains the child, typically to commit another offense against the child.
Short-term abductions may end with a crime being committed against the child, with them being returned, or culminate with the death of the child.

LONG-TERM ABDUCTIONS

There were approximately 350,000 abductions committed by a family member in 1988 (Finklehor, Hotaling, & Sedlak, 1991). In these cases, a family member is usually a parent that takes a child in violation of a family court decree and tries to conceal the taking of the child and moves the child to another state permanently, or alters the custodial arrangements. These abductions were most likely to occur during January and August, when school vacations and parental visits end. Additionally, they commonly occur during weekend visitation hours, when the abducting parent had legal rights during a particular time frame and failed to return the child to the rightful custodial guardian.

THE REDUCTION OF PARENTAL ABDUCTION RISKS

There is no amount of precaution that can completely protect you from a spouse or ex-spouse who intends in taking the children. You can take some steps to reduce the risks:

1. Obtain legal, permanent, or temporary custody of your child. If no legal custody has been obtained, the abducting spouse has not violated any laws.
2. Once you have obtained legal custody, secure a passport for your children and notify the passport office that your children are not to be taken out of the country without your written permission.
3. If the spouse or ex-spouse is threatening to abduct, have the threats witnessed or tape-recorded with discretion.
    a. The parent who is seeking visitation can be ordered to post a sizable bond. If he or she leaves, the bond is defaulted to you.
    b. Make sure that your custody order details police procedure. If the order is violated, the police have specific authorization by the court to retrieve the child if necessary.
    c. Place restrictions upon where visitations may take place.
4. Know and maintain current vital information about your spouse or ex-spouse, such as social security, driver's license number, license plate number, and credit information.
5. Don't frustrate or manipulate the ex-spouse's visitation time if he or she is behaving responsibly in accordance with the custody agreement. The frustration and anger can cause the parent to contemplate snatching the children.
6. Attempt to maintain a friendly or at least civil relationship with your spouse or ex-spouse for the well-being of the children.
7. If your child is school age or attends a day care center, or stays with a babysitter, submit a certified copy of the custody order with a photo of the other parent.
8. Talk with your children, and teach them what to do in a case of an abduction. Tell them that you will always want them and that you are alive and you are searching for them.

STRANGER ABDUCTIONS—REDUCING THE RISKS

The abduction of your child by a stranger is every parent's nightmare. Fortunately, there are precautions you can teach your child to help reduce the risks of being abducted.

1. Never leave the child unattended in a car, supermarket, or shopping center, or at home alone.
2. Instruct your child not to go with any stranger.
3. Don't purchase or dress your child in a T-shirt with his or her name printed on it. Knowing a child's name is a first step to familiarity.

4. Teach your children that a stranger is also somebody they don't know.
5. Encourage children to have buddies. Children like to do things in pairs.
6. Have the children do a project in which they write their entire name, address, and telephone number with area code.
7. Show your children how to use a telephone, explain what an area code means and what it does.
8. Tell the children that most adults will help them rather than hurt them.
9. Teach your children to be alert. If someone is hanging around, or driving around in a car, take a good look at the person's face and car.

AMBER ALERTS

AMBER is the acronym for *America's Missing: Broadcast Emergency Response,* it's warning system was developed to enhance the likelihood of locating missing children. AMBER is also named after nine-year old Amber Hagerman, who was abducted in Texas and viciously murdered (United States Department of Justice, 2017). These are alerts transmitted through partnerships with law enforcement and media to trigger critical announcements for children who are not only abducted, but are known to be at serious risk. In 2005, every state in the United States of America adopted AMBER Alert procedures for activating recovery methods for kidnapped children at risk (Miller & Clinkinbeard, 2006).

AMBER alerts are designed to incorporate diverse methods to transmit critical information. Officials use traffic billboards, social media, reverse 911 calls, television, radio, and other means to distribute physical descriptions of abducted children, their abductors, and vehicle information. Subscribers of certain text messaging services can have this information sent directly to their smartphones. It is a timely, holistic effort to locate the endangered child as fast as possible and all means are used.

AMBER alerts are only used in the circumstances where the child is in *imminent danger* and the United States Department of Justice outlines the recommended standards. They are:

- There is reasonable belief by law enforcement that an abduction has occurred.
- The law enforcement agency believes that the child is in imminent danger of serious bodily injury or death.
- There is enough descriptive information about the victim and the abduction for law enforcement to issue an AMBER Alert to assist in the recovery of the child.

- The abduction is of a child aged seventeen years or younger.
- The child's name and other critical data elements, including the Child Abduction flag, have been entered into the National Crime Information Center (NCIC) system.

(U.S. Department of Justice, 2017)

Law enforcement and search teams must move swiftly to locate these endangered children. Most children abducted by strangers who intend to kill do so in approximately three hours (Hanfland, Keppel, & Weiss, 1997; Sicafuse & Miller, 2010). AMBER alerts attempt to reach the most amount of people in the least amount of time to find children who are in extreme danger.

CART (CHILD ABDUCTION RESPONSE TEAM)

A Child Abduction Response Team (CART) is a group composed of professionals who are gathered for their expertise to investigate and recover an abducted child. The strength in CART teams lies in its diversity of skills organized rapidly to address specific child kidnapping cases (Swager, 2007). CART teams use a multi-disciplinary method, including experienced detectives, prosecutors, patrol officers, crime scene experts, social workers, victim assistance professionals, and media specialists.

© Jo millington/Shutterstock.com

The CART team leaders receive standardized training for guiding investigations of abduction children, generally under the age of thirteen. When CART teams assemble, a collaborative investigative search effort commences with any and all relevant law enforcement agencies. In state CART programs, procedures are distributed for guiding investigations, outlining the resources available to teams' members when attempting to locate a missing child. Additionally, in terms of best practices, "After Action Reports" are required for criminal justice executives to review for identification of what "worked" and what will need improvement or adjustment for future missing children investigations (New Jersey Office of the Attorney General, 2009).

SUMMARY

Many groups of victims face special problems that require special solutions. The distraught parents of missing children need to convince authorities that their youngsters were truly victims of foul play and to take immediate action. There are numerous child-search organizations that are operated by volunteers that can help to mobilize manhunts, and state-clearing houses for information about missing children can coordinate activities.

Most states now require police officers to take on how to investigate missing children cases, to interact with their families, and activate AMBER alerts. In addition the valuable AMBER alert resource, state legislators realize the need for expert response and have assembled local Child Abduction Response Teams (CART) to swiftly respond to children who have been abducted and are in danger.

VICTIMS OF CHILD ABUSE

Children are more vulnerable to victimization because of their age, size, and dependence on adults. Children have little or no control over the lives in their home or who associates with members of the household. There are certain children who are targeted more frequently; including the shy, lonely, and compliant children, as well as pre-verbal and very young children. Those kids are labeled as "bad kids." Children with physical, emotional, or developmental disabilities are particularly vulnerable to victimization.

DEFINITION OF CONCEPTS

1. Maltreatment: Acts of omission as well as commission, including, neglect, physical abuse, sexual abuse and emotional abuse.
2. Neglect: The range of abandonment to the failure to meet a child's three basic requirements:
    a. Physical—basic supervision
    b. Emotional—nurturing and affection
    c. Educational—providing support for academic or educational learning
3. Physical Abuse: Involved assaults—punching, kicking, scalding, suffocating, shaking, extended confinement, and excessive punishments.
4. Sexual Abuse: Are recognized as incest, fondling, sodomy, intercourse, rape, and impairment of the child's morals.
5. Emotional Abuse: Serious or mental disorder.
6. Prevalence: Proportion of people in some population being studied who have ever suffered this form of victimization.
7. Incidence: New cases that come to light each year.
8. Pedophiles: Child molesters.

SIGNS AND SYMPTOMS OF CHILD ABUSE

Some signs and symptoms of child abuse include:

1. Head injury and/or multiple injuries to the body.
2. Frequent bacterial infection, genital rash, and vaginal discharge.
3. Fractures or bruises in an infant who has not started to learn how to walk.
4. Immersion burns from scalding hot water and cigarette burns.
5. Injury to buttocks or scalp (bruising or hair loss).
6. Injury to thin body parts (chins, knee, elbows, and etc.).
7. Dramatic academic changes, disruptive or overly aggressive behavior.
8. Emotional/behavioral changes, runaway, truancy, and drug abuse.
9. Interest in sexual acts or display of sexual knowledge beyond the child's years.
10. Masturbatory behavior.
11. Extremely passive.
12. Withdrawn or hostile towards authority figures.

CHILD INTERVIEWS AND INVESTIGATION

When responding to a report of child abuse (sexual assault, neglect, etc.), it's vital that specially trained personnel conduct the investigation. As in all investigations, all pertinent information must be gathered. In terms of a child abuse case, investigators must contact family (if not the accused perpetrator), school employees, child services, neighbors, etc. to get an overall view of the child's behavior and psyche. Does the child tend to lie or embellish frequently? Is the child constantly being addressed for unacceptable behavior, or is there an absence of these issues? All these questions must be answered along with a development of an extensive background to truly understand the life of the child prior to conducting an interview to discover if any crime has been committed against the child.

Interviewing children is a difficult assignment. Strip away any emotional feelings the investigator might sense (empathy, anger, horror), child interviews must be conducted in a manner putting the child first amongst all, with the overall goal of gaining an understanding what actually took place during the incident in the child's own words. If a child freely discloses criminal behavior, the interview must be conducted legally and without coercion, so the child's statement and residual evidence gained from the dialogue can be used in a court of law to punish the offender.

Past approaches towards child interviewing came under scrutiny in the mid 1980's, highlighted by cases where children were reported to be sexually abused and arrests made with the assistance of child interviews. One such case of national notoriety was at Wee Care Day Nursery, in Maplewood, NJ, where a care giver was reported to have sexually abused multiple children (115 counts on nineteen children). Margaret Michaels was convicted of these crimes in 1987, only to have her conviction turned over under appeal. The appeal stated and the courts agreed, the case was wrought with "prosecutorial abuses, including the questioning of children that planted suggestions, tainting their testimony." (Nieves, 1994). Cases like these were being scrutinized across the United States attacking the techniques of interviewers and the credibility of child witnesses.

According to The Cornerhouse Forensic Interview Protocal (RATAC), child interviews must be a "fact-finding" mission, "legally defensible," and in a "child-friendly environment." (Anderson, et. al, 2009). This interview style was developed and introduced to help interviewers acquire credible statements, respect the dignity of the child, and also preserve the civil rights of the accused. RATAC is an acronym which stands for rapport, anatomical drawings, touch inquiry, abuse scenario, and closure. Also known as *Finding Words*, this method employed by trained interviewers has been widely accepted as credible by the courts across the United States. This interview technique is planned and organized, however it maintains itself as a "semi- structured" method allowing for flexibility in terms of adjusting to the development of the child (Anderson, et. al., 2009).

First, child forensic interviewing is not conducted in your typical police station interview and interrogation room. The environment is set to put the child at ease. Typically, there are carpeted benches allowing the interviewer to be eye-level with the child. Additionally, an easel and marker are located in the room for drawing by the interviewer to enhance communication and record things important to the child's life. For instance, depending on age and development, the interviewer may draw the child's face and ask, "Where should I put your nose?" This opens dialogue with the draws and builds rapport. The ancillary benefit to this method is that the interviewer is getting to understand the child's verbal and cognitive abilities.

Interview Instructions

Prior to beginning the interview and building rapport, the interviewer gives instructions for the interview and provides the child with information. The child is assured that they are not in any trouble and they are only in the room to talk about some things. The child is asked, "Do you know what the truth is? This is called the *truth statement*. The interviewer will allow the child to answer. The child provides their version. The interviewer will follow with "the truth is what really happens, and we are only here to talk about the truth today, do you think we can do that?

Additionally, the interviewer may set *ground rules* say, "I may ask you a question you don't know the answer to, it's okay if you say I don't know." Or, the interviewer may say, "If I say something that you think is wrong I want you to tell me." These *ground rules* and *truth statements* give credibility to the interview and the child, especially when they correct you about something in the interview that is a mistake. It shows they are freely giving information and comprehending (Anderson, et. al, 2009).

Rapport

The first component of *Finding Words* is to come to a common ground with the child and form a rapport. This allows for the child to become comfortable and is an important barrier to breach. Interviewers use techniques such as the face drawing and family circles. Family circles are important and are typically written in the easel with the marker. This allows the child to provide information to the interviewer regarding where the live, what type of residence they live in, who lives with them, do they have pets, where to they go to school, etc. All of this information is important to the investigation, and again, the child is slowly becoming more comfortable with the interviewer and the interviewer is beginning to understand what the verbal and cognitive abilities are for the child.

Anatomical Drawings

The second portion of the interview involves anatomical drawings. Anatomical drawings are presented to children to ascertain what names "they" use to identify different parts of the body. Although children can be at multiple cognitive and verbally levels, cultural and social differences affect thinking and communication. It is important for the interviewer to know what words the child uses to identify different body parts so they know exactly what the child is saying in their own words. Also, the child will know what the interviewer is referring to when they use the word the child provided. Additionally, the interviewer is still analyzing cognition and perception as they are gathering more information from the child. This also becomes helpful further in the interview when the interviewer can refer to a body part name to clarify the child's statement.

Touch Inquiry

Touch inquiries or "good touch, bad touch," is the part of the interview process, after body parts are identified, where the interviewer will ask the question, "Are there touches that you like and don't like?" Some touches the child may say they like are kisses from mommy, hugs from daddy, etc. A question may be posed, "Is there anywhere on your body people are not allowed to touch?" Often children will identify the penis or vagina (in their own words) as portions of the body which are not allowed to be touched by others. This can be followed with, "Has anybody ever touched in those places?" If the answer is "yes," the interviewer will follow with an open-ended question designed to get the child's response with no coercion such as, "Can you tell me more about that?" At this point, the interviewer is transitioning into the abuse scenario.

Abuse Scenario

The interviewer explores abuse scenarios only if the child discloses anything that may resemble some type of abuse. The purpose of the abuse scenario portion is to get a full understanding in detail of what the child has experienced. Importantly, the interviewing must use as much open-ended questions as possible to guard against leading or influencing the child. "Tell me more about that..., And then what happened?...and "Tell all you remember about that time," are all questions designed for the interviewer to explore as much information as possible from the free recall of events (Anderson, et. al, 2009). In an audio and video recorded statement, after all of the events have transpired in the interview (carefully planned, systematic, non-leading questioning), the child's free and voluntary statement is free of coercion and loaded with credibility. The interview is designed to get the information from the child without the interference or suggestiveness of the interviewer. Ultimately, the child's free statement is taken in an effort to corroborate the information with additional statements, facts, and physical evidence.

Closure

The closure process is designed to "educate the child, to explore safety options, and to provide a respectful end to the interview." (Anderson, et. al, 2009). In this phase, it's important to let the child know they can talk to their parents, teachers, police officers, family friends, etc. about these situations. The interviewer encourages the child to name and identify people of trust they can tell if something happens to them. By naming these people and authority figures, the interviewer emphasizes security precautions that are anchored with notifying someone of trust. This can be an appropriate time to discuss how to call 911. In addition, it's important for the interviewer to praise the child if they did tell a parent or relative about the abuse and to encourage them to do the same in the future. It is significant to note, even if the child did not disclose an abuse scenario, to reinforce safety measures and communicate what children should do if they are put in these situations.

The RATAC process is used across the world for the purpose of respecting the child, enhancing credibility, and respecting civil rights. The process is designed to gather facts and statements directly in concert with the child's ability. Additionally, the method seeks to obtain this information freely, without being persuaded by the interviewer, to successful obtain a clear view of the child's experience during an acute incident or over time.

PREVENTION STRATEGIES

What can be done to ensure that all children have a safe home and a loving atmosphere in which to grow and develop? Parents Anonymous is a nonprofit organization that have local chapters throughout the

United States. They offer a unique and effective approach to strengthening families based upon the subsequent principles and its importance:

1. Mutual Assistance: The parents take the lead in achieving personal and family growth. Parents are responsible for their own growth, as well as for reaching out to others.
2. Empowerment: Parents have the ability to take charge of their lives by seeking solutions for their problems.
3. Support: Mutual learning and individual growth is achieved by providing a non-threatening environment.
4. Ownership: The group belongs to its members and they control the content of the weekly meetings.
5. Caring: Group members create an atmosphere of belonging and acceptance in which healthy-family interacts.
6. Non-violence: No violence is permitted among family members.
7. Anonymity and Confidentiality: Parents have the right to withhold their names from others.

COUNSELING

Another avenue for dealing with child abuse cases emphasizes a treatment or rehabilitation approach. This response seeks to help both the victim and the offender, often involving the entire family. Most treatment interventions resolve around individual and group counseling. The counseling helps to open-up the lines of communication. The communication helps the individuals to cope with their problems.

EDUCATION

The education efforts aim to demystify child rearing by providing parents with instruction in child development. Many advocate the continuing of adult education projects at hospitals, schools, churches, and social service agencies. Moreover, once this approach is in place, it would require several years before yielding positive dividends.

CONCLUSION

It has taken our society a great deal of time to recognize that child abuse exists. The state has enacted legislation forbidding the victimization of children. Child abuse tends to take place behind closed doors. It often involves victims who are unable to defend themselves, making detection difficult.

There are numerous coping strategies; however, they suggest that the eradication of child abuse and neglect is everybody's responsibility. Finally, somewhere in this country, another child died from abuse or neglect in time it took to read this chapter.

DISCUSSION QUESTIONS

1. Why was the Lindbergh Law enacted?

2. Explain the key differences between short-term abductions, stranger abductions, and parental abductions?

3. What is the fundamental reasoning for interviewing children with a different approach?

4. Who are the different members of CART and why is it important to have members from separate professional expertise?

REFERENCES

Anderson, J., Ellefson, J., Lashley, J., & Miller, A. L. (2009). The CornerHouse forensic interview protocol: RATAC. *TM Cooley J. Prac. & Clinical L.*, *12*, 193.

Diamond, J. L. (1985). Kidnapping: A modern definition. *Am. J. Crim. L.*, *13*, 1.

Finkelhor, D., Hotaling, G., & Sedlak, A. (1991). Children abducted by family members: A national household survey of incidence and episode characteristics. *Journal of Marriage and the Family*, 805–817.

Hanfland, K. A., Keppel, R. D., & Weis, J. G. (1997). *Case management for missing children homicide investigation*. Olympia: Attorney General of Washington.

Karmen, A. 2007). Crime Victims: An Introduction to Victimology, 5th ed. Belmont, CA: Wadsworth Publishing Company.

Miller, M. K., & Clinkinbeard, S. S. (2006). Improving the AMBER Alert system: Psychology research and policy recommendations. *Law & Psychol. Rev.*, *30*, 1.

Nieves, E. (1994, Dec 3). Prosecutors Drop Charges From Abuse Case From Mid-1980's. *The New York Times*. Retrieved from http://www.nytimes.com/1994/12/03/nyregion/prosecutors-drop-charges-in-abuse-case-from-mid-80-s.html.

New Jersey Office of the Attorney General (2009) Attorney General Law Enforcement Directive No. 2008-4. Retreived from http://www.nj.gov/oag/newsreleases08/pr20081201a-Cart-Directive.pdf.

Sicafuse, L. L., & Miller, M. K. (2010). Social psychological influences on the popularity of AMBER alerts. *Criminal Justice and Behavior*, *37*(11), 1237–1254.

Swager, B. (2007). Tampa's Child Abduction Response Team. *Law and Order*, *55*(9), 134–138.

United States Department of Justice (2017). AMBER Alert Guidelines. Retrieved from https://www.amberalert.gov/guidelines.htm.

United States Department of Justice (2017). AMBER Alert Legislation. Retrieved from https://www.amberalert.gov/legislation.htm.

Villanti, C. A. (2012). A Game of Hold'em: Critiquing United States v. Gabaldon's "All-In" Approach to Federal Kidnapping. *St. John's Law Review*, *81*(3), 8.

Name: _____   Date _____

You must use this form and turn in the original to the instructor. No other form will be accepted.

CHAPTER ASSIGNMENT

With the policies and procedures in place for interviewing children in a different manner than regular questioning, why do you think it is important for specially trained individuals to be charged to complete this task?

_____

_____

_____

_____

_____

_____

_____

_____

_____

_____

_____

_____

_____

_____

_____

_____

_____

Chapter Seven

VICTIMS OF BULLYING, CYBER-BULLYING, AND HAZING

LEARNING OBJECTIVES

After exploring Chapter Seven (7), the student will be able to:

1. Define harassment, intimidation, and bullying
2. Provide examples of cyber-bullying and hazing
3. Demonstrate the link between dating violence and bullying
4. Describe peer victimization experiences, differentiating between male and female victims
5. Distinguish relational victimization and overt victimization
6. Demonstrate the causal relationship between bullying and anxiety, specifically referring to longitudinal studies
7. Describe the relationship between youth aggression and partner violence

KEY TERMS

Bullying, Intimidation, Cyber-bullying, Dating violence, Domestic violence, Hazing, Victimization, Power and control issues, Casual relationship, Batterer

© StockPhotoAstur/Shutterstock.com

INTRODUCTION

There is a clear relationship between bullying and domestic violence. Domestic violence is centered upon power and control issues. Bullying is centered on power and control issues.

The statistics demonstrate that those who bully are 70 percent more likely to have a conviction by the time they are twenty-four than non-bullies. (*Bullying at School: What We Know What We Can Do 1993*) Also, ALL domestic violence abusers were bullies in school. (Spivak H, Prothrow-Stith D. The need to address bullying in violence prevention. 2001)

The statistics show that 65 percent of domestic violence occurs in the presence of children. (CDC). In fact, 85 percent of batterers learn how to use violence in their own homes. Therefore, it has been shown that in homes were children were the victims of abuse, at least 50 percent of those households suffered incidents of domestic violence (CDC) .So, the end result can be children who continue the cycle of child abuse, domestic violence and that just witnessing the incidents of domestic violence leads to increased use of drugs/alcohol and teenage pregnancies. We have also seen that children exposed to domestic violence kill themselves at six times the National rate of suicide (CDC).

Dating violence is a precursor to domestic violence. Hitting, threatening, or violence in small forms leads to larger violence. Most abusers do not wake up one day and decide it is a good day to start domestic violence. The abusers start at an early age and the behavior is likely to come about as bullying. A little shove or a veiled threat turns uglier if the partner in the relationship tolerates it. The abusers use the playground as a testing ground. The abusers hone their skills at an early age.

© Amir Ridhwan/Shutterstock.com

- ▶ **Harassment, Intimidation, and Bullying**—"harassment, intimidation and bullying" means any gesture—written, verbal, or physical that:
    - ◆ Is motivated by any actual or perceived characteristic such as race, color, religion, ancestry, national origin, gender, sexual orientation, gender identity and expression, or a mental, physical, or sensory disability.
    - ◆ Will have the effect of harming someone else (physically or emotionally), harming their property, or putting them in fear they or their property may be harmed.
    - ◆ Have the effect of insulting or demeaning someone else in such a way as to cause substantial disruption in, or substantial interference with their learning and the orderly operation of the school. (Hazing.)
    - ◆ Threaten (written, verbal, or physical).
    - ◆ Extort/coerce (verbal, written, or physical intimidation or threats meant to force an individual to act in a way that he or she may not want to).
    - ◆ Instigate—verbal, written, or physical taunting, baiting, inciting, and/or encouraging a fight, disruptions, or other violation of school rules. (Hazing.)

The above includes sexual harassment.

Defining bullying has been very nebulous, as no single definition covers all aspects of bullying. Despite this, it has been identified as a willful, conscious desire to hurt another or put him/her under stress. The stress is created not only by what actually happens but also by fear of what might happen. However, bullying is not the same as harassment or assault. It tends to involve many incidents that accumulate over time, rather than a single incident or a few of them. Bullying can also be as direct as teasing, hitting, or threatening, or as indirect as exclusions, rumors, or manipulations.

Technology has evolved the process of bullying. The use of social media to instill fear or espouse a desire to another or put him/her under stress has made the ability to accumulate many instances (often with anonymity) in a short period of time; with a very broad/wide audience.

Direct hazing and bullying has been attributed to many suicides in young adults. In fact, the rise of suicide in college-age persons continues to grow exponentially. Identifying and dealing with incidents of hazing/bullying are becoming much more of a focus to school officials, the news media, and law enforcement.

© serato/Shutterstock.com

Dan Olweus, a pioneer in the systematic study of bullying, identifies hallmark features of this behavior as deliberate aggressiveness and marked inequality of power. Tactics employed in these acts include harsh teasing, constant criticisms, insults, gossip, and unreasonable demands. According to this definition, victims experience injury or distress in the face of repeated attacks against which they are unable to defend themselves.

In the arena of bullying is the development of digital or cyber-bullying, the sending of menacing text messages via cell phones and emails, posting, comments via computers. In addition, hate-filled web pages about a victim often include their personal information. This form of cyber-bullying is extraordinarily damaging to the person who is being victimized by it.

Although studies of prevalence rates of bullying in the United States are few, several studies indicate that bullying may be the most prevalent form of violence in the schools and the form that is likely to affect the greatest number of students. Data from the U.S. Department of Education's National Center for Education Statistics indicate that the percentage of students aged twelve to eighteen who reported being bullied at school increased from 1999 to 2001 and remained stable from 2001 to 2003. A study of bullying behaviors in a large, nationally representative sample of American youth in grades six–ten found that 29.9 percent of students reported moderate or frequent involvement in bullying. That means that approximately 3.2 million children in those grades are victims of moderate to serious bullying every year. As bullying tends to decline with age, the number is likely to be higher in elementary students. However, the process often turns to hazing and cyber-bullying for older teens to young adults.

Bullying leads to serious, ongoing problems for both bullies and victims. Involvement in bullying as either bully or victim has been associated with school dropout, poor psychosocial adjustment, and other persisting negative outcomes. Some researchers have found that bullies and victims have lower self-esteem than do their non-involved peers. Victims have been found to suffer from emotional and academic difficulties, problems with social relationships, low self-esteem, and increased risk for depression. In extreme cases, running away, refusing to attend school, and attempting suicide have been linked to victimization through bullying.

EFFECTS OF BULLYING

In 2003, The National Association of School Psychologists reported that every day more than 160,000 American school children miss school because they fear being bullied. In other situations, targets of bullying may stop talking about school, get to school late each day, miss classes, or make up excuses to miss school entirely as a result of fear of attack or intimidation. Hazing, though, tends not to generate absences; rather, the victims internalize their victimization. Often, feeling the need to belong to a group is paramount to the degradation or even physical injuries they might suffer.

Victims of bullying feel sad, unhappy, hurt, or rejected as a reaction to peer victimization. They often feel bad about themselves based on comments that were made by bullies and some even report losing relationships as a result of the victimization. Persistent bullying may erode a victim's self-confidence, induce serious health problems, and even ruin his/her career. Victims may also experience headaches, sleeplessness, anxiety. and depression. Some may even develop Post-Traumatic Stress Disorder.

Such behavior not only happens in educational settings, but occurs in the modern workplace. The "office bully" is commonplace in corporate America.

The most extreme consequence of bullying for victims and society is violence including

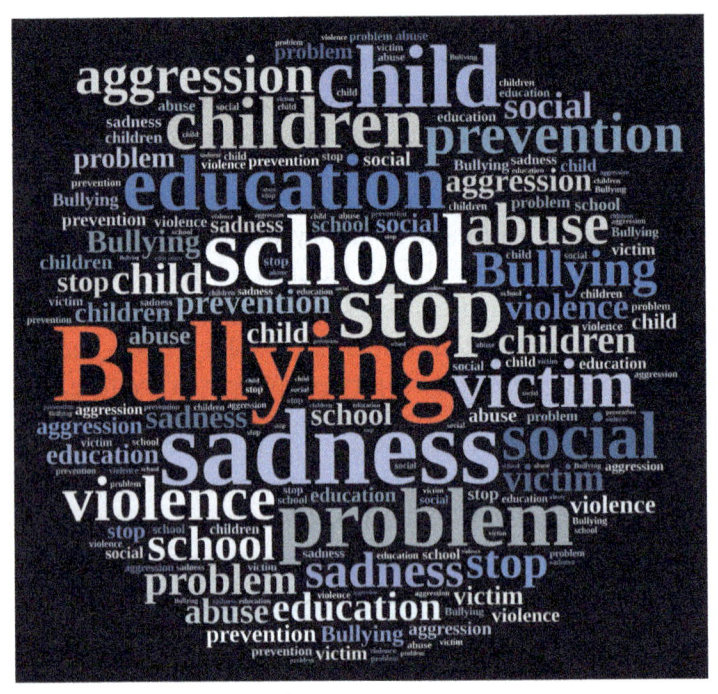

© StockPhotoAstur/Shutterstock.com

suicide and murder. The sense of powerlessness experienced by people who are victimized can be so profound that some victims of bullying react with self-destructive acts or lethal retaliation. Often this behavior is seen in the school setting. In addition, victims of bullying often become more easily identifiable because they become moody, irritable, frustrated, or act tired and withdrawn. It is important to note that everyone should be able to help qualify that type behavior. Many of the "infamous" school shootings (perhaps, other mass violence) can have the perpetrator's actions traced to many pre-indicator actions. Social media, talks of violence, saying goodbye to friends, or alike, have been found to be the mode for many of these violent offenders. In other cases, victims may even become aggressive with those at home or with peers and friends and typically exhibit later difficulties in intimate relationships.

Bullying also has effects on the bullies themselves. Numerous studies have demonstrated that if not stopped in childhood, bullies would likely grow up to bully others at home or in the workplace. In fact, it is common knowledge that those who had been bullies at childhood developed behavior patterns that endured into adult life and are more likely to have criminal records than those who were not bullies.

According to Olweus' (1999) research, more than half of the children identified as bullies in school had criminal convictions by the time they were in their twenties. In addition, although the bullies themselves may not suffer any initial consequences, they are most likely to suffer from long-term consequences. If they do not change behaviors, the pattern of bullying behavior often becomes a habit as the bully gets older. These bullies at adulthood become aggressive adults and have a higher chance of court intervention, criminal convictions, alcoholism, and personality disorders. Research suggests that both victims and bullies have more depressive and suicidal thoughts than their peers not involved in bullying. Huesmann (1997) suggests that home dysfunction may contribute to depressive feelings for bullies, whereas for victims, being bullied is the reason they are depressed.

STATUS OF CURRENT RESEARCH

Peer victimization among children and adolescents has been the focus of hundreds of studies over the last three decades. Defined as repeated exposure "to negative actions on the part of one or more other persons," large scale community studies suggest that as many as 20 to 30 percent of children and adolescents are chronically victimized by peers. Whereas in the past, peer victimization was viewed as an inevitable part of childhood or rite of passage, attention to this phenomenon has increased as parents, school personnel, and health professionals have recognized the relationship of being victimized to numerous psychosocial adjustment problems.

In early investigations of peer relations, victimization was thought to primarily occur through physical or verbal attacks such as hitting, pushing, cursing, or threatening. Not surprisingly, this research found that boys were victimized more frequently than girls. Such findings, however, contradicted common knowledge about the peer experiences of girls and boys. More recent research has revised this conceptualization to include forms of peer maltreatment such as shunning, ignoring, and spreading rumors. The shift in the definition of what constitutes a victimizing act has had significant implications on applied practice and empirical study. By broadening the definition of peer victimization to include gender normative aggressive behaviors, a more balanced picture of boys' and girls' peer experiences has been captured. The newer technology advances and the newer attention to "initiations" in colleges have broadened the conceptual picture even further.

Many who are teased/hazed are frequently seen as socially unassertive and submissive, often physically weak (if male), and low in self-esteem. Some victims also display externalizing problems, such as disruptiveness, aggression, and socially inappropriate behaviors, which are thought to irritate and provoke bullies. For example, numerous studies have shown that victims typically make repeated attempts to interact with their victimizer, which frequently would lead to fights. Interpersonally, the friendships of teased/hazed victims tend to be fraught with conflict and betrayal. Overall, relationships of those who are teased are characterized as less positive, both behaviorally (e.g., cooperating, sharing) and affectively (e.g., smiling, acceptance) than those of non-victims.

Research on bullies has focused on their tendency to attribute hostile intentions to others, often resulting in conflict. Olweus (1978) wrote that the aggressor is "characterized by an aggressive personality pattern, with a tendency to react aggressively in many different situations, with fairly weak controls or inhibitions against aggressive tendencies, and with a positive attitude towards violence." Aggressors are noncompliant with authority figures and use physically assertive behaviors to display dominance over rivals or weaker peers. There is some evidence that aggressive people may differ from others in the way that they process social information. Data suggest that aggressive people interpret environmental cues differently (e.g., a friendly shove may be perceived as an aggressive act) and generate more hostile responses to neutral stimuli. As well, aggressive youth, as compared to non-aggressive and socially competent youth, are more likely to pursue dominance and revenge goals and less likely to pursue afflictive goals.

There are three types of studies to consider in examining the impact of peer victimization on psychosocial adjustment. Cross-sectional studies look at the relationship between current victimization and current psychosocial adjustment. While these studies are the most practical to carry out, the findings they yield can be difficult to interpret since correlation does not equal causation. Longitudinal studies ameliorate this problem by following the same group of over time, looking at their psychosocial functioning at baseline and then collecting data on victimization experiences and psychosocial functioning at later time-points. Finally, retrospective studies ask adults about recalled victimization experiences during childhood and examine the relationship between recalled memories and current psychosocial functioning. This kind of study also provides valuable information, but there is disagreement about the reliability of retrospective recall, with some researchers finding it to be a relatively accurate method of assessment of childhood experiences and others calling it into question.

As noted earlier, males and females often suffer from different kinds of peer victimization experiences, calling into question whether they also react to peer victimization in different ways. Cross-sectional studies show that for females, the relationship between peer victimization and anxiety is mediated by feelings of low self-worth. For males, feelings of self-worth moderate the relationship between peer victimization and anxiety. While high levels of self-worth served as a protective factor against anxiety following victimization experiences, low levels of self-worth serve as a risk factor for anxiety. These findings suggest that women may internalize negative feedback from peers to a greater degree than males, leading to a direct negative effect on self-worth. Some males (those with high self-worth), on the other hand, might see bullying as a normal part of their peer relations and not be distressed by it or might actually derogate the bully, serving to make themselves feel better.

Other cross-sectional studies have compared the relative impact of overt and relational victimization. In these studies, relational victimization (shunning, gossip) was more strongly related to internalizing problems for women than overt victimization (hitting, pushing, and threatening) was. Relational victimization was found to be associated with internalizing symptoms (depression, loneliness, and poor self-worth) for males and females, while overt victimization was found to be associated with depression symptoms for males only.

There are conflicting findings on how victimized children interact with peers. While some cross-sectional studies suggest that victims interact in a passive, submissive way, others suggest that they are more aggressive than non-victimized peers. It is possible that these conflicting data emerge owing to the use of differing methodologies (e.g., teacher report, child report, parent report). They also could be indicative of the broad range of coping behaviors the victimized child displays, such as sometimes being overly-aggressive or at other times unduly submissive when confronted by a bully. There seems to be agreement, however, that victimized children have difficulties managing confrontations with peers. Rather than seeking out additional information to resolve a problem, victimized children tend to let situations escalate quickly. These findings can be applied to actions when older. Hazing can be related and compared to actions of passive acceptance, while the victim internalizes the issues or acts out on others in a different venue.

Mirroring results from cross-sectional studies, longitudinal studies consistently find victimization to be predictive of a variety of internalizing problems including anxiety, depression, and loneliness. Various predictors have been found to influence the relationship between peer victimization and later psychosocial problems. One study by Storch (2006) found that increased negative mood from one school year to the next was influenced not only by an increase in actual victimization but also by the belief (of the victim) that aggression is a legitimate and warranted form of social behavior.

While most longitudinal studies in this body of literature extend from a few months to a few years, several long-term studies have shown that victimization during childhood and early adolescence was predictive of depressive tendencies and poor self-esteem into early adulthood, suggesting that the negative consequences of victimization might be quite far reaching.

Consistent with this, self-worth has also been found to be related to victimization in longitudinal studies. Several studies have explored the relationship between self-regard and victimization over the course of a school year. While victimization was related only to low perceived social competence at the beginning of the year, it came to be associated by the end of the year with poor global self-worth and a sense that children could not stand up for themselves once victimized. Further examination of these studies suggest that poor self-concept invited increased victimization over time, even when overt triggers for victimization that were visible to peers were partial led out (e.g., internalizing behaviors, physical weakness, etc.). Leading to the conclusion why some accept hazing in a college setting. Further, these studies may indicate why those who were continued victims turned to violence or suicide in a college/university.

Being victimized by peers has also been found to be strongly associated with externalizing problems. The research suggests a strong connection between victimization and later aggressive behavior, attention problems, and later delinquency. Both cross-sectional and longitudinal studies have shown that peer victimization predicts later interpersonal difficulties, including peer rejection. Children who are victimized tend to gravitate toward friends who are similar to them, and associating with other victimized children (who also have internalizing problems) probably sets the scene for even more victimization from peers.

© lkeskinen/Shutterstock.com

Longitudinal studies have also found victimization to also be associated with academic problems. Several studies report the relationship between self-perceived victimization and poor school outcomes was moderated by poor psychological adjustment (self-worth, loneliness, and depression); Victimization, in and of itself, did not negatively impact school performance.

Less attention has been paid to the relationship between peer victimization and later difficulties with mood and anxiety. The limited available research suggests, however, that the experience of peer victimization during childhood is associated with later psychological distress. In several studies that specifically examined the impact

© marimedi/Shutterstock.com

of recalled childhood teasing, college students who recalled frequently having this experience reported being more anxious, more fearful of negative evaluation from others, more depressed, and more lonely. Perhaps, reaching out to be accepted by others and "inviting" hazing.

Other retrospective studies that looked at peer victimization, more broadly defined, reported similar findings. In one study by Roth (2002), patients in an anxiety disorders clinic were asked whether or not they had ever been bullied or severely teased. Eighty-five percent of the participants with social anxiety disorder responded affirmatively to this question. Furthermore, participants with social anxiety disorder were significantly more likely to report that they had been bullied or severely teased than participants with panic disorder (25 percent) or obsessive-compulsive disorder (56 percent) were. In other words, recalled peer victimization seems particularly related to later difficulties in the social domain.

Recalled victimization has also been found to be associated with later problems with mood. In two studies by Gibb and colleagues (2004), college students were asked about victimization experiences by peers and boyfriends/girlfriends during childhood and adolescence. Students at high risk for depression (as assessed by psychological instruments) reported significantly more victimization experiences, particularly by boyfriends/girlfriends, than students at low risk for depression did. The relationship held even when controlling for a number of relevant parental variables (parental cognitive style, parental history of depression).

Taken together, these findings imply that childhood victimization is related to later interpersonal problems as well. Although being teased in the social domain was found to be most strongly associated with later psychological distress (depression, anxiety, and loneliness), being teased about social behavior, performance, and appearance all seemed to have roughly equal (negative) effects on later interpersonal functioning. Although recalled teasing was not found to be related to the number of friends that participants had during early adulthood, it was found to be related to lower social self-esteem and to difficulties in romantic relationships. Specifically, recalling frequent teasing during childhood was found to be associated with less comfort with intimacy and closeness, less of an ability to trust and depend on others, as well as a greater degree of worry about being unloved or abandoned in relationships.

THE RELATIONSHIP BETWEEN YOUTH AGGRESSION AND PARTNER VIOLENCE

During middle school, peer-directed aggressive behaviors peak among both boys and girls and then decline from ninth through twelfth grade. In the 2003 Youth Risk Behavior Survey (YRBS), for example, 39 percent of 9th graders report being in a fight, compared to 26 percent of twelfth graders, and weapons carrying dropped slightly from 18 percent to 16 percent. During the high school years, however, young people also become involved in dating and intimate partner relationships, and problems dealing with aggression in these relationships emerge. Partner violence is widespread, with the prevalence increasing rapidly between the ages of fifteen and twenty-five years. Once initiated, aggressive patterns of interacting and resolving conflict, especially with intimate partners, can be very difficult to break.

Violence often begins in dating relationships of adolescents and continues through courtships, longer-term relationships, and marriage, when more serious violence may occur. In a national sample of young adults, Morse (1995) found that both males and females reported engaging in frequent minor assaults on their partner, but that young men were more likely to repeatedly beat their partner and to cause injury requiring medical treatment. This pattern often continues through adulthood. Data suggests that although women, in general, may strike as often, men hit harder, and women may underestimate the potential risk of being seriously injured or killed. Women who engage in the use physical force often report that their use of force was primarily or exclusively in self-defense, though aggression between partners can also be interactive and reciprocal.

There are relatively few longitudinal studies that begin prior to adulthood and examine multiple forms of violence (i.e., bullying, school violence, intimate partner abuse) and perpetration by males and females. In a cohort of New Zealand Youth followed from birth through age twenty-one, individuals with histories of early antisocial behavior problems were more likely to behave violently toward their partners and to be victims of violence. In a twenty-year prospective study on intergenerational transmission of partner violence, adolescent conduct disorders were a strong predictor of partner violence perpetration for both genders. Associations have also been reported between adolescent violence assessed at ages fifteen to eighteen and subsequent relationship aggression among adults assessed at twenty-five and twenty-nine years of age.

Other cross-sectional and shorter-term longitudinal research provides an inconsistent picture of the relationship of early aggression to partner violence. Using cross-sectional analyses from the National Study of Adolescent Health, Roberts (2003) concludes that early aggressive behaviors are associated with later reports of intimate partner abuse. In a study of the co-occurrence of peer violence and dating violence among European and Mexican American adolescents interviewed at sixteen–twenty years of age and again one year later, males who engaged in peer violence perpetration were more likely to be at risk for dating violence and sexual aggression; this finding did not hold for females. In annual surveys with eighth and ninth grade urban youth, having been in physical fights with a peer predicted onset of serious physical dating violence victimization for males, but not for females. The study of Foshee et al. (2004) provides evidence that bullying behaviors and perpetration of violence during middle school predicts subsequent partner victimization.

OTHER RISK FACTORS FOR PARTNER VIOLENCE

As research shows time and time again, one of the most consistent findings for both genders is the relationship between childhood victimization, including verified child abuse and neglect, and involvement in or witnessing parental domestic violence episodes.

Therefore, the early intervention and education of students will play a large role in stemming the cycle of violence. In a sample of college students, those who were physically abused or who witnessed domestic violence in childhood were at greater risk for partner violence during high school, and those who were victimized during high school were at greater risk for victimization as young adults. Young men who assaulted partners had also experienced more family violence than other men. However, other studies have found that reports of friends engaging in dating violence, but not inter-parental violence, predicted report of one's own dating violence.

Although much of the existing research on intimate partner violence has focused primarily on acts of physical violence, psychological abuse should also be considered as it is closely intertwined with physical abuse. Past research has shown that verbal abuse is related to physical aggression and that psychological abuse may precede physical abuse. Threatening, controlling, and terrorizing behaviors are likely to explain at least part of the reason that women remain in abusive situations. Furthermore, most research suggests that the long-term effects of psychological abuse on physical and mental health may be quite serious.

When investigating early indicators of intimate partner violence, three variables are consistently reported as being related to subsequent partner abuse. These are reports of early conduct problems (prior to age fifteen), early delinquency, and early substance abuse (prior to age fifteen). The correlations of partner abuse with earlier conduct problems and physically violent delinquent offending suggest that young persons who have a lengthy history of solving interpersonal problems in a coercive manner are likely to use similar tactics in their primary adult relationships. The correlation of partner abuse and earlier substance abuse is consistent, as well as other research showing that early onset substance abuse is closely linked with aggressive behavior, and often precedes it.

SEX-BASED HARASSMENT

Title IX of the Education Amendments of 1972 prohibits discrimination on the basis of sex in schools that receive federal funding. All forms of sex-based harassment are prohibited, including sexual harassment, harassment based on a student's failure to conform to gender stereotypes, and sexual assault. It does not matter whether the harasser intends to harm or not, the harasser and target do not need to be of different sexes, and severe harassment does not necessarily require repeated incidents.

Title IX protects every person—boys and girls; men and women; students and employees—from sex-based harassment in schools and colleges that receive federal funding. This means that school districts or colleges may violate Title IX when sexual- or gender-based harassment by classmates (or peers) is so serious that it interferes with or limits a student's ability to participate in or benefit from the school or school activities, and such harassment is encouraged, tolerated, not adequately addressed, or ignored by school employees.

Despite efforts to curb sexual- and gender-based harassment in schools, including sexual assault, these forms of sex discrimination are still prevalent in K–12 schools and colleges around the nation. The problem begins as early as elementary school. In a 2010 nationwide survey of elementary schools, nearly half of all teachers (48 percent) reported that they hear students make sexist remarks at their school. Harassment based on failure to conform to sex stereotypes, which Title IX prohibits, is also prevalent in students' early years. The same study found that one-third of students (33 percent) have heard kids at school say that girls should not do or wear certain things because they are girls, and 38 percent have heard their peers say that boys should not do or wear certain things because they are boys. Indeed, students who do not conform to traditional gender norms are more likely than their peers to say they are called names, made fun of, or bullied at school (56 percent versus 33 percent).[1]

Sex-based harassment continues into middle and high school. In a nationwide survey of students in grades eight–eleven, 81 percent reported experiencing sexual harassment during their school lives.[2] And in a recent survey of seventh–twelfth grade students, nearly half (48 percent) experienced some form of sexual harassment during the 2010–11 school year, with a vast majority of those students (87 percent) reporting that the harassment had a negative effect on them.[3] Both studies found that girls were more likely than boys to have experienced harassment.[4]

And among lesbian, gay, bisexual, and transgender (LGBT) students, the numbers are even higher—in a study of LGBT students in grades six–twelve, 85 percent of respondents reported being verbally harassed and 40 percent reporting being physically harassed at school because of their sexual orientation. Close to two-thirds (64 percent) were verbally harassed because of their gender expression.[5] Another study found that LGBT youth were twice as likely to have been verbally harassed at school as their non-LGBT peers.[6]

Sexual harassment, including assault, on college campuses is also a widespread problem. In a nationwide survey of college students, most respondents (89 percent) stated that sexual harassment occurs among students at their school, and nearly two-thirds (62 percent) said they had been sexually harassed.[7]

Sex-based harassment can be very damaging to the lives of women and girls, both in its emotional impact and in its impact on their education. Feeling unsafe at school has been correlated with declining academic performance, skipping school, and dropping out.[8] To illustrate, a recent survey found that nearly one-third (32 percent) of students who experienced harassment reported not wanting to go to school as a result of the harassment, and girls were more likely than boys to report harassment affecting them in this way.[9]

For girls and young women who drop out of school due to sexual- or gender-based harassment, the long-term economic impact can be devastating. Young women who don't graduate from high school have higher rates of unemployment than men who drop out;[10] those who do get jobs make significantly lower wages than male dropouts.[11] Women lacking a high school degree are also more likely to have to rely on safety net programs than their male peers or men and women who have graduated from high school and college.[12] And although men at every level of education make more than women with similar educational backgrounds, the wage gap is particularly high among high school dropouts: the typical woman who starts but does not finish high school is paid only 71 percent of what her male counterpart is paid.[13] Female dropouts are more likely to live in poverty than both men and women with higher educational attainment.[14] And children raised in such situations may find it difficult to escape poverty themselves;

studies have shown that being poor at birth is a strong predictor of future poverty status, and children in poverty have lower odds of experiencing upward mobility across generations.[15] Thus, the economic impact of sex-based harassment on women and their families can be overwhelming.

Title IX and other federal civil rights laws do not explicitly prohibit discrimination in schools on the basis of sexual orientation or gender identity, but when LGBT students are subjected to harassment because of failure to conform to gender stereotypes—meaning harassment or bullying because a student does not conform to stereotyped notions of masculinity or femininity—Title IX applies. For example, gender-based harassment can include harassing a female student based on the belief that a girl should not take shop classes, or be a math whiz, or play a particular sport, or harassing a male student because he is on the dance team or exhibits effeminate mannerisms.

Cyber-bullying

Many forms of what people might consider bullying, hazing, or cyberbullying are actually sex-based harassment that is prohibited under Title IX. For example, prohibited harassment may include common behaviors such as using cell phones or the Internet to target students by calling them sexually charged epithets like "slut" or "whore"; spreading sexual rumors; rating students on sexual activity or performance; disseminating compromising photographs or videos of a student; or circulating, showing, or creating emails or websites of a sexual nature. Conduct often dismissed as just "boys being boys" or "mean girls," when severe, persistent, or pervasive, can actually be prohibited harassment.

In order to clarify schools' obligations under Title IX with regard to harassment, the U.S. Department of Education's Office for Civil Rights ("OCR") issued a Guidance document in October 2010 specifying that Title IX prohibits sex-based bullying and harassment that interferes with a student's education, whether it is conducted in person or in electronic form. The Guidance states that "bullying fosters a climate of fear and disrespect that can seriously impair the physical and psychological health of its victims and create conditions that negatively affect learning, thereby undermining the ability of students to achieve their full potential."[16]

© ricochet64/Shutterstock.com

Some schools question whether they can react to cyberbullying that is done "off campus," from home computers, cell phones, or elsewhere, because of concerns about students' rights to free speech. However, Title IX applies to all programs and activities of the school, and includes, for example, conduct that takes place on school buses, during extracurricular activities, and when students are participating in a school's athletics program.[17] In addition, courts have held that schools may discipline students for truly off-campus cyberspeech consistent with the First Amendment if it was reasonably foreseeable that the speech would create a substantial disruption in the school environment.[18]

Endnotes

1. GAY, LESBIAN AND STRAIGHT EDUCATION NETWORK (GLSEN), PLAYGROUNDS AND PREJUDICE: ELEMENTARY SCHOOL CLIMATE IN THE UNITED STATES xvi-xvii (2012), *available at* http://www.glsen.org/binary-data/GLSEN_ATTACHMENTS/file/000/002/2027-1.pdf.
2. AAUW EDUC. FOUND., HOSTILE HALLWAYS: BULLYING, TEASING, AND SEXUAL HARASSMENT IN SCHOOL 4 (2001), *available at* http://www.aauw.org/learn/research/upload/hostilehallways.pdf.
3. CATHERINE HILL & HOLLY KEARL, AAUW, CROSSING THE LINE: SEXUAL HARASSMENT AT SCHOOL 2 (2011), *available at* http://www.aauw.org/learn/research/upload/CrossingTheLine.pdf.
4. HOSTILE HALLWAYS, *supra* note 2, at 4 (observing girls were more likely than boys to report experiencing harassment often or occasionally (83 percent versus 79 percent) or often (24 percent versus percent)); CROSSING THE LINE, *supra* note 3, at 2 (reporting 56 percent of girls reported being sexually harassed in the past school year, compared to 40 percent of boys).
5. GAY, LESBIAN & STRAIGHT EDUC. NETWORK (GLSEN), THE 2009 NATIONAL SCHOOL CLIMATE SURVEY: THE EXPERIENCES OF LESBIAN, GAY, BISEXUAL AND TRANSGENDER YOUTH IN OUR NATION'S SCHOOLS vxi (2010), *available at* http://www.glsen.org/binary-data/GLSEN_ATTACHMENTS/file/000/001/1675-2.pdf.
6. HUMAN RIGHTS CAMPAIGN, GROWING UP LGBT IN AMERICA: HRC YOUTH SURVEY REPORT KEY FINDINGS (2012), *available at* http://www.hrc.org/files/assets/resources/Growing-Up-LGBT-in-America_Report.pdf.
7. CATHERINE HILL & ELENA SILVA, AAUW EDUC. FOUND., DRAWING THE LINE: SEXUAL HARASSMENT ON CAMPUS 14 (2005), *available at* http://www.aauw.org/learn/research/upload/DTLFinal.pdf.
8. HOSTILE HALLWAYS, *supra* note 2, at 36–38.
9. CROSSING THE LINE, *supra* note 3, at 22 (reporting 37 percent of girls did not want to go to school versus 25 percent of boys).
10. Bureau of Labor Statistics, Current Population Survey, *available at* http://data.bls.gov/cgi-bin/srgate (last visited May 10, 2012). In 2011, women twenty-five and older without a high school diploma had an unemployment rate of 14.8 percent, compared to 13.6 percent for men twenty-five and older without a high school diploma. Data were accessed using codes LNU04027675 (men) and LNU04027679 (women).
11. U.S. Census Bureau, Current Population Survey (CPS), 2011 Annual Social and Economic Survey, Table PINC-03:Educational Attainment—People Twenty-five Years Old and Over, by Total Money Earnings in 2010, Work Experience in 2010, Age, Race, Hispanic Origin, and Sex, *available at* http://www.census.gov/hhes/www/cpstables/032011/perinc/new03_000.htm [hereinafter Educational Attainment Table]. Earnings data are for men and women twenty-five–sixty-four who worked full time, year round. The typical woman who started, but did not finish high school had earnings of $20,779, just 71 percent of her male counterpart's earnings ($29,076).

12. NWLC calculations using U.S. Census Bureau, Current Population Survey, 2011 Annual Social and Economic Survey, public-use microdata files. Calculations based on receipt of WIC, SSI, and TANF. Medicaid data from U.S. Census Bureau, Current Population Survey, CPS Table Creator, *available at* http://www.census.gov/cps/data/cpstablecreator.html (last visited May 10, 2012).
13. Educational Attainment Table, *supra* note 11.
14. U.S. Census Bureau, Current Population Survey, CPS Table Creator, *available at* http://www.census.gov/cps/data/cpstablecreator.html (last visited May 10, 2012). Data are for women ages twenty-five–sixty-four. In 2010, women without a high school diploma had a poverty rate of 39 percent compared to 18 percent for women with a high school diploma, and less than 5 percent for women with a bachelor's degree or higher. At all education levels, women were more likely than men to live in poverty.
15. *See* Harry J. Holzer, *Penny Wise, Pound Foolish: Why Tackling Child Poverty During the Great Recession Makes Economic Sense*, HALF IN TEN (Ctr. for Am. Progress, Washington, D.C.), Sept. 2010, at 3, *available at* http://www.americanprogress.org/issues/2010/09/pdf/hit_child poverty.pdf; *Poverty Among Women and Families, 2000-2010: Extreme Poverty Reaches Record Levels as Congress Faces Critical Choices* (Nat'l Women's Law Center, Washington, D.C.), Sept. 2011, at 1, *available at* http://www.nwlc.org/sites/default/files/ pdfs/povertyamongwomenand-familiesin2010.pdf.
16. *U.S. Department of Education, Office For Civil Rights, Dear Colleague Letter On Bullying and Harassment 1* (Oct. 26, 2010), available at http://www2.ed.gov/about/offices/list/ocr/letters/colleague-201010.pdf.
17. Ibid.
18. See, e.g., *Kowalski v. Berkeley Cmty. Schs.*, 652 F.3d 565, 572-74 (4th Cir. 2011), cert. denied by 132 S. Ct. 1095 (No. 11-461, Jan. 17, 2012) (upholding school's discipline of student for creating a website off campus that ridiculed a fellow classmate, since it was foreseeable that the speech would reach the school and the website involved substantial disruption and interference with the school's work); *J.S. ex rel. Snyder v. Blue Mountain Sch. Dist.*, 650 F.3d 915, 926 (3d Cir. 2011) (en banc), cert. denied by *Blue Mountain Sch. Dist. v. J.S. ex rel. Snyder*, 132 S. Ct. 1097 (No. 11-502, Jan. 17, 2012) (assuming without deciding that a student may be disciplined by a school consistent with the First Amendment for cyber-speech created off-campus which causes a substantial disruption in school, or which could reasonably lead school officials to fear substantial disruption in school, though the speech in that particular case did not create such a disruption or fear of disruption); *Doninger v. Niehoff*, 527 F.3d 41, 50-53 (2d Cir. 2008), cert. denied by 132 S. Ct. 499 (No. 11-113, Oct. 31, 2011) (holding plaintiff did not demonstrate a clear likelihood of success on the merits of her First Amendment claim based on school's sanctions against her for off-campus blog post regarding school event because it created a foreseeable risk of substantial disruption to the work and discipline of the school); *J.S. v. Bethlehem Area Sch. Dist.*, 807 A.2d 847, 850 (Pa. 2002) ("[A] school district may, consistent with the First Amendment . . . , discipline a student for creating at home, and posting on the Internet, a web site that . . . contained derogatory, profane, offensive and threatening statements directed toward of the student's teachers and principal."); cf. *D.J.M. v. Hannibal Pub. Sch. Dist. #60*, 647 F.3d 754, 765-66 (8th Cir. 2011) (holding school did not violate First Amendment in disciplining student for instant messages sent from his home in which he talked about getting a gun and shooting fellow students and himself, both because it was reasonably foreseeable that the threats would cause a substantial disruption and because they constituted a true threat).

DISCUSSION QUESTIONS

1. Provide a definition of bullying. Be certain to include specific wording that covers the types and means in which bullying occurs.

2. Explain hazing and parameters for both victims and abusers.

3. Why has cyber-bullying become such a concern for all age groups? Provide Examples of how cyber-bullying can differ among age groups.

4. Describe some of the effects bullying produces for victims and the bullies.

5. Provide examples of "signs" that someone might be on the verge of committing violence in the school/workplace based upon the studies in the chapter.

6. Describe some ways that victimized children interact with their peers.

7. Provide specific examples of the differences in methods of bullying/hazing based upon gender.

Name: _____   Date _____

You must use this form and turn in the original to the instructor. No other form will be accepted.

CHAPTER ASSIGNMENT

Using studies and research contained in the text compare your independent research on the effects of hazing in a college setting and likely outcomes. Include codes of conduct, rules on campus and housing, laws and if hazing behavior has negative impacts on academics and personal well-being.

_____
_____
_____
_____
_____
_____
_____
_____
_____
_____
_____
_____
_____
_____
_____
_____
_____

Chapter Eight

VICTIMS OF CRIMES PERPETRATED BY JUVENILES—RIGHTS AND THE JUVENILE JUSTICE PROCESS

© hafakot/Shutterstock.com

LEARNING OBJECTIVES

After exploring Chapter Eight (8), the student will be able to:

1. Describe the federal juvenile justice system.
2. Define juvenile offender.
3. Explain the difference between the state juvenile justice process and the federal juvenile justice process.
4. Identify gang statutes under federal law.
5. List the steps in the New Jersey juvenile justice system.

KEY TERMS

Juvenile Justice System, Gang, State system, Federal system, Juvenile delinquency, Disposition hearing, Crisis intervention, Diversion

FEDERAL JUVENILE DELINQUENCY PROSECUTION—INTRODUCTION

Nearly two-thirds of all youth arrested are referred to a court with juvenile jurisdiction for further processing. "Juvenile Offenders and Victims: A National Report", National Center for Juvenile Justice (August, 1995). Cases that progress through the system may result in adjudication and court-ordered supervision or out-of-home placement, or may result in transfer for criminal (adult) prosecution. Over the five-year period from 1988 through 1992, the juvenile courts saw a disproportional increase in violent offense cases and weapon law violations.

Many gang members and other violent offenders are under the age of eighteen when they commit criminal acts. Therefore, under 18 U.S.C.A. § 5031, these offenders are classified as "juveniles" for purposes of federal prosecution. Federal crimes committed by the juveniles which would be crimes if committed by an adult or violations of 18 U.S.C.A. § 922(x) are classified as acts of "juvenile delinquency." Gang members are treated as adults for federal criminal prosecutions if they have attained their eighteenth birthday when they commit federal crimes.

At common law, one accused of a crime was treated essentially the same whether he was an infant or an adult. It was presumed that a person under the age of seven could not entertain criminal intent and thus was incapable of committing a crime. One between the ages of seven and fourteen was presumed incapable of entertaining criminal intent but such presumption was rebuttable. A person fourteen years of age and older was prima facie capable of committing crime.

Prior to 1938, there was no federal legislation providing for special treatment for juveniles. In 1938, the Federal Juvenile Delinquency Act was passed with the essential purpose of keeping juveniles apart from adult criminals. The original legislation provided juveniles with certain important rights including the right not to be sentenced to a term beyond the age of twenty-one. This early law also provided an individual could be prosecuted as a juvenile delinquent only if the Attorney General in his discretion so directed. The 1938 Act gave the Attorney General the option to proceed against juvenile offenders as adults or as delinquents except those allegedly committing offenses punishable by death or life imprisonment. The Juvenile Delinquency Act was amended in 1948, with few substantive changes.

In 1974, Congress adopted the Juvenile Justice and Delinquency Prevention Act (hereinafter referred to as "the Act"). Its stated purpose was "to provide basic procedural rights for juveniles who came under federal jurisdiction and to bring federal procedures up to the standards set by various model acts, many state codes and court decisions." The purpose of the Act is to remove juveniles from the ordinary criminal process to avoid the stigma of a prior criminal conviction and to encourage treatment and rehabilitation. This purpose, however, must be balanced against the need to protect the public from violent offenders. The intent of federal laws concerning juveniles are to help ensure that state and local authorities would deal with juvenile offenders whenever possible, keeping juveniles away from the less appropriate federal channels since Congress' desire to channel juveniles into state and local treatment programs is clearly intended in the legislative history

© Artem Samokhvalov/Shutterstock.com

of 18 U.S.C.A. § 5032. Therefore, referral to the state courts should always be observed except in the most severe of cases.

REFERRAL TO STATE AUTHORITIES

First, if a juvenile is arrested by federal authorities for acts of juvenile delinquency, he or she may be surrendered to the state unless proper certification is made for federal proceedings. If an alleged juvenile delinquent is not surrendered to state authorities, any proceedings against the juvenile shall be in an appropriate district court of the United States.

JUVENILE DELINQUENCY PROCEEDINGS—CERTIFICATION

It may be deemed appropriate to proceed against the juvenile(s) in federal court. This process is divided into two (2) distinct methods depending upon whether the juvenile will be treated as a juvenile delinquent or a criminal (adult). Juvenile adjudication is presumed appropriate unless the government establishes that prosecution as an adult is warranted. Prosecution by either method can proceed by information, although seeking to transfer juvenile cases to adult status could begin with a complaint and result in an indictment if such transfer is granted by the court. Certification is not required prior to the filing of a complaint and issuance of an arrest warrant. Perhaps, when arrests are made by federal investigators and later it is determined that the arrestee is a juvenile.

The certification requirement is a prerequisite to the district court's subject matter jurisdiction in cases where the government proceeds against juveniles accused of performing acts which would be federal crimes if committed by adults. The information for juvenile offenders is similar to informations filed for adult offenders, although it is a good idea to include language stating the charges are generally based upon the authority to proceed against juveniles under 18 U.S.C.A. § 5032, as well as, particularly setting forth the actual criminal offense(s).

© Mark Van Scyoc/Shutterstock.com

The United States Attorney may wish to prosecute the juvenile as a juvenile delinquent rather than treating him as an adult or criminal. Certification by the United States Attorney must be made to the United States District Court that (1) the juvenile court or other appropriate state court does not have jurisdiction over the juvenile with respect to the alleged act of juvenile delinquency, (2) the state does not have available programs and services adequate for the needs of juveniles, or (3) the offense charged is a violent felony or an offense described in 21 U.S.C.A. §§ 841, 952(a), 955, 959, 960(b)(1), (2), (3); 18

U.S.C.A. § 922(p) or (x), or 18 U.S.C.A. § 924(b), (q) or (h), and there is a substantial federal interest in the case or the offense to warrant the exercise of federal jurisdiction. The third certification reason as described in the preceding sentence will probably be most appropriate when dealing with gang violence.

While Section 5032 does not define crime of violence, the phrase is defined in Title 18, United States Code, Section 16. The term "crime of violence" means:

a. an offense that has as an element the use, attempted use, or threatened use of physical force against the person or property of another, or

b. any other offense that is a felony and that, by its nature, involves a substantial risk that physical force against the person or property of another may be used in the course of committing the offense." 18 U.S.C.A. § 16 (West Supp. 1995).

Conspiracy to commit a violent crime is a crime of violence as contemplated by Sections 16(b) and 5032. Conspiracies that may properly be deemed crimes of violence include those whose objectives are violent crimes or those whose members intend to use violent methods to achieve the conspiracy's goals. A conspiracy to commit a non-violent crime is not a crime of violence under the applicable provisions.

Thus, conspiracies to commit drug trafficking under 21 U.S.C.A. § 846 are not transferable.

HEARING TO DETERMINE DELINQUENCY

A juvenile is accorded all due process rights at a juvenile hearing which includes the right to contest the value of the evidence offered by the government. Although juvenile adjudications are adjudications of status rather than criminal liability, the government must still prove beyond a reasonable doubt that a juvenile is a delinquent.

Proceedings for adjudication of a juvenile as a delinquent shall be in district court. The court may convene at any time and place within the district, in chambers or otherwise, to take up the proceedings of juvenile delinquency. A juvenile may consent to having a magistrate judge preside over cases involving a Class B or C misdemeanor, or an infraction. There is a certain advantage to the juvenile in exercising this option since a magistrate judge cannot impose a term of imprisonment in these situations. Proceedings in misdemeanor cases can be ordered to be conducted before a district judge rather than a magistrate judge by the court's own motion or upon petition with good cause by the United States Attorney.

© Rob Wilson/Shutterstock.com

ADJUDICATION AS A JUVENILE DELINQUENT

Adjudication of a juvenile as a delinquent under the Act is not deemed a conviction of a crime, but rather a determination of status. The manifest purpose of the Act is to aid in the rehabilitation of juveniles who have been determined to have engaged in crime. The purpose of the federal juvenile delinquency proceeding is to remove juveniles from the ordinary criminal process in order to avoid the stigma of a prior criminal conviction and to encourage treatment and rehabilitation.

DISPOSITION HEARING

If the court finds a juvenile to be a delinquent, a disposition hearing shall be held. It must be held within twenty days of the finding of delinquency unless a "further study" of the juvenile is ordered by the court.

At the disposition hearing, and after considering any pertinent policy statements promulgated by the Sentencing Commission, the court may suspend the findings of juvenile delinquency, order restitution, place the juvenile on probation, or commit him to official detention. Generally, any term of probation or custody will not extend past the juvenile's twenty-first birthday or the maximum term that would be authorized if the juvenile had been tried and convicted as an adult, whichever occurs first.

© Junial Enterprises/Shutterstock.com

If a juvenile found to be delinquent is between eighteen and twenty-one and has committed a Class A, B, or C felony, the district court may order official detention for up to five years. The court may impose detention for up to three years in the case of other crimes. The maximum authorized term refers to the maximum length of sentence to which a similarly situated adult would be subjected if convicted of the adult counterpart of the offense and sentenced under the Guidelines. A court has no authority under the Act to sentence an adjudicated juvenile delinquent to supervised release in addition to a term of official detention.

Sentencing Guidelines do not directly apply to juvenile delinquency proceedings. However, the sentencing and reviewing courts will have to determine an appropriate guideline range in juvenile delinquency proceedings which will be used solely to determine the upper limit in setting the maximum term for which a juvenile may be committed to official detention, absent circumstances that would warrant departure under 18 U.S.C.A. § 3553(b).

NEW JERSEY JUVENILE JUSTICE SYSTEM—COMPARISON WITH THE FEDERAL SYSTEM

According to—**http://www.nj.gov/oag/jjc/thru_system.htm**

Arrest/Police Diversion

A juvenile enters the juvenile justice system when a complaint charging the commission of a delinquent act is signed. A law enforcement officer may take a juvenile into custody when there is probable cause to believe that the juvenile is delinquent. In lieu of signing a delinquency complaint, the officer may divert the case through several means, including releasing the juvenile to a responsible parent or guardian (with or without a reprimand and warning) or conduct a station house adjustment. Once a delinquency complaint is signed, a juvenile can be held in a secure detention facility if certain statutory criteria are met. The officer refers the case to court intake service to request admission into detention.

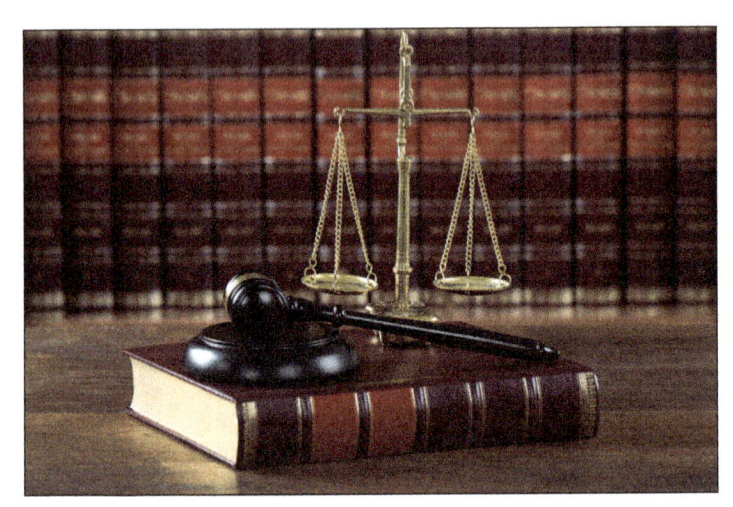

© Andrey_Popov/Shutterstock.com

Juvenile/Family Crisis Intervention Units

Juvenile/Family Crisis Intervention Units (JFCIUs) were authorized to divert from court proceedings, matters involving family related problems, e.g., incorrigibility, truancy, runaway, and serious family conflict. The JFCIUs provide short-term, crisis intervention services with the goal of stabilizing the family situation and/or referring the juvenile and family to available community agencies.

Court Diversion

Juvenile Conference Committees (JCCs) and Intake Service Conferences (ISCs) are diversion procedures established by the court and utilized in select first and second offenses of a minor nature. JCCs are comprised of community residents appointed by the court to review certain delinquency complaints. ISCs are conducted by court intake staff to review slightly more serious delinquency allegations. Both diversion procedures occur after delinquency complaints have been signed and filed with the court.

Secure Detention

Secure juvenile detention is the temporary placement of juveniles charged with a delinquent act, in a locked facility, prior to the disposition of their case. New Jersey law mandates that the court can detain

From *In Summary*, 2006 compiled by Patrick Griffin by National Center for Juvenile Justice. Copyright © 2006 by National Center for Juvenile Justice. Reprinted by permission.

juveniles only if they are considered a danger to the community or if they are deemed a risk not to appear in court. (N.J.S.A. 2A:4A-34). In addition, some juveniles are detained post-disposition while awaiting program placement. Several counties have also developed a short-term commitment program, which serves as a dispositions option.

In New Jersey, counties are generally responsible for operating and financing detention facilities. The State's role is primarily limited to standard setting, monitoring, and technical assistance through the JJC's Compliance Monitoring Unit. In 1999 there were eighteen juvenile detention facilities statewide, with a capacity of 910 beds.

Court Process

The Family Court / Court Process

The Family Court is required to hold hearings for juveniles charged as delinquents, with specific mandated time limitations, particularly regarding juveniles held in secure detention (N.J.S.A. 2A:4A-38).

In sequential order, they are as follows:

1. An initial detention hearing is to be held within twenty-four hours of admission.
2. For juveniles remanded to detention, the initial probable cause hearing and second detention hearing are to be held within two court days. If probable cause is not found, the juvenile is released from detention pending an adjudicator hearing.
3. Review hearings are held for detained juveniles at intervals of fourteen and twenty-one court days. At each of these hearings, the juvenile's detention status is reconsidered by the judge.
4. At the adjudicator hearing, the court makes a determination on the delinquency charges. A juvenile may be adjudicated delinquent on one or more of the charges; the other charges are dismissed. After an adjudication of delinquency (at that time or at a separate disposition hearing), the judge will order a disposition.
5. In detained cases, the disposition hearing is to occur within sixty court days of admission to detention unless extended by the court for good cause.

Disposition Hearings and Options

The Juvenile Code allows judges a wide array of dispositions in adjudicated cases. The most common disposition is probation supervision. Probation is often ordered along with other dispositions requirements such as performing community service or paying financial restitution. In addition, probation is ordered along with more restrictive requirements such as entering a residential program or undergoing counseling. Probation is a major resource to the Family Court and the Juvenile Justice System.

Short of waiving juveniles to the adult system, commitment to the JJC for incarceration is the most severe disposition available to the Family Court. The average sentence in committed cases is two years, although terms range from thirty days to twenty years or more. In cases where commitment is suspended, adjudicated youth are often placed on probation and, in addition, ordered into a JJC non-institutional residential program.

Classification and Placement

Following the commitment of a juvenile by the court, each juvenile is assigned to a specific custody level and treatment program based on assessments of the offenders' supervision requirements and service needs. For the Commission, this means first determining whether juveniles are appropriate for institutional or structured non-institutional placement.

Mobile Classification / Waiver to Adult Court

The Mobile Classification team begins the classification process by visiting the county detention centers within a designated region in order to review court, detention, and prior placement documents and histories, and to interview juveniles upon their commitment. Through this process the team identifies specific sanctions and services that have been utilized for the youth, as well as ongoing or new service needs, and makes a recommendation regarding an appropriate placement for the juvenile. Using this information, the team completes a unified intake assessment packet, which includes the recommendation for either institutional care or structured non-institutional program placement, and submits it to the JJC's Centralized Intake and Classification Office.

Waiver to Adult Court / Mobile Classification

Waiver is the practice of transferring jurisdiction over a juvenile from Family Court to adult Criminal Court. (N.J.S.A. 2A:4A-26). Once waived, the juvenile is treated in the same manner as an adult. The juvenile can be held in an adult jail and, if found guilty, is subject to the same penalties as an adult. For those sentenced to a term of incarceration, the sentence is served in either an adult or (in some instances) a juvenile facility.

The prosecutor initiates the process by filing a waiver motion; the court then determines probable cause and decides whether or not to waive. A juvenile must be fourteen or older at the time of the charged delinquent act to be considered for waiver. Juveniles fourteen or older also may elect to have their cases waived to adult court.

New Jersey Juvenile Justice Commission

Juvenile Gang Intervention and Prevention Project **http://www.nj.gov/oag/jjc/aboutus_intro.html#ganginter**

The New Jersey Juvenile Justice Commission (JJC) understands that gangs and gang-related activities impact every community in our state. The JJC has responded with a comprehensive program that addresses youth gangs at all levels.

CHAPTER 8 Victims of Crimes Perpetrated by Juveniles—Rights and the Juvenile Justice Process   125

juvenile justice commission
NJ JJC moving through the system

Allegation of Delinquency or Juvenile / Family Crisis

- **Taken Into Custody by Law Enforcement Officer**
  - Law Enforcement Diversion
  - Delinquency Complaint Signed
    - Request to Detain
    - No Request to Detain
- **Non-Law Enforcement Complaintant**
  - Delinquency Complaint Signed
- **Family Crisis Intervention Unit Referral**
  - Initial Response
    - Short-Term Services
    - Crisis Resolved
    - Referral for Long-Term Services
    - Voluntary Out-of-Home Placement
    - Unsuccessful Diversion

FAMILY COURT INTAKE

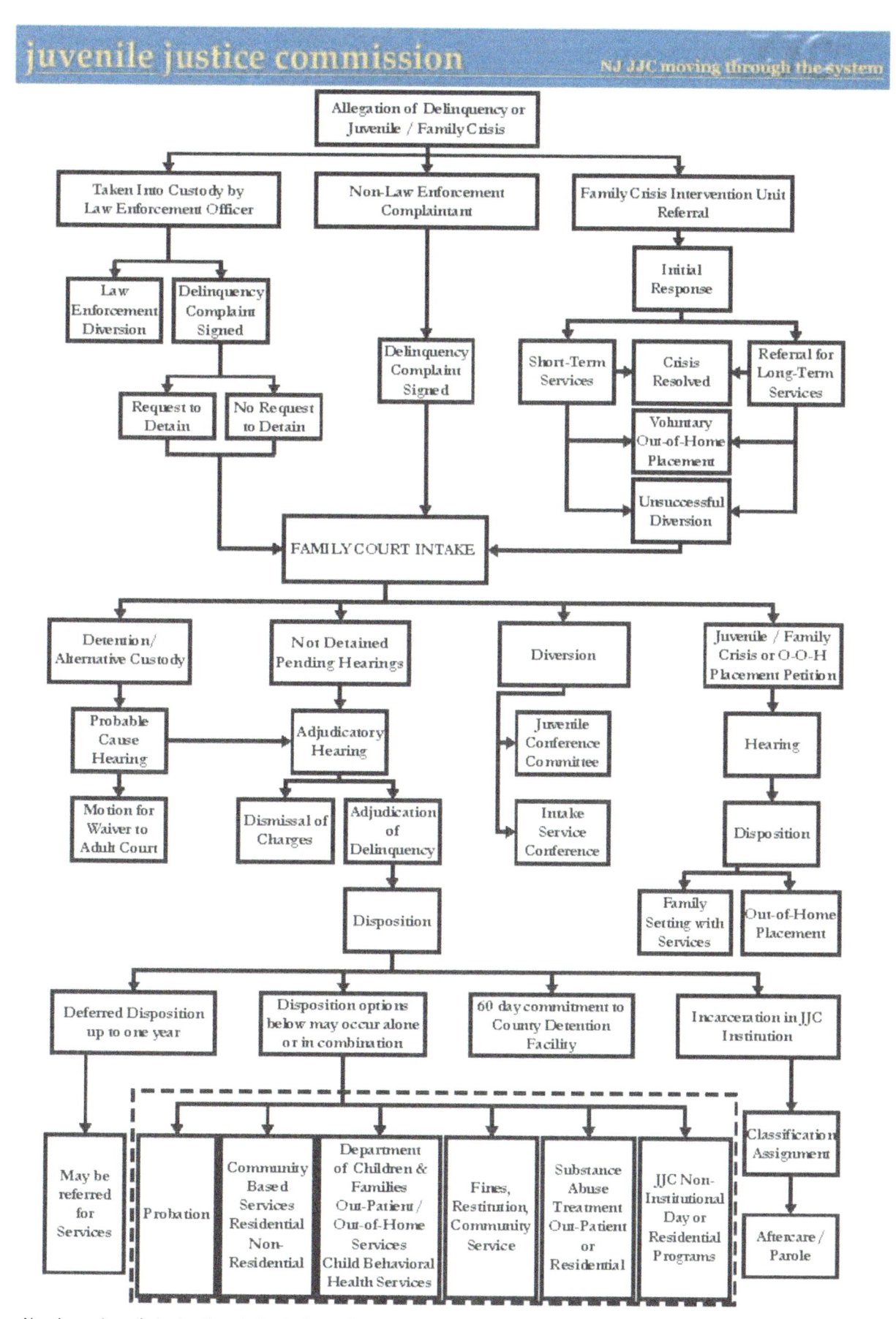

- **Detention/Alternative Custody**
  - Probable Cause Hearing
    - Motion for Waiver to Adult Court
    - Adjudicatory Hearing
- **Not Detained Pending Hearings**
  - Adjudicatory Hearing
    - Dismissal of Charges
    - Adjudication of Delinquency
      - Disposition
- **Diversion**
  - Juvenile Conference Committee
  - Intake Service Conference
- **Juvenile / Family Crisis or O-O-H Placement Petition**
  - Hearing
    - Disposition
      - Family Setting with Services
      - Out-of-Home Placement

Disposition:
- Deferred Disposition up to one year
  - May be referred for Services
- Disposition options below may occur alone or in combination:
  - Probation
  - Community Based Services Residential Non-Residential
  - Department of Children & Families Out-Patient / Out-of-Home Services Child Behavioral Health Services
  - Fines, Restitution, Community Service
  - Substance Abuse Treatment Out-Patient or Residential
  - JJC Non-Institutional Day or Residential Programs
- 60 day commitment to County Detention Facility
- Incarceration in JJC Institution
  - Classification Assignment
  - Aftercare/Parole

From New Jersey-Juvenile Justice Commission by State of New Jersey. Copyright © 2017 by State of New Jersey. Reprinted by permission.

General Rights

Crime Victims' Rights in the Juvenile Justice System apply to the victim of an offense, as well as, to the parent or legal guardian of a minor victim.

- ▶ Your right to justice includes the right to a meaningful role in the juvenile justice process, to be treated with dignity and respect, to fair and impartial treatment, and to reasonable protection from the youth offender.
- ▶ Many victims' rights are automatic although you may need to "tell" someone you want to receive them.
- ▶ Other rights you must specifically request to receive the right. One way to do this is to contact your District Attorney or Juvenile Department to request these rights.
- ▶ You, your attorney, or, upon your request, the District Attorney, may assert your rights in court.

Automatic Rights

- ▶ You have the right to have a support person with you.
- ▶ If your case involved physical harm or death, you may be able to get financial help for counseling, medical, or death related costs.
- ▶ You can attend open court proceedings.
- ▶ You can get a copy of a transcript or recording of open court proceedings if one is already made. You may be charged for the transcript or recording.
- ▶ Most "personal identifiers" can usually be protected from an alleged youth offender. These include your phone number, address, social security number, date of birth, bank account, and credit card account numbers.
- ▶ You or the District Attorney can ask the court to limit distribution of information and recordings in cases involving sexual or invasion of personal privacy offenses.

Rights that Must be Requested

- ▶ To get certain criminal history information about the youth offender (alleged or adjudicated).
- ▶ That the youth offender adjudicated in your case get testing for HIV if the crime involved the transmission of bodily fluids.

AFTER A YOUTH IS TAKEN INTO CUSTODY

Automatic Rights

- ▶ The judge will consider your safety at a release hearing.
- ▶ You can refuse to speak to an attorney or private investigator for the alleged youth offender or adjudicated youth offender.
- ▶ Some cases may be handled informally rather than through the court process. You can ask to be notified of this decision. These can include:
- ▶ Formal Accountability Agreement
- ▶ Diversion
- ▶ Teen or Peer Court

From North Carolina Criminal Law Blog by LaToya Powell. Copyright © 2014 by School of Government, UNC-Chapel Hill. Reprinted by permission.

Rights that Must be Requested

- To be notified of certain open court proceedings.
- To be notified in advance about the release hearing.
- To be consulted about the plea in a violent felony case.
- If you did not have notice of, or an opportunity to be heard at, certain hearings in which the youth offender was released, you can request a hearing to reconsider the release decision.

IF YOUR CASE GOES TO ADJUDICATION AND DISPOSITION

Automatic Rights

- The court will take your schedule into account when setting trial dates or hearings that you need to attend.
- Rape shield laws may apply in your case.
- You have a right to agree or disagree to personal service being performed for you as a condition of probation for a youth offender.
- If your property is damaged by graffiti, you can allow or refuse to allow, a youth offender on your property to clean it up.
- You can ask to know the outcome in your case.

Rights that Must be Requested

- To express your views at a detention or shelter hearing or at a hearing to review placement of the youth or youth offender.
- To express your views at a disposition (sentencing) in person or in writing.
- For the court to exclude media television, photography, or recording equipment during sex offense proceedings. The court may deny this request.

AFTER DISPOSITION

Automatic Rights

- To receive prompt restitution.
- To be heard at a hearing on a motion to set aside, vacate, or dismiss a case.
- The District Attorney will notify you if the youth offender in your case applies for expunction.
- To attend an expunction hearing.
- To be heard at an expunction hearing.
- For youth found Responsible Except for Insanity (REI) there may be additional victim services available (state or federal specific).

Rights that must be requested

- To be notified about juvenile review hearings including hearings where probation may be revoked.
- To be notified about expunction hearings.
- To be notified of hearings for relief from sex offender reporting requirements.

In Sex Offense Cases

- You have a right to not be contacted by the sex offender adjudicated in your case.
- For information about registered sex offenders call: (state or federal specific).

Rights that Must be Requested

- To be notified when the adjudicated youth is released from a facility. You must give your contact information directly to (State or Federal Specific) and keep this information up to date with any changes.
- For more information concerning victim services while a youth offender is in (state or federal specific) custody, contact: (state or federal specific)
- You may also receive automated notifications of youth releases from a (state or federal specific) facility by registering with (state or federal specific) VINE (Victim Information Notification Everyday). For more information contact: (state or federal specific).

Rights that Must be Requested: (State or Federal Specific)

Other Legal Information

The following information applies to the victim, or to the legal guardian of a minor child who is the victim.

- If you are a victim of stalking, you can go to the police or to court and ask for a stalking protective order.
- If you are a victim of sexual assault, a hospital must give you accurate information and access to emergency contraception. (state or federal specific).
- If you are a victim of domestic violence, you may be able to get financial help from (state or federal specific).
- If you are a victim of domestic violence, sexual assault or stalking, you may be able to:
  - Take leave from work to attend court proceedings (state or federal specific).
  - Take leave from work for medical or counseling appointments
  - Get unemployment benefits
  - End a rental agreement early
  - Have your locks changed
  - Get special arrangements for public housing
  - Set up a payment plan with the phone company
- Your immigration status should not affect your rights as a crime victim.
- Immigrant victims may have additional legal options.
- If your constitutional rights are not honored, you can assert a claim of violation of crime victims' rights.

There are time limits for this right. For more information visit: **www.doj.state.or.us/victims**

Please contact your (state or federal specific) agency for more information about your rights.

Some victims' rights become rights only if you request them.

Definitions—Examples from the Ohio Victim's Bill of Rights

Generally, the juvenile court has jurisdiction over persons under the age of eighteen who commit acts that if committed by an adult would be a crime. This includes violations of city, county, or state laws.

- "Adjudication"—When the youth offender is found "guilty" in a fact-finding hearing (trial) or has admitted guilt.
- "Disposition"—The sentence. This can include conditions of probation or commitment.
- "Dispositional Hearing"—When the youth is "sentenced."
- "Diversion"—May include a youth court, mediation program, crime prevention or chemical substance abuse education program or other program established for the purpose of providing consequences and reformation and preventing future delinquent acts.
- "Formal Accountability Agreement (FAA)"—A voluntary contract between a youth and a juvenile department whereby the youth agrees to fulfill certain conditions in exchange for not having a petition (formal charging document) filed and going in front of the juvenile court.
- "REI"—Responsible Except for Insanity.
- "Serious Physical Injury"—Physical injury which creates a substantial risk of death or which causes serious and protracted disfigurement, protracted impairment of health or protracted loss or impairment of the function of any bodily organ.
- "Taken into Custody"—Arrested and charged with a crime. The youth may be lodged in detention OR released to parent or guardian.
- "Teen Court or Peer Court"—Youth courts, where a youth panel hears the case and recommends consequences.
- "Victim"—Any person determined by the District Attorney, the juvenile department or the court to have suffered direct financial, psychological or physical harm as a result of the act that has brought the youth or youth offender before the juvenile court. When the victim is a minor, "victim" includes the legal guardian of the minor.
- "Violent Felony"—Any offense that, if committed by an adult, would constitute a felony and involves actual or threatened serious physical injury or is a sexual offense.

Victim Services Contact Information

Oregon Department of Justice Crime Victims' Services Division
1162 Court Street NE, Salem, OR 97301
503-378-5348
(Salem and surrounding areas)
800-503-7983
(statewide toll free)
www.doj.state.or.us/victims

Crime Victims' Compensation Program 800-503-7983

Statewide Legal Aid Information www.oregonlawhelp.org

Oregon Crime Victims Law Center 503-208-8160

Oregon State Bar 800-452-7636

www.osbar.org/public

Oregon Psychiatric Security Review Board 503-229-5598

Oregon State Police—Sex Offender Registry 503-934-1258

Oregon Youth Authority 503-373-7205

Call to Safety

Statewide Referral to Local Crisis Programs 888-235-5333

Immigration Counseling Service (ICS) 503-221-1689

Catholic Charities Immigration Legal Services 503-542-2855

State of Oregon Department of Justice
Crime Victims' Services Division
1162 Court St. NE
Salem, OR 97301
(503) 378-5348
(800) 503-7983
www.doj.state.or.us/victims

DISCUSSION QUESTIONS

1. Why are most juvenile criminal cases heard in state courts?

2. Do victims of crimes committed by juveniles have less rights than those that were victims of adult perpetrated crimes?

3. How does the juvenile justice system operate in New Jersey?

4. Is gang activity a major source of criminal activity for youth?

Name: _____ Date _____

You must use this form and turn in the original to the instructor. No other form will be accepted.

CHAPTER ASSIGNMENT

The text makes a comparison between the Juvenile Justice System federally and in the states. Why do you believe there exists such a disparity in the systems?

_____
_____
_____
_____
_____
_____
_____
_____
_____
_____
_____
_____
_____
_____
_____
_____
_____

Chapter Nine

VICTIMS OF DRUNK/DRUGGED DRIVERS

LEARNING OBJECTIVES

After exploring Chapter Nine (9), the student will be able to:

1. Define drunk and drugged driving.
2. Identify resources available to help victims of drunk/drugged driving.
3. Describe several statistical impacts drunk/drugged driving has on the American public.
4. Discuss the recidivism rate among drunk/drugged driving offenders.
5. List several law enforcement initiatives to combat drunk/drugged driving.

KEY TERMS

Drunk driving, Drugged driving, Impairment, Intoxication, Victims of Crime Act, Crime Victims Fund, MADD, SADD, Drug Recognition Expert, National Highway Traffic Safety Bureau, Blood Alcohol Concentration Level, IDRC, Interlock device

INTRODUCTION

In 1984, Congress created the Victims of Crime Act (VOCA) and the Crime Victims Fund, which provides funds to organizations for victim assistance and compensation programs that offer support and services to those affected by violent crimes. Since the Crime Victims Fund comes entirely from criminal fines and other penalties, spending from the fund does not add to the national debt or deficit and does not hurt taxpayers.

MADD relies on VOCA funds to help serve drunk driving victims in many states. Last year, MADD served over 63,000 drunk and drugged driving victims at no charge—one person every eight minutes. Although drunk driving has been cut in half in the thirty years since the founding of MADD, there are still over 10,000 people killed and 350,000 injured each year due to drunk and drugged driving accidents.

50 to 75 percent of convicted drunk drivers continue to drive on a suspended license.

(Peck, R.C., Wilson, R. J., and Sutton, L. 1995). "Driver license strategies for controlling the persistent DUI offender, strategies for dealing with the intent drinking driver." Transportation Research Board, Transportation Research Circular No. 437. Washington, D.C. National Research Council: 48–49 and Beck, KH, et al. "Effects of Ignition Interlock License Restrictions on Drivers with Multiple Alcohol Offenses: A Randomized Trial in Maryland." American Journal of Public Health, 89 vol. 11 (1999): 1696–1700.)

Only time will sober a person up. Drinking strong coffee, exercising, or taking a cold shower will not help.

(Michigan State University. "Basic Alcohol Information." East Lansing, MI: Michigan State University, 2003.)

Every two minutes, a person is injured in a drunk driving crash.

National Highway Traffic Safety Administration. "The Economic and Societal Impact of Motor Vehicle Crashes, 2010." National Highway Traffic Safety Administration, May 2014, DOT HS 812 013. http://www-nrd.nhtsa.dot.gov/Pubs/812013.pdf

On average, two in three people will be involved in a drunk driving crash in their lifetime.

National Highway Traffic Safety Administration. "The Economic and Societal Impact of Motor Vehicle Crashes, 2010." National Highway Traffic Safety Administration, May 2014, DOT HS 812 013. http://www-nrd.nhtsa.dot.gov/Pubs/812013.pdf

In 2013, 28.7 million people admitted to driving under the influence of alcohol—that's more than the population of Texas.

Substance Abuse and Mental Health Services Administration, results from the 2013 National Survey on Drug Use and Health: Summary of National Findings. Rockville, MD: Substance Abuse and Mental Health Services Administration, 2014. http://www.samhsa.gov/data/sites/default/files/NSDUHresultsPDFWHTML2013/Web/NSDUHresults2013.pdf

The rate of drunk driving is highest among twenty-six to twenty-nine year olds (20.7 percent).

Substance Abuse and Mental Health Services Administration, results from the 2013 National Survey on Drug Use and Health: Summary of National Findings. Rockville, MD: Substance Abuse and Mental Health Services Administration, 2014. http://www.samhsa.gov/data/sites/default/files/NSDUHresultsPDFWHTML2013/Web/NSDUHresults2013.pdf

© angkrit/Shutterstock.com

Every day in America, another twenty-seven people die as a result of drunk driving crashes.

National Highway Traffic Safety Administration. "Traffic Safety Facts 2014: Alcohol-Impaired Driving." Washington DC: National Highway Traffic Safety Administration, 2016. http://www-nrd.nhtsa.dot.gov/Pubs/812231.pdf

In the United States, the number of drunk driving deaths has been cut in half since MADD was founded in 1980.

National Highway Traffic Safety Administration. "Traffic Safety Facts 2014: Alcohol-Impaired Driving." Washington DC: National Highway Traffic Safety Administration, 2016. http://www-nrd.nhtsa.dot.gov/Pubs/812231.pdf

An average drunk driver has driven drunk over eighty times before first arrest. Arrest data: Federal Bureau of Investigation, "Crime in the United States: 2014"

https://www.fbi.gov/about-us/cjis/ucr/crime-in-the-u.s/2014/crime-in-the-u.s.-2014/tables/table-29 Incidence data: Centers for Disease Control and Prevention. "Alcohol-Impaired Driving Among Adults—United States, 2012." Morbidity and Mortality Weekly Report. August 7, 2015 / 64(30);814-817. http://www.cdc.gov/mmwr/preview/mmwrhtml/mm6430a2.htm

Drunk driving costs each adult in the United States over $500 per year.

MADD 5th Anniversary Report to the Nation, 2011. http://www.talklikemadd.org/books/statereport/#/4/

Drunk driving costs the United States $132 billion a year.

MADD 5th Anniversary Report to the Nation, 2011. http://www.talklikemadd.org/books/statereport/#/4/

Adults drank too much and drove about 121 million times per year—over 300,000 incidents of drinking and driving a day.

Centers for Disease Control and Prevention. "Alcohol-Impaired Driving Among Adults—United States, 2012." Morbidity and Mortality Weekly Report. August 7, 2015 / 64(30);814–817. http://www.cdc.gov/mmwr/preview/mmwrhtml/mm6430a2.htm

In 2015, 10,265 people died in drunk driving crashes—one every fifty-one minutes—and 290,000 were injured in drunk driving crashes.

National Highway Traffic Safety Administration. "Traffic Safety Facts 2015: Alcohol-Impaired Driving." Washington DC: National Highway Traffic Safety Administration, 2016. http://www-nrd.nhtsa.dot.gov/Pubs/812231.pdf

Drunk driving involvement in fatal crashes in 2014 was almost four times higher at night than during the day (34 versus 9 percent).

National Highway Traffic Safety Administration. "Traffic Safety Facts 2014: Alcohol-Impaired Driving." Washington DC: National Highway Traffic Safety Administration, 2016. http://www-nrd.nhtsa.dot.gov/Pubs/812231.pdf

In 2014, 16 percent of all drivers involved in fatal crashes during the week were drunk, compared to 29 percent on weekends.

National Highway Traffic Safety Administration. "Traffic Safety Facts 2014: Alcohol-Impaired Driving." Washington DC: National Highway Traffic Safety Administration, 2016. http://www-nrd.nhtsa.dot.gov/Pubs/812231.pdf

In 2013, a total of 1,149 children fourteen and younger were killed in motor vehicle traffic crashes. Of those 1,149 fatalities, 200 (17 percent) occurred in alcohol-impaired-driving crashes. Out of

those 200 deaths, 121 (61 percent) were occupants of vehicles with drivers who had BACs of .08 or higher, and another twenty-nine children (15 percent) were pedestrians or pedal cyclists struck by drivers with BACs of .08 or higher.

NHTSA data query, 2013.

Impairment is not determined by the type of drink, but rather by the amount of alcohol drunk over time.

(Insurance Institute for Highway Safety. "Q&A: Alcohol: General." Arlington, VA: National Highway Insurance Institute for Highway Safety, March 2012.)

A standard drink is defined as 12 ounces of beer, 5 ounces of wine, or 1.5 ounces of distilled spirits, which contain the same amount of alcohol.

(National Highway Traffic Safety Administration. "Alcohol Screening and Brief Intervention in the Medical Setting." DOT HS 809 467. Washington, DC: National Highway Traffic Safety Administration, July 2002.)

The average person metabolizes alcohol at the rate of about one drink per hour.

(Michigan State University. "Basic Alcohol Information." East Lansing, MI: Michigan State University, 2003.)

In fatal crashes in 2014, the highest percentage of drunk drivers was for drivers ages twenty-one to twenty-four (30 percent), followed by ages twenty-five to thirty-four (29 percent) and thirty-five to forty-four (24 percent).

National Highway Traffic Safety Administration. "Traffic Safety Facts 2014: Alcohol-Impaired Driving." Washington DC: National Highway Traffic Safety Administration, 2016. http://www-nrd.nhtsa.dot.gov/Pubs/812231.pdf

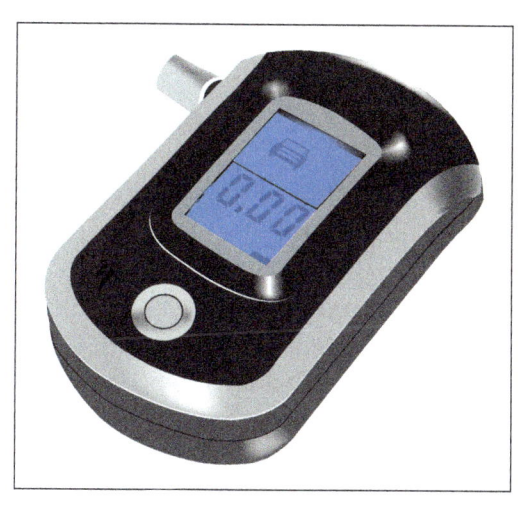

© stanga/Shutterstock.com

In 2014, three times as many males were arrested for drunk driving as females (401,904 v 130,480).

Federal Bureau of Investigation, Crime in the United States: 2014. https://www.fbi.gov/about-us/cjis/ucr/crime-in-the-u.s/2014/crime-in-the-u.s.-2014/tables/table-33

Each day, people drive drunk more than 300,000 times, but only about 3200 are arrested.

Arrest data: Federal Bureau of Investigation, "Crime in the United States: 2014"

https://www.fbi.gov/about-us/cjis/ucr/crime-in-the-u.s/2014/crime-in-the-u.s.-2014/tables/table-29
Incidence data: Centers for Disease Control and Prevention. "Alcohol-Impaired Driving Among Adults—United States, 2012." Morbidity and Mortality Weekly Report. August 7, 2015 / 64(30); 814–817. http://www.cdc.gov/mmwr/preview/mmwrhtml/mm6430a2.htm

Over 1.1 million drivers were arrested in 2014 for driving under the influence of alcohol or narcotics.

Federal Bureau of Investigation, "Crime in the United States: 2014." https://www.fbi.gov/about-us/cjis/ucr/crime-in-the-u.s/2014/crime-in-the-u.s.-2014/tables/table-29

About one-third of all drivers arrested or convicted of drunk driving are repeat offenders.

(Fell, Jim. "Repeat DWI Offenders in the United States." Washington, DC: National Department of Transportation, National Highway Traffic Safety Administration Traffic Tech No. 85, February 1995.)

BLOOD ALCOHOL CONCENTRATION (G/DL)[1]

The most common level of BAC which is the legal benchmark for drunk driving is .08

Alcohol decreases a person's ability to drive a motor vehicle safely. The more you drink, the greater the effect. The amount of alcohol required to become impaired differs according to how fast you drink, your weight, your gender, and how much food you have in your stomach. Because of these variables, the safest choice is always not to drink and drive.

.02

- Some loss of judgment
- Relaxation
- Slight body warmth
- Altered mood
- Decline in visual functions (rapid tracking of a moving target)
- Decline in ability to perform two tasks at the same time (divided attention)

.05

- Exaggerated behavior
- May have loss of small-muscle control (e.g., focusing your eyes)
- Impaired judgment
- Usually good feeling
- Lowered alertness
- Release of inhibition
- Reduced coordination
- Reduced ability to track moving objects
- Difficulty steering
- Reduced response to emergency driving situations

.08

- Muscle coordination becomes poor (e.g., balance, speech, vision, reaction time, and hearing)
- Harder to detect danger
- Judgment, self-control, reasoning, and memory are impaired
- Concentration
- Short-term memory loss
- Speed control
- Reduced information processing capability (e.g., signal detection, visual search)
- Impaired perception

.10

- Clear deterioration of reaction time and control
- Slurred speech, poor coordination, and slowed thinking
- Reduced ability to maintain lane position and brake appropriately

.15

- Far less muscle control than normal
- Vomiting may occur (unless this level is reached slowly or a person has developed a tolerance for alcohol)
- Major loss of balance
- Substantial impairment in vehicle control, attention to driving task, and visual and auditory information processing

[1] The information shows the BAC level at which the effect usually is first observed, and has been gathered from a variety of sources including the National Highway Traffic Safety Administration, the National Institute on Alcohol Abuse and Alcoholism, the American Medical Association, the National Commission Against Drunk Driving, and www.webMD.com.

In 2015, 10,265 people died in drunk driving crashes—one every fifty-one minutes—and 290,000 were injured in drunk driving crashes.

Over half of all children killed in drunk driving crashes are killed while riding with the drunk driver. Most of the time, that person is old enough to be a parent or caregiver.

Black's Law Dictionary defines child abuse as:

When a child's parent or custodian, by reason of cruelty, mental incapacity, immorality or depravity, is unfit to properly care for him or her, or neglects or refuses to provide necessary physical, affectional, medical, surgical or institutional care for him or her or is under such improper care or control as to endanger his or her morals or health.

© Rei and Motion Studio/Shutterstock.com

Clearly, driving under the influence with a child in the vehicle—child endangerment—is "improper care . . . so as to endanger his or her morals or health" and thus constitutes child abuse. Therefore, additional sanctions should be placed on those who drive under the influence of alcohol or drugs with a child in the vehicle—regular sanctions and treatment are not enough.

Forty-thee states and the District of Columbia have laws enhancing penalties for those who drive drunk with a child passenger in a vehicle. The laws vary widely in severity and definition of a child passenger. For example in New York it is a felony to drive drunk with a child passenger under the age of sixteen, whereas in Wisconsin, the same offense is a misdemeanor.

References

Drunk driving fatalities (.08 BAC or higher): 111 representing 0.2% of all total traffic deaths, a 31.1% decrease from last year.

DUI arrests: 22,201

Taxpayer subsidy of drunk driving fatalities: $992 million

DRUG RECOGNITION EXPERTS

The Drug Evaluation and Classification (DEC) program was created through a collaboration between the National Highway Traffic Safety Administration (NHTSA) and the International Association of Chiefs of Police (IACP).

The DEC program, also referred to as the Drug Recognition Expert (DRE) program, was developed to help officers identifying drug-impaired drivers. To become a DRE, officers must follow a rigorous three-phase training curriculum and learn to conduct a standardized and systematic twelve-step evaluation consisting of physical, mental and medical components.

© u3d/Shutterstock.com

Currently, there are thirty-seven states plus the District of Columbia participating in the program with about 8,000 officers trained nationwide.

For more information on the DEC/DRE program, contact the International Association of Chiefs of Police (IACP).

ARIDE

For those agencies who lack the funding to employ a full time DRE, an alternative training has been established—the Advanced Roadside Impaired Driving Enforcement (ARIDE) program.

ARIDE was created by NHTSA to address the gap between the traditional Standard Field Sobriety Test training given to officers to assist in detecting impaired drivers and the DEC/DRE program. The class requires sixteen hours of classroom training versus the three-phase curriculum required to become a certified DRE.

There are currently more than 36,000 officers ARIDE certified.

For more information on the ARIDE program, contact the International Association of Chiefs of Police (IACP).

SFST

Standardized Field Sobriety Testing (SFST) remains the foundation of impaired driving detection and enforcement for some 800,000 officers across the country. Some states, however, do not require SFST training for officers assigned to patrol functions. MADD expects all officers to have the basic SFST skills to detect an impaired driver on the roads.

© Lightspring/Shutterstock.com

How to Help

According to MADD, here are some ways that you can help a loved one struggling with the holidays:

1. Stay in touch, sometimes loved ones distance those who are grieving, they may be trying to protect them, but when contact is lost the victim or survivor can feel abandoned. Offer to come visit; even if they don't feel like going out, they may want to have you visit or call to check in on them.
2. Invite victims and survivors to social outings. Don't assume he or she should go or wouldn't go. Simply ask, and accept the response. It won't hurt to ask a second time a few days later if the first response was negative, but the decision is still theirs.
3. Invite those who are grieving to attend a holiday vigil to honor their loved one.
4. Ask to help with specific tasks. "Call me if you need me" is not always a useful offer as often those grieving don't want to burden others. Instead say, "I'd love to do some shopping for you when I do mine. May I?" or "I imagine decorating the house will be hard this year. May I come help you or do it for you some morning?"
5. Be a good listener. The holidays will draw out deep feelings for surviving families. Many will feel they must talk about their loved one. Hear their feelings and accept them. Learn to be comfortable with silences and don't feel you need to interrupt them. If you don't know what to say it's ok to be quiet or tell them you care about them.
6. Write a holiday letter. Many things can be said on paper which may be difficult to say in person. A letter can be treasured, read again and again, and kept forever.
7. Give a gift or make a donation in honor of the victim or survivor to their favorite charity.
8. If a loved one has been killed, it's good to speak their name often. It is important for someone who is bereaved to speak and hear their loved one's name. It may be painful, but the pain is already there and the opportunity to talk about the one they miss so much will be cherished.

Costs that may be compensated:
- Funeral expenses
- Medical, rehabilitation and prescription expenses

- Lost wages
- Counseling services
- Child care
- Crime scene cleanup

MADD advocates for states to provide a source of compensation funds for the financial losses and expenses of all victims of violent crime, including DWI/DUI victims and survivors of loved ones killed by an impaired driver. These programs should be funded by fees assessed to offenders, as well as, from other sources.

http://www.madd.org/victim-services/

https://ojp.gov/ovc/

http://www.nj.gov/mvc/Violations/dui_Intoxicated.htm

DUI: DRIVING UNDER THE INFLUENCE

The only scientific way to determine whether a driver is under the influence is through blood alcohol concentration (BAC). Your BAC can be tested with a simple Breathalyzer test.

In New Jersey, a person with a BAC of 0.08 percent or greater who operates a motor vehicle or a boat is considered to be driving under the influence (DUI).

Being convicted of a DUI is a serious offense, carrying heavy penalties including: fines, fees and surcharges license suspension, ignition interlock device, jail time, and community service.

Notes: IDRC—Intoxicated Driver Resource Center

AERF—Alcohol Education and Rehabilitation Fund

Underage drinking may cause a six-month delay in getting a license

Alcohol and drug-related offenses require completion of an alcohol screening and evaluation program

© designer491/Shutterstock.com

Failure to pay DUI surcharges will result in

- Indefinite suspension of driving privileges
- Action filed in State Superior Court by MVC. This may include securing a lien against your property, garnishing your wages or other similar action

In New Jersey, a person is guilty of drunk driving if he/she operates a motor vehicle with a Blood Alcohol Concentration (BAC) of 0.08 percent or greater. BAC refers to the amount of alcohol in your blood.

Although the law refers to a 0.08 percent BAC, you can be convicted of driving while under the influence of intoxicating liquor even when your BAC is below 0.08 percent. Consuming even small amounts of alcohol dulls the senses, decreases reaction time, and hampers judgment, vision, and alertness. If you consume any amount of alcohol and your driving is negatively impacted, you can be convicted of drunk driving.

PARENTS AND GUARDIANS

A parent or guardian who is convicted of driving while intoxicated and had a passenger in the motor vehicle seventeen years of age or younger, is also guilty of a disorderly persons offense. In addition, a person forfeits the right to operate a motor vehicle for a maximum of six months and must perform community service for up to five days.

The Penalties

First Offense

Under New Jersey Law (P.L. 2003, CHAPTER 314), if an offender's BAC is 0.08 percent or higher, but less than 0.10 percent, or if an offender permits another person with a BAC over 0.08 percent, but less than 0.10 percent to operate a motor vehicle, the penalties are:

- A fine of $250–$400*
- Imprisonment for up to thirty days*
- 3 months license suspension*
- A minimum of six hours a day for two consecutive days in an Intoxicated Driver Resource Center
- An automobile insurance surcharge of $1,000 a year for three years.

If the offender's BAC is 0.10 percent or higher, or the person operates a motor vehicle while under the influence of a narcotic, hallucinogenic, or habit-producing drug, or permits another person with a BAC of 0.10 percent to operate a motor vehicle, the penalties are:

- A fine of $300–$500*
- Imprisonment for up to thirty days*
- A license suspension between seven months and one year*

- A minimum of six hours a day for two consecutive days in an Intoxicated Driver Resource Center
- An automobile insurance surcharge of $1,000 a year for three years

Offenders with a BAC of 0.15 percent or higher must install an ignition interlock device in any vehicle they principally operate during the license suspension period and for a period of six months to one year after license restoration.

Second Offense

- A fine of $500–$1,000*
- Imprisonment of at least forty-eight consecutive hours, and up to ninety days*
- Two-year license suspension*
- Forty consecutive hours detainment in a regional Intoxicated Driver Resource Center.
- An automobile insurance surcharge of $1,000 a year for three years.
- Installation of an ignition interlock device for a period of one year to three years after license restoration.

Third Offense

- A fine of $1,000*
- Imprisonment of 180 days*
- Ten-year license suspension*
- Detainment in an in-patient alcoholism treatment program
- A fee to be paid to the Intoxicated Driver Resource Center dependent upon court sentence
- An automobile insurance surcharge of $1500 a year for three years
- Installation of an ignition interlock device for a period of one year to three years after license restoration.

Any Offense Also Carries

- $100 surcharge to be deposited in the Drunk Driving Enforcement Fund
- A Motor Vehicle Commission restoration fee of $100 and an Intoxicated Driving Program fee of $100
- A Violent Crimes Compensation Fund fee of $50
- A Safe and Secure Community Program fee of $75
- Registration Revocation/Ignition Interlock

In addition to these penalties, judges may order the revocation of the vehicle registration (Public Law 2000, Chapter 83).

The ignition interlock device, which measures the driver's blood alcohol level, may be required for up to three years following license restoration after a DWI conviction. Any person may start a motor vehicle equipped with an interlock device for safety reasons or to repair the device or motor vehicle, but the convicted offender may not operate the vehicle.

A person who, on behalf of the convicted offender, blows into an interlock device to start a motor vehicle or tampers with the device to circumvent its operation may be charged with a disorderly persons offense.

CONSEQUENCES OF UNDERAGE DRINKING AND DRIVING

In New Jersey, you must be at least twenty-one years of age to purchase, possess or consume alcoholic beverages. Underage drinking is illegal and can have severe consequences for young people who drink and for adults who provide alcoholic beverages to those under twenty-one.

If you are under twenty-one and buy or drink alcohol in a place with an alcohol beverage license, you may be fined $500 and lose your driver license for six months. If you do not have your driver license, the suspension starts when you are first eligible to receive a license. Also you may be required to participate in an alcohol education or treatment program.

If you are under twenty-one, drive with any detectable amount of alcohol in your system (.01 BAC or above), and are convicted for violating New Jersey's zero tolerance law, the penalties are:

- Loss or postponement of driving privileges for thirty to ninety days
- Fifteen to thirty days of community service
- Participation in an alcohol and traffic safety education program

Driving with a Suspended License Due to Driving While Intoxicated—The Penalties are:

- A fine of $500*
- Ten to ninety days imprisonment*
- One to two years added to license suspension*

If you are involved in a crash while your license is suspended and someone is hurt, you face

- Mandatory forty-five day jail sentence*
- Revocation of motor vehicle registration*

© Muskoka Stock Photos/Shutterstock.com

Refusal to Submit to Breath Test—The Penalties are:

- 1st offense—$300–$500 fine and a license suspension of not less than seven months or more than one year*
- 2nd offense—$500–$1,000 fine and a two-year license suspension*
- 3rd offense—$1,000 fine and a ten-year license suspension*
- Installation of an ignition interlock device for a period of six months to one year after license restoration for the 1st offense, one year to three years for the second and third offenses.
- Automobile insurance surcharge of $1,000 a year for three years for first and second offenses, $1,500 for third offense
- $100 surcharge to be deposited in the Drunk Driving Enforcement Fund Referral to an Intoxicated Driver Resource Center

Possessing an Open Container in the Passenger Compartment—The Penalties are:

- 1st offense—$200
- 2nd offense—$250 fine or 10 days of community service

* If occurring within a school zone or school crossing, this penalty is increased under Public Law 99, Chapter 185.

https://www.aaim1.org/victim.asp

IMPAIRED DRIVING

In 2009, 10,839 people were killed in crashes involving alcohol-impaired drivers in the United States.[1]

In 2009, the holidays on which alcohol-related crashes represented the highest percentage of total fatalities were Memorial Day (42 percent), New Year's Day and the Fourth of July (40 percent each), and Labor Day (38 percent).[2]

About three in every ten Americans will be involved in an alcohol-related crash at some time in their lives.[3]

In 2009, an average of one alcohol-related fatality occurred every forty-eight minutes in the United States.[4]

In 2009, 14 percent of child traffic fatalities—181 deaths—were caused by alcohol-impaired drivers.[5]

In 2009, 32 percent of traffic fatalities involved drivers with a BAC of 0.08 grams per deciliter or higher. An additional 6 percent involved drivers with a BAC of between .01 and .07 grams per deciliter.[6]

What Is Impaired Driving?

Alcohol and other drugs, when used in excess or incorrectly, impair driving by altering the brain's ability to function. Vision and depth perception become distorted, coordination is slowed, and judgment is negatively affected. A driver commits the crime of *impaired driving* whenever his or her ability to safely operate a vehicle is impaired by the effects of illegal drugs, prescription medications, or over-the-counter medications, or by having a blood alcohol concentration (BAC) of 0.08 grams per deciliter or higher.

Victims of impaired driving crashes are not hurt accidentally. They are victims of a crime that is the result of two choices made by a driver: (1) to use alcohol or other drugs incorrectly or in excess, and (2) to operate a vehicle (a car, motorcycle, boat, jet ski, etc.) while under the influence of these substances. These choices are as dangerous to the public as using a deadly weapon and can be just as lethal.

If You Are the Survivor of an Impaired Driving Crime

If you or a loved one is a victim of an impaired driving crime, you may be affected emotionally and physically. For injured victims and family members of those killed or injured, often the most difficult step is to begin processing what has happened. If a loved one has been killed, this sudden, traumatic death probably feels unlike any other loss you have ever experienced. Coming to terms with such profound grief will take time.

The injustice of the death and involvement with the criminal justice system as a result of the crime may complicate your grief. If the case is treated as an accident by the offender, rather than a crime resulting from the offender's choice to drive while impaired, you may feel even more angry and frustrated.

Everyone has a different way of processing grief and loss, and everyone does so in their own timeframe. You may experience extreme swings in emotion. You may feel guilty for not being able to protect your loved one even though the crime and its consequences were beyond your control. You may feel depressed or hopeless. The emotions you experience may seem to use up all of your energy.

This emotional suffering may also affect your physical routines. Your eating habits may change. You may have difficulty sleeping or be unable to sleep at all. You may have nightmares about the crash or have difficulty riding in or driving an automobile. You may lose interest in activities you once enjoyed. You may have lingering physical injuries, which can serve as painful physical reminders of your emotional pain.

Victims of impaired driving crashes cope with the profound loss and changes in their lives differently. But no matter how they grieve, most victims of impaired driving crashes are, after a time, able to face life with new understanding and meaning.

Where Can You Get Help?

Advocates can provide you with information and a full range of victim support services. Victim assistance programs and trained professionals can help you learn about crime victims' rights in your state. You may want to call your local or state MADD chapter to seek counselors who understand the grief that follows this kind of loss and trauma. Such organizations may also provide support through court accompaniment and advocacy services.

When a loved one has been injured or killed, the financial impact can compound your sense of loss. The costs of medical care, phone bills, counseling, lost wages, and funerals can be overwhelming. All states have crime victim compensation programs that reimburse victims' families for certain out-of-pocket expenses, including funeral, counseling, medical expenses, and lost wages. Many states provide emergency funds that are available within weeks of the crash. To be eligible for compensation, the crime must be reported to the police, and the victim and victim's family must cooperate with the criminal justice system.

Victim assistance programs in your community can provide you with compensation applications and additional information.

Resources for Information and Assistance

Mothers Against Drunk Driving
1-800-GET-MADD or 1-800-438-6233
www.madd.org

National Center for Victims of Crime
202-467-8700
www.ncvc.org

National Organization for Victim Assistance
1-800-TRY-NOVA or 1-800-879-6682
www.trynova.org

Students Against Destructive Decisions
1-877-SADD-INC (723-3462)
www.sadd.org

Endnotes

1. National Highway Traffic Safety Administration, 2010, *2009 Traffic Safety Facts,* Washington, DC.
2. U.S. Department of Transportation, 2011, *Fatality Analysis Reporting System/General Estimate System (FARS/GES) 2009 Data Summary,* Washington, DC.
3. National Highway Traffic Safety Administration, March 2001, *The Traffic Stop and You: Improving Communications Between Citizens and Law Enforcement,* Washington, DC.
4. National Highway Traffic Safety Administration, 2010, *2009 Traffic Safety Facts,* Washington, DC.
5. Ibid.
6. U.S. Department of Transportation, 2011, *FARS/GES 2009 Data Summary,* Washington, DC.

DISCUSSION QUESTIONS

1. Why is the recidivism rate so high among drunk/drugged drivers?

2. What are some ways to reduce the drunk/drugged driving related motor vehicle accidents?

Name: _____   Date _____

| **You must use this form and turn in the original to the instructor. No other form will be accepted.** |

CHAPTER ASSIGNMENT

The text discusses several law enforcement initiatives to combat drunk/drugged driving in the United States. What do you think are the most effective methods and why?

_____
_____
_____
_____
_____
_____
_____
_____
_____
_____
_____
_____
_____
_____
_____
_____
_____
_____

Chapter Ten

VICTIMS OF SEXUAL ABUSE

LEARNING OBJECTIVES

After exploring Chapter Ten (10), the student will be able to:

1. Define sexual assault.
2. Discern the differences between the Wetterling Act and Megan's Law.
3. Explain the common trauma symptoms experience after a sexual assault occurs.
4. Understand the functions performed by the Sexual Assault Nurse Examiner (SANE).
5. Discuss the importance of the Sexual Assault Examination Kit.

KEY TERMS

Sexual assault, Rape trauma syndrome, the Wetterling Act, Megan's Law, Sexual Assault Response Team, SANE nurse, Sexual Assault Advocate, SAFE kits

INTRODUCTION

This chapter studies the crime of sexual assault and the responses enacted to aid victims during the criminal justice process and help them through recovery from the traumatic event. After an explanation of sexual assault in general, the chapter explains sex offender registry and notification systems. Additionally, a multi-disciplinary coordinated response is also given attention as services are provided to the victims of sexual assault. There are a variety of services available to the victims of this particular crime. This chapter outlines a few of the different types of assistance available.

HISTORICAL DEVELOPMENT

Rape or sexual assault is the most underreported crime in America. There have been significant changes to improve the treatment of sexual assault victims have occurred in the last several decades. The impact of reforms led by the women's movement can be seen in the legal, medical, mental health, and victim services arenas. During the 1970s the first rape crisis center was established to assist victims of sexual assault.

EVOLUTION OF THE DEFINITION OF SEXUAL ASSAULT AND RAPE

Prior to the 1960s the legal definition of rape was generally a common law definition which was used throughout the United States and it was defined: rape as "carnal knowledge of a woman not one's wife by force or against her will." In 1962, the definition was updated, and defined rape as a man who has sexual intercourse with a female not his wife is guilty of rape, if he compels her to submit by force or threat or threat of imminent death or serious bodily injury.

© ibreakstock/Shutterstock.com

However, most statutes retained a marital-rape exemption, and it focused on the victims consent rather than the perpetrator's forcible conduct.

In the 1970s and 1980s extensive rape reform laws were enacted throughout the United States and the legal definition of rape changed considerably. The states enacted rape statutes, which were called criminal sexual conduct, and sexual assault statutes. These statutes broaden the definition of rape and they possess the following characteristics:

1. Rape is defined as gender neutral, which broadens the earlier definition of rape to include men as well as women.
2. They include acts of sexual penetration other than vaginal penetration by a penis.
3. Threats as well as overt force are recognized as means to overpower the victim.

THE MEASUREMENT OF RAPE—SEXUAL ASSAULT

There is a major difference between rape cases and rape victims because women can be raped more than once. Also, there is a difference between the incidence of rape and the prevalence of rape. Incidence refers to the number of cases that occur in a given period of time, (usually a year), and incidence statistics are often reported as rates (the number of rapes per 100,000 women in the population). In contrast, prevalence, it refers to the percentage of women who have been raped in a specific period of time (within the past year or throughout their life time). Moreover, there is a difference between estimates based on reported versus non-reported rape cases. Finally, the estimates of rape are derived from two basic types of sources: official governmental sources and studies conducted by private researchers, which are often supported by grants from federal agencies.

SEXUAL ASSAULTS

Sexual assault involves any act of sexual violence including date rape, spousal rape, stranger rape, unwanted touching, or any sexual behavior exhibited toward a child under the age of fifteen. There is a major misconception about sexual assault and most people believe these violent acts are carried out only by strangers. However, sexual assault is the fastest rising violent crime in America today; stranger rape is not the leading form of sexual assault. The majority of victims involved in non-fatal, violent sexual assault know and more than likely trust the offender.

© ibreakstock/Shutterstock.com

In many cases, the sexual offender and/or the victim had been drinking and/or using drugs.

The use of alcohol or drugs is never an excuse to commit unwarranted sexual acts.

FACTS ABOUT DATE RAPE

Date rape is when someone you are dating forces you to have sex. However, examine the subsequent facts of date rape:

1. Date rape can happen on a first date or long into a relationship.
2. No matter who it is, if someone does not listen when you say no to sex, it is rape.
3. Rape is not about sex, it is about power and control.
4. Date rape often does not involve weapons or physical force: but rather threats to you or someone you care about if you refuse to have sex. This is considered to be rape.
5. You can always say no to having sex—even if you have been kissing or have had sex with that person in the past.
6. You can always change your mind about having sex. No matter what, NO means NO!
7. While there are others, alcohol is the original and most common date rape drug.

8. The highest number of rape victims is between the ages eleven–seventeen.
9. Nothing entitles someone to sex, not if they pay for your dinner, not if they buy you gifts, not if they become sexually aroused—Nothing.
10. Men are also victims of rape and sexual assault.

RAPE TRAUMA SYNDROME

The following are common responses to sexual assault and may be symptoms of the rape trauma syndrome.

1. Shock
2. Denial
3. Humiliation
4. Embarrassment
5. Self-blame
6. Guilt
7. Shame
8. Anger
9. Emotional Numbness
10. Nightmares
11. Phobias
12. Stomach Problems
13. Headaches

MYTHS ABOUT RAPE

MYTH #1: Rape is a street crime that only happens to women who put themselves in bad situations.

WRONG: Every eight minutes, someone is raped or assaulted, more often than not by someone they know and often in their own home. It can happen to you.

MYTH #2: Guys are sometimes oversexed and get carried away. WRONG AGAIN: There is nothing romantic about sexual assault. Real love and intimacy are not expressed through force, power, or humiliation. Rape is an act of hostile aggression, not uncontrollable passion.

MYTH #3: Girls who flirt or dress in sexy clothes are asking for it. WRONG AGAIN: Like men, women have the right to dress as they please and flirting is an accepted part of most cultures.

PREVENTING DATE RAPE

There are various ways to reduce your chances of being sexually assaulted.

1. Know your date. Besides asking his name and address, get to know more about his ideas about women and relationships. If he is someone you do not know, arrange to meet in a public place.

2. Keep a clear head. Excessive use of alcohol or drugs can decrease your awareness and make you more vulnerable.
3. Be assertive. Do not be afraid to speak up if a situation makes you uncomfortable. Make it clear to your date that his paying for things doesn't give him rights to your body. It is always a good idea to have some money of your own with you.
4. Express yourself and expect to be respected. It may seem awkward at first, but tell your date how far you will go. If kissing is enough, say so, it can help avoid feelings of rejection or anger.
5. Trust your instincts. Do not deny danger signals around you. If someone displays a violent temper, tries to control you, or will not take "no" for an answer, listen to what that behavior is telling you. Do not become a puppet.

RAPE PREVENTION IN YOUR HOME

1. Make sure that your home has a door viewer and a deadbolt lock.
2. All entrances and garages should be well-lighted.
3. Never hide a key over a door or in a flowerpot.
4. If single, don't put your first name on your mailbox or in the telephone book.
5. Do not admit strangers to you home under any circumstances.

RAPE PREVENTION IN YOUR AUTOMOBILE

1. Always lock your car when leaving and entering it.
2. Always look in the back seat before entering the vehicle.
3. Have your keys in hand so you don't' have to linger before entering.
4. If you have car trouble, raise the hood, lock yourself in, and wait for the police.
5. Do not stop to offer a ride to a stranded motorist: stop at the nearest phone booth and call the police.
6. If you suspect that someone is following you, drive to the nearest public place and blow your horn.

MEGAN'S LAW

Megan's Law is the result of the sexual assault and murder of Megan Kanka, age seven, in Hamilton Township, New Jersey. She was a victim of Jesse Timmendequas, who was a twice-convicted sex offender. His previous sexual deviancy targeted small children, who he sexually assaulted. Timmendequas lived across the street of the Kanka family. The parents of Megan Kanka, used the national attention given to this horrific case to persuade the community and the federal government to make changes to sex offender registration law. They contended that if they had an awareness about the criminal activity of the their neighbor that he would never have had the opportunity to kill their daughter. Shortly after the death of Megan Kanka, New Jersey passed Megan's Law. This law demands convicted sex offenders to register, the state to maintain an archive of the records, and law enforcement to relentlessly follow-up with compliance. In addition, the location of sex offenders with the high risk of reoffending is now made public to the surrounding neighborhood, schools, and businesses. This process is based on a tiered system, which increases notifications, as the offender is deemed more or less dangerous to the public (Wright, 2014).

Megan's Law was not the first legal requirement regarding registration required for sexual offenders, it's actually an amendment to previous federal law. Its precursor was a federal law named the Jacob Wetterling Act of 1994. This law mandated every state to design a system for sexual offenders and certain other offenses against children to register with the local law enforcement authorities of the jurisdiction where the offender lives. Sound familiar? It should. The major difference between the Jacob Wetterling Act and Megan's Law is community notification (Wright, 2014). In the wording of the Wetterling Act, registry information was exclusive for law enforcement eyes only. A caveat did exist. Law enforcement, with their own determination, was allow to inform the public on a "case-by-case" basis about sex offenders in their municipality if they deemed the offenders a public safety threat. The next section discusses the notification process.

SEX OFFENDER NOTIFICATION FOR NEIGHBORHOODS AND COMMUNITIES (MEGAN'S LAW)

A sex offender is a person who has been convicted of a violation or attempted violation of any of the subsequent offenses, including, but not limited to:

1. Sexual abuse if the victim is under the age of eighteen.
2. Sexual conduct with a minor.
3. Sexual assault.
4. Molestation of a child.
5. Child prostitution.
6. Criminal sexual contact.

Prior to releasing the convicted sex offender from confinement, the Department of Corrections will notify the following:

1. County Sheriff
2. State Attorney General
3. County Prosecutor or District Attorney
4. Local Law Enforcement

5. County Probation Department
6. Division of Parole
7. Victims and family
8. Local community

GUIDELINES

A committee consisting of criminal justice personal will implement specific community notification guidelines. The guidelines provide for levels of notification based on the risk that a particular sex offender poses to the community. Level three poses a high risk to re-offend. Level two an intermediate, and level one is a low risk.

The level three offenders require notification to the surrounding neighborhood, area schools, appropriate community groups, and offender prospective employer and the County Prosecutor or District Attorney Officer. A flyer will include a photo of the offender's status and criminal background. Also, the prior information is placed on the Internet. If a level three offender fails to register, a warrant is issued and the community is notified. The County Prosecutor or District Attorney will prosecute the offender for the failure to register.

For level two offenders, the notification should be sent immediately to the neighbors, schools, appropriate community groups, and prospective employers.

If the offender fails to register, the County District Attorney or the County Prosecutor will prosecute the offender.

The level one offender, the local law enforcement agency is responsible for the notification and shall maintain information about the offender. Information may be forwarded to the people with whom the offender resides. Once again, failure to register, the offender will be prosecuted.

SEXUAL ASSAULT PROTOCOLS

Sexual violence is a grave subject. The lifelong effects remain with the victims of these offenses, repeatedly. Precise laws differ from state to state in regard to sexual assault. All states have criminalized sexual assault; however, the definitions of this behavior and acts considered to fall in this category will vary as well. The United States Department of Justice (DOJ) uses the following definition: "Sexual assault is any type of sexual contact or behavior that occurs without the explicit consent of the recipient. Falling under the definition of sexual assault are sexual activities as forced sexual intercourse, forcible sodomy, child molestation, incest, fondling, and attempted rape." (Retrieved from **https://www.justice.gov/ovw/sexual-assault.**)

© PhotoMediaGroup/Shutterstock.com

Sexual assault crimes have a massive effect on victims and their families, often leaving lasting emotional and psychological wounds. Even as physical wounds may heal rather quickly, the psychological/emotional impact may be sustained unremittingly for the rest of the victim's life. With this in mind, it is important to recognize the clear need of a systematic approach to help these victims. The methodology must be holistic with empathy and compassion as the principal focus.

Creating and renewing a safe environment for the victim allows for the healing process to begin. It's critical to form this atmosphere so the victim can feel comfortable with accepting support from the assistance programs and services that are available to them. Many states have protocols and procedures developed to tend to victims of sexual assault. Victims of sexual assault can start receiving assistance from a variety of outlets. The victim may be identified from hospital staff, educational facilities, counselors, law enforcement, etc. Typically, states and counties create multidisciplinary teams with representatives from organizations that will eventually be involved in providing assistance to victims. Sexual assault response teams will respond to provide services to the victim to assistance with medical treatment, counseling, and evidence collection should the victim decide to pursue the matter and report the incident as a crime.

A COORDINATED SEXUAL ASSAULT RESPONSE

For a sexual assault response team to be activated, naturally a victim must report the incident to some channel. Most likely, this ensues when a victim travels to an emergency room or informs a local law enforcement agency about the crime. At this point, the method to address this issue becomes triggered with generally two goals: 1) insuring the victim receives counseling and medical assistance and 2) coordinate resources for effectual investigation and prosecution of the criminal.

Local police and emergency room personnel are provided with contact information for neighboring shelters or centers for counseling that have trained professionals to attend to victims of sexual assault. Police and emergency room personnel are typically instructed to call a hotline number, which is monitored 24-hours, for the victim to speak with a representative of sexual assault response units. The victim will be asked questions about the incident in private. The hotline staff determines what types of response are required to assists the victim. For example, questions arise such as, "When did the assault occur?" or "Are you wearing the same clothing?"

The hotline staff evaluates if there is still an opportunity for evidence collection, along with determining what services are available for this specific victim (medical treatment, psychological screening, counseling, evidence collection, etc.) After hotline staff speaks with the victim, they will direct medical personnel or law enforcement how to proceed in respect of the wishes of the victim. Obviously, medical treatment for injuries sustained during the assault take precedence over anything else. After the victim is determined to be in stable physical condition, the victim may chose to go to a specific hospital to have evidence collected in a medical setting by a Sexual Assault Nurse Examiner (SANE) or SANE nurse. Typically, there are designated hospital sites that are

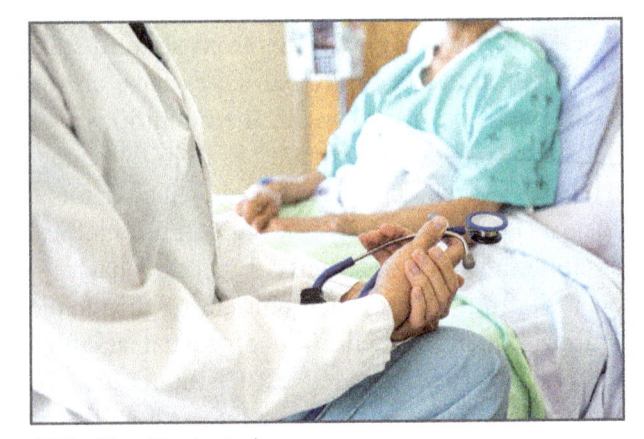

© Tyler Olson/Shutterstock.com

equipped and selected to are these examinations performed. Regardless, it is important the victim is taken to the closest emergency room where instant medical care is needed. Also, the victim must be informed of the standard operating procedures necessary for the collection of evidence for sexual assault investigations, and if they so desire, to proceed with process.

ROLE OF THE ADVOCATE

Victims must be informed of their right to speak with a rape care advocate or counselor that is trained with tending to victims of sexual assault. This is done prior to any treatment (except for necessary medical), formal interviews conducted by law enforcement, or evidence collection.

Advocates generally explain to the victim the process of a sexual assault investigation and the victim's options moving forward in a compassionate manner. They have formal training that is focused on putting the victim first. Advocates also explain the significance of the forensic exam conducted by the SANE nurse and how it applies to criminal investigations of sexual assault.

In many states, it is required all hospitals and law enforcement agencies provide sexual assault victims with information about the local designated rape care program, regardless of when or where the incident occurred, or whether or not the victim has reported the incident to police.

Additionally, these agencies must afford the victim the opportunity to contact the rape care program and to have a rape care advocate present during any medical treatment or law enforcement interview. These guidelines are set for the State of New Jersey in the New Jersey Statutes Annotated (See N.J.S.A. 52:4B-22) that outlines victim's rights.

The following is information from New Jersey's Office of the Attorney General's Standards for providing services to the victims of sexual assault: The victim will be afforded the opportunity to speak privately with a rape care advocate prior to investigative and sexual assault medical forensic interviews or procedures. The rape care advocate will explain the advocate's role and the services of the rape care program. The victim will have the opportunity to have the rape care advocate present to provide crisis intervention and emotional support throughout the medical and investigative process. The rape care advocate may be present to provide emotional support at the victim's request; however, the rape care advocate will not participate with evidence collection or law enforcement interviews. The rape care advocate will ensure that the victim is informed regarding all procedures, options and resources, including rape care services, the importance of seeking medical attention, and the value of immediate evidence collection and early police reporting. The rape care advocate will provide the victim a safe, neutral and confidential avenue to explore and weigh options. The rape care advocate will support the victim's choices and decisions. The rape care advocate will maintain the confidentiality of all communications occurring solely between the advocate and the victim unless otherwise instructed by prior written consent of the victim. See N.J.S.A. 2A:84A-22.15. The services of the rape care program are available to the victim throughout the entire healing process including accompanying the victim during all legal and court proceedings. The rape care program is available to provide support for non-offending family members and friends (New Jersey Department of Criminal Justice, 2004).

SEXUAL ASSAULT NURSE EXAMINER (SANE)

SANE nurses are specially trained medical examiners, who are skilled in collecting evidence and conducting investigations during sexual assaults. SANE nurses use specially designed sexual assault evidence collection kits to conduct forensic examinations to collect any evidence transfer, document any injuries via photographs, and create a formal written report of their observations. All victims of sexual assault will have the opportunity to discuss their medical condition, treatment options, and medical referral plan privately with the SANE, SAE ,or other health care provider before or during the course of treatment.

The SANE, SAE, or other health care provider who is examining and providing care for a victim of sexual assault is responsible for obtaining appropriate written consents and continually validating verbal consent with the victim throughout the examination and evidence collection process.

The SANE, SAE, or other health care provider is responsible for documenting information pertaining to the victim's complaint of sexual assault, obtaining a pertinent medical history, performing the sexual assault medical forensic examination, ensuring that necessary medical treatment is provided, providing patient education, and making all necessary referrals for follow-up care.

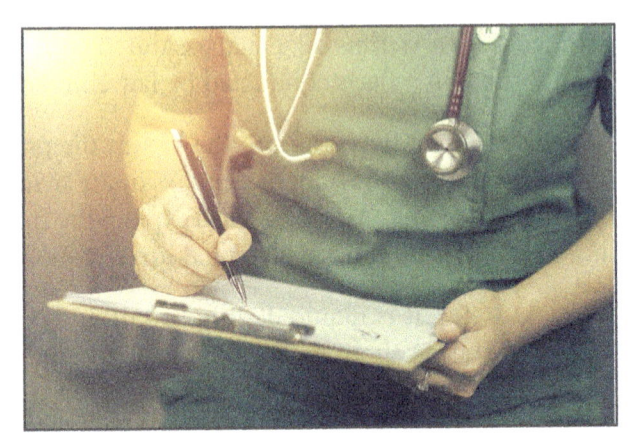

© Have a nice day Photo/Shutterstock.com

In accordance with the American College of Emergency Physicians's (ACEP) policy on the Evaluation and Management of Sexually Assaulted or Sexually Abused Patients, it is recommended that health care providers ensure that every victim is offered information about sexually transmitted infections and available treatment options. Health care providers should also provide every female victim with information about emergency contraception.

At the conclusion of the sexual assault medical forensic examination, any evidence collected will be packaged and protected in a manner to ensure the integrity of specimens and the appropriate chain of custody of the evidence. It is recommended that health care facilities work cooperatively with the County Prosecutor's Office to develop a written protocol to ensure proper handling of any identified and collected evidence.

SEXUAL ASSAULT EXAMINATION KITS

Every victim of sexual assault who reports the incident within five days of when it occurred is entitled to request a sexual assault medical forensic examination for the purpose of identifying injuries and collecting forensic evidence. The County Prosecutor's Office will provide the New Jersey Sexual Assault Forensic Evidence (SAFE) Collection Kits and Examination Forms to every emergency health care facility in the county. Kits will be kept on-site and may only be used for sexual assault medical forensic examinations.

Every sexual assault medical forensic examination should be completed using the New Jersey SAFE Collection Kit and Examination Forms, regardless of the jurisdiction in which the crime is reported to have occurred. All individuals age thirteen or older reporting sexual assault victimization should be advised of the value of immediate evidence collection. All victims have the right to consent or to decline any or all parts of a sexual assault medical forensic examination. The consent of the victim will be obtained prior to the performance of any examination. No examination will be conducted without the consent of the victim. In the case where a victim is a minor, his or her consent must be obtained before an examination is conducted. In a situation where the victim is unable to consent due to permanent mental incapacity, the consent of the victim's medical proxy will be obtained prior to the performance of the examination.

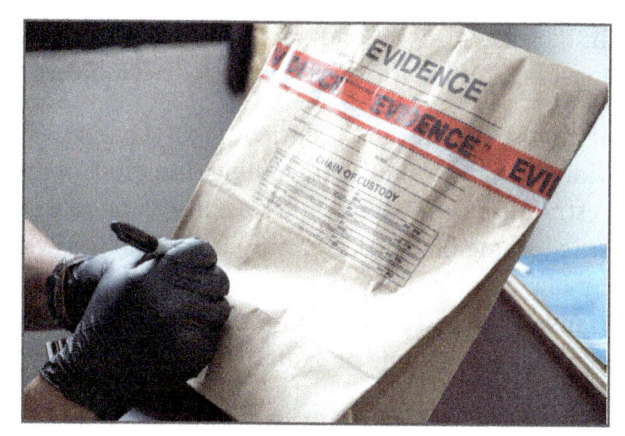

© Prath/Shutterstock.com

The health care provider conducting the examination will make the determination as to which items of evidence should be collected in each case, based upon the history and circumstances of the incident as reported by the victim.

At the conclusion of the medical forensic examination, the evidence collected will be packaged and protected in a manner to ensure the integrity of each specimen and appropriate chain of custody. Every victim will be afforded a minimum of ninety days in which evidence will be held pending the victim's decision to release evidence to law enforcement. The victim will be apprised of county policy regarding time frames for the storage and possible destruction of evidence.

Upon notification of the imminent destruction of a SAFE kit, the SANE coordinator will contact, or attempt to contact, the victim to determine if the victim wants returned any clothing items collected during the examination.

SAFETY PLANS FOR VICTIMS OF SEXUAL ASSAULT

Every victim of sexual assault will have the benefit of a discharge plan that addresses personal safety, medical follow-up and emotional needs. All individuals who provide services to a victim immediately after a sexual assault will assess if the victim feels safe returning to his or her residence. If the victim does not feel safe, then assistance in developing a safety plan will be provided. Alternatives to returning to their residence may include seeking temporary housing in the home of a relative or friend or, in the case of a domestic violence incident, at a local domestic violence shelter.

© arka38/Shutterstock.com

In the case of child and adolescent victims sexually assaulted by family members or caretakers, DYFS must be notified for that agency to determine appropriate placement.

If the sexual assault occurred in the context of a domestic violence incident, the victim will be provided with information regarding domestic violence victim's rights including information on temporary restraining orders and other means of increasing safety. The victim will be given assistance to safely reach home or an alternative location. If the victim does not have transportation, it will be arranged by law enforcement. It is recommended that the examination facility staff have a plan for arranging transportation for the victim who has not utilized the services of the SART or is not reporting to law enforcement at time of exam.

Victims will be assisted in identifying personal support systems such as relatives, friends, clergy, or others who may provide emotional, financial, or physical assistance in the days following the assault. Victims will also be given information regarding professional resources for counseling which will include the contact number of the local rape care program and how to access those services.

Following medical treatment for a sexual assault, victims will receive information regarding recommended follow-up to address medical concerns that may arise. This information will be provided by the SANE, SAE, or other medical personnel who provided care.

If requested, victims will be advised of the investigative process and provided with the name of a contact person from the local law enforcement agency and/or the prosecutor's office. Every victim will be provided with the Crime Victims Bill of Rights and contact information for the County Prosecutor's Office Victim-Witness Advocacy Unit and the Victims of Crime Compensation Board.

© Rawpixel.com/Shutterstock.com

EVALUATION AND FOLLOW-UP

Victims of sexual assault who choose to utilize SART services will be afforded an opportunity to evaluate the services provided. Participating members of the SART will also be afforded an opportunity to evaluate the services provided and to recommend improvements.

At the conclusion of the SART activation, victims will be provided with a short, preprinted standardized victim survey form. The victim will be asked to complete and return the self-addressed, stamped survey to the New Jersey Coalition Against Sexual Assault (NJCASA). These standardized survey forms are anonymous.

Results of the victim surveys will be forwarded to each county SART Coordinator on a regular basis. The SART Coordinator will take appropriate action to address any reported issues.

Aggregate data for all counties will be provided to the SART/SANE Coordinating Council and the county SART Advisory Boards.

The SANE, SAE, and/or the rape care program should offer victims the opportunity to consent to follow-up telephone contact. The purpose of this contact is to evaluate the victim's well-being and to offer further opportunities for referral for follow-up care and services. If the victim agrees, this contact should be made, or attempted, within fourteen days after the SART activation.

At the conclusion of a SART activation, each participating team member will be provided with a SART survey form and asked to complete and return the form to the county SART coordinator within seven days.

The SART Coordinator will address any issues reported by the team members. The SART coordinator will discuss any issues with the reporting team member and will apprise that person of what steps, if any, were taken. Results of the SART survey, and any actions taken to address identified issues, will be reported to the county SART Advisory Board at the next regularly scheduled meeting.

CONCLUSION

Sexual assault is a damaging crime to the victim, physically, mentally, and emotionally. It is critical for victims to understand there is help and hope. They are not broken. This chapter sketches the different available resources for victims. Sex offender notification systems are in place to prevent future victimizations. A multidisciplinary approach is designed to assist victims in a personal manner and guided by decisions made by the victims along with criminal justice practitioners and mental health professionals. The victim-assistance component in a sexual assault response to is crucial to recovery for the victim.

DISCUSSION QUESTIONS

1. What are some of the symptoms of the rape trauma syndrome and how can they affect a person's everyday life?

2. SANE nurses are extensively trained. What services do they provide to the victim's of sexual assault and why is this of particular concern to the criminal justice system?

3. Sexual Assault Response Teams (SART) are multidisciplinary. Why is this important to the victim? In your view, what do you think are the most important components of this response and why?

REFERENCES

The New Jersey Department of Criminal Justice. Office of the Attorney General. Attorney General Standards for Providing Services to Victims of Sexual Assault. Retrieved from http://www.nj.gov/oag/dcj/agguide/standards/standardssartsane.pdf on January 19, 2017.

The United States Department of Justice. Office of Violence Against Women-Sexual Assault. Retrieved from https://www.justice.gov/ovw/sexual-assault on January 17, 2017.

Wright, R. G. (2014). *Sex offender laws: failed policies, new directions* (Second ed.). Springer Publishing Co. Inc. pp. 50–65.

Name: _____   Date _____

> **You must use this form and turn in the original to the instructor. No other form will be accepted.**

CHAPTER ASSIGNMENT

People who are obligated to register for Megan's Law (at a certain tier) have their criminal history basically broadcasted to the surrounding community. These individuals have served their punishment and have completed the requirements to be released back into society. With civil rights in mind, do you think this is fair? …Why?

_____
_____
_____
_____
_____
_____
_____
_____
_____
_____
_____
_____
_____
_____
_____
_____
_____
_____

Chapter Eleven

VICTIMS OF HATE CRIMES

LEARNING OBJECTIVES

After exploring Chapter Eleven (11), the student will be able to:

1. Define hate crime.
2. Provide examples of a bias crime.
3. Explain how the FBI investigates hate crimes.
4. Describe how legislation can enhance penalties for certain crimes if categorized as biased or hate crimes.
5. Discuss the evolution of how hate crimes became laws in the United States.

KEY TERMS

Hate crime, Bias crime, Shepard-Byrd Act, Church Arson Prevention Act, Hate Crime Working Groups, National Crime Victimization Survey, Penalty Enhancements Statutes

INTRODUCTION

Since 1968, when Congress passed, and President Lyndon Johnson signed into law, the first federal hate crimes statute, the Department of Justice has been enforcing federal hate crimes laws. The 1968 statute made it a crime to use, or threaten to use, force to willfully interfere with any person because of race, color, religion, or national origin and because the person is participating in a federally protected activity, such as public education, employment, jury service, travel, or the enjoyment of public accommodations, or helping another person to do so. In 1968, Congress also made it a crime to use, or threaten to use, force to interfere with housing rights because of the victim's race, color, religion, sex, or national origin; in 1988, protections based on familial status were added. In 1996, Congress passed the Church Arson Prevention Act, 18 U.S.C. § 247. Under this Act, it is a crime to deface, damage, or destroy religious real property, or interfere with a person's religious practice, in situations affecting interstate commerce. The Act also bars defacing, damaging, or destroying religious property because of the race, color, or ethnicity of persons associated with the property.

In 2009, Congress passed, and President Obama signed, the Matthew Shepard and James Byrd Jr. Hate Crimes Prevention Act, expanding the federal definition of hate crimes, enhancing the legal toolkit available to prosecutors, and increasing the ability of federal law enforcement to support the Department of Justice's state and local partners. This law removed then existing jurisdictional obstacles to prosecutions of certain race- and religion-motivated violence and added new federal protections against crimes based on gender, disability, gender identity, or sexual orientation. Before the Civil Rights Division prosecutes a hate crime, the Attorney General or someone the Attorney General designates must certify, in writing, that (1) the state does not have jurisdiction; (2) the state has requested that the federal government assume jurisdiction; (3) the verdict or sentence obtained pursuant to state charges did not demonstratively vindicate the federal interest in eradicating bias-motivated violence; or (4) a prosecution by the United States is in the public interest and necessary to secure substantial justice. In the seven years since the passage of the Shepard-Byrd Act, the Justice Department has charged seventy-two defendants and convicted forty-five defendants under this statute. In total, as of July 15, 2016, the department has charged 258 defendants for hate crimes under multiple statutes over the last seven years.

© LANTERIA/Shutterstock.com

The Matthew Shepard and James Byrd Jr. Hate Crimes Prevention Act of 2009, 18 U.S.C. § 249

The Shepard Byrd Act makes it a federal crime to willfully cause bodily injury, or attempt to do so using a dangerous weapon, because of the victim's actual or perceived race, color, religion, or national origin.

The Act also extends federal hate crime prohibitions to crimes committed because of the actual or perceived religion, national origin, gender, sexual orientation, gender identity, or disability of any person, only where the crime affected interstate or foreign commerce or occurred within federal special maritime and territorial jurisdiction. The Shepard-Byrd Act is the first statute allowing federal criminal prosecution of hate crimes motivated by the victim's actual or perceived sexual orientation or gender identity.

James Byrd Jr. was born in Beaumont, Texas, one of nine children, to Stella and James Byrd Sr. In 1967, Byrd, who was African American, graduated from the last segregated class at Jasper's Rowe High School. Byrd went on to marry and have three children. In the pre-dawn hours of June 7, 1998, Byrd was walking home in Jasper, Texas, when he was stopped by three white men who offered him a ride home. Byrd got in the bed of their pick-up truck, but the men did not take him home. Instead, they drove him to a desolate, wooded road east of town, beat him severely, chained him to the back of the truck by his ankles and dragged him for more than three miles. The murderers drove on for another mile before dumping his torso in front of an African-American cemetery in Jasper. Byrd's lynching-by-dragging gave impetus to passage of a Texas hate crimes law.

Matthew Shepard was a twenty-one-year-old freshman at the University of Wyoming where he studied political science, foreign relations, and languages. On October 7, 1998, a few hours after he had attended a planning meeting for Gay Awareness Week events on campus, Shepard was tortured and murdered by two men in a remote area east of Laramie, Wyoming, the victim of a heinous hate crime. The son of Judy and Dennis Shepard, Shepard attended public school in Casper, Wyoming until his junior year of high school when he moved with his family to Saudi Arabia. He finished high school at The American School in Switzerland because there were no American high schools in Saudi Arabia at the time. In both Wyoming and Switzerland, he was elected by his peers to be a peer counselor. He was easy to talk to, made friends easily, and actively fought for the acceptance of all people. Shepard had a great passion for equality. His experiences abroad fueled his love for travel and gave him the chance to make many new friends from around the world.

Shepard's life and untimely death changed the way we talk about, and deal with, hate in America. Since his death, Matt's legacy has challenged and inspired millions of individuals to stand up to hate in all its forms. Although Matt's life was too short, his story continues to have a great impact on young and old alike. His legacy lives on in thousands of people who actively fight to replace hate with understanding, compassion, and acceptance.

Criminal Interference with Right to Fair Housing, 42 U.S.C. § 3631

This statute makes it a crime to use, or threaten to use force to interfere with housing rights because of the victim's race, color, religion, sex, disability, familial status, or national origin.

Damage to Religious Property, Church Arson Prevention Act, 18 U.S.C. § 247

This statute prohibits the intentional defacement, damage, or destruction of religious real property because of the religious nature of the property, where the crime affects interstate or foreign commerce, or because of the race, color, or ethnic characteristics of the people associated with the property. The statute also criminalizes the intentional obstruction by force, or threat of force of any person in the enjoyment of that person's free exercise of religious beliefs.

Violent Interference with Federally Protected Rights, 18 U.S.C. § 245

This statute makes it a crime to use, or threaten to use force to willfully interfere with any person because of race, color, religion, or national origin and because the person is participating in a federally protected activity, such as public education, employment, jury service, travel, or the enjoyment of public accommodations, or helping another person to do so.

Conspiracy Against Rights, 18 U.S.C. § 241

This statute makes it unlawful for two or more persons to conspire to injure, threaten, or intimidate a person in any state, territory, or district in the free exercise or enjoyment of any right or privilege secured to him or her by the Constitution or the laws of the U.S.

DEFINING A HATE CRIME

A hate crime is a traditional offense like murder, arson, or vandalism with an added element of bias. For the purposes of collecting statistics, the FBI has defined a hate crime as a "criminal offense against a person or property motivated in whole or in part by an offender's bias against a race, religion, disability, sexual orientation, ethnicity, gender, or gender identity." Hate itself is not a crime—and the FBI is mindful of protecting freedom of speech and other civil liberties.

These efforts serve as a backstop for investigations by state and local authorities, which handle the vast majority of hate crime cases throughout the country.

© Mark Van Scyoc/Shutterstock.com

THE FBI'S ROLE

Investigative Activities: The FBI is the lead investigative agency for criminal violations of federal civil rights statutes. The Bureau works closely with its local, state, tribal, and federal law enforcement partners around the country in many of these cases.

Law Enforcement Support: The FBI works closely with state/local/tribal authorities on investigations, even when federal charges are not brought. FBI resources, forensic expertise, and experience in identification and proof of hate-based motivations often provide an invaluable complement to local law enforcement. Many cases are also prosecuted under state statutes such as murder, arson, or more recent local ethnic intimidation laws. Once the state prosecution begins, the Department of Justice monitors the proceedings in order to ensure that the federal interest is vindicated and the law is applied equally among the ninty-five U.S. Judicial Districts.

Prosecutive Decision: The FBI forwards results of completed investigations to local U.S. Attorneys Offices and the Civil Rights Division at the Department of Justice, which decide whether a federal prosecution is warranted. Prosecution of these crimes may move forward, for example, if local authorities are unwilling or unable to prosecute a crime of bias.

Hate Crimes Working Groups (HCWGs): The majority of the FBI's field offices participate in local Hate Crime Working Groups. These Working Groups combine community and law enforcement resources to develop strategies to address local hate crime problems.

Public Outreach: The FBI has forged partnerships nationally and locally with many civil rights organizations to establish rapport, share information, address concerns, and cooperate in solving problems. These groups include such organizations as the American-Arab Anti-Discrimination Committee, American Association of University Women, Anti-Defamation League, Asian American Justice Center, Hindu American Foundation, Human Rights Campaign, The Leadership Conference on Civil and Human Rights, National Association for the Advancement of Colored People, National Center for Transgender Equality, National Council of Jewish Women, National Disability Rights Network, National Gay and Lesbian Task Force, National Organization for Women, Sikh American Legal Defense and Education Fund, The Sikh Coalition, Southern Poverty Law Center, and many others.

Training: The FBI conducts hundreds of operational seminars, workshops, and training sessions annually for local law enforcement, minority and religious organizations, and community groups to promote cooperation and reduce civil rights abuses. Each year, the FBI also provides hate crimes training for new agents, hundreds of current agents, and thousands of police officers worldwide.

The term "hate crime" was coined in the 1980s by journalists and policy advocates who were attempting to describe a series of incidents directed at Jews, Asians, and African-Americans. The Federal Bureau of Investigation defines hate crime (also known as bias crime) as "a criminal offense committed against a person, property, or society that is motivated, in whole or in part, by the offender's bias against a race, religion, disability, sexual orientation, or ethnicity/national origin."[1] Washington and Oregon were the first states to pass hate crime legislation in 1981; today, forty-nine states have hate crime statutes. States vary with regard to the groups protected under hate crime laws (e.g., religion, race or ethnicity, and sexual orientation), the range of crimes covered, and the penalty enhancements for offenders. Most states and large cities now have hate crime task forces coordinating across several levels of government and working with community organizations.

UNEVEN DATA COLLECTION MAKES ESTIMATING PREVALENCE DIFFICULT

Accurate estimates of the prevalence of hate crime remain elusive because of differences in data collection efforts across jurisdictions. In addition to varying state definitions, differences in law enforcement training, statistical reporting provisions and attitudes toward hate crime as a legitimately separate class of crime all make it harder for law enforcement and researchers to establish the scope of the problem.

© Palto/Shutterstock.com

REPORTING UNDER THE HATE CRIME STATISTIC ACT

In 1990, Congress passed the Hate Crime Statistics Act, which required the U.S. Department of Justice to acquire crime data from law enforcement agencies and publish an annual summary of findings. The FBI led a coordinated effort to collect hate crime data via the Uniform Crime Reporting (UCR) system.

In 2008, law enforcement agencies voluntarily reported 6,598 single-bias hate crime incidents (involving 7,775 offenses, 8,322 victims, and 6,219 known offenders) to the FBI. Almost half (48.5 percent) were racially motivated and 19.7 percent were motivated by religious bias. Bias against sexual orientation and ethnicity or national origin accounted for another 18.5 percent and 11.8 percent, respectively.[1]

VICTIMIZATION SURVEY REPORTS HIGHER NUMBERS

Estimates from victim interviews reported as part of the National Crime Victimization Survey (NCVS) far exceed the numbers reported by police agencies in the URC. NCVS indicates that approximately 191,000 hate crime incidents occur annually. Results from victim interviews indicate that only 44 percent of victimizations were reported to the police.[2] Only about 20 percent of these were validated by law enforcement as bias related.

IMMIGRANTS AS VICTIMS

In late 2009, NIJ was tasked by Congress to "evaluate trends in hate crimes against new immigrants, individuals who are perceived to be immigrants, and Hispanic-Americans, and to assess the underlying causes behind any increase in hate crimes against such groups."[3] NIJ has funded Abt. Associates to conduct this evaluation, which is ongoing.

WHAT MOTIVATES HATE OFFENDERS?

According to the Bureau of Justice Statistics, race is the most common motivating factor in hate crime offending reported to the police (61 percent), followed by religion (14 percent), sexual orientation (13 percent), ethnicity (11 percent), and victim disability (1 percent). In racially motivated offenses, 60 percent targeted blacks and 30 percent targeted whites.[4]

One study classified hate crime offenders into four categories that differ with respect to the psychological and situational factors that lead to hate crime offending.[5] This typology is widely used by law enforcement for training officers in the investigation and identification of hate crime.

Hate Crime Offender Typology

Offender Type/Characterization	Percent of Offenders
Thrill-seeking. Motivated by the desire for excitement.	66
Defensive. Commit hate crimes to protect their neighborhood from perceived outsiders.	25
Retaliatory. Acting in response to a hate crime — either real or perceived.	8
Mission. So strongly committed to bigotry that they make hate a career.	1

Federal Bureau of Investigation, Hate Crime Statistics Page

Hate Crime Statistics presents data regarding incidents, offenses, victims, and offenders in reported crimes that were motivated in whole or in part by a bias against the victim's perceived race, religion, ethnicity, sexual orientation, or disability.

Office for Victims of Crime

Enhances the nation's capacity to assist crime victims and provides leadership in changing attitudes, policies, and practices to promote justice and healing for all crime victims. OVC's Hate and Bias Crimes web pages link to numerous resources about, and organizations that serve hate crime victims.

National Criminal Justice Reference Service

A federally funded resource offering justice and substance abuse information to support research, policy, and program development worldwide. Spotlight on Hate Crime provides information about bias legislation, grants, publications, training, and technical assistance.

OTHER NATIONAL HATE CRIME RESOURCES

Anti-Defamation League

ADL fights against anti-Semitism and other types of bigotry; helps victims of discrimination or bias-motivated violence achieve redress of grievances through mediation, administration, or judicial means; and trains law enforcement agencies on responding to victims of bias crimes.

Center for the Prevention of Hate Violence

CPHV produces research-driven reports on bias, discrimination, and violence against targeted groups, and develops and implements training and education programs to assist businesses, nonprofit organizations, schools, and law enforcement agencies in preventing hate crimes.

Southern Poverty Law Center

Provides legal services in hate crimes, civil rights, and class action cases and works to educate the public through films and publications. Its *Intelligence Report* monitors white supremacist groups and hate crimes in the United States.

Overview of UCR Hate Crime from FBI 2015

- In 2015, 14,997 law enforcement agencies participated in the Hate Crime Statistics Program. Of these agencies, 1,742 reported 5,850 hate crime incidents involving 6,885 offenses.
- There were 5,818 single-bias incidents that involved 6,837 offenses, 7,121 victims, and 5,475 known offenders.
- The thirty-two multiple-bias incidents reported in 2015 involved forty-eight offenses, fifty-two victims, and eighteen known offenders.

Single-bias Incidents

Analysis of the 5,818 single-bias incidents reported in 2015 revealed that:

- 56.9 percent were motivated by a race/ethnicity/ancestry bias.
- 21.4 percent were prompted by religious bias.
- 18.1 percent resulted from sexual-orientation bias.
- 2.0 percent were motivated by gender-identity bias.
- 1.3 percent were prompted by disability bias.
- 0.4 percent (twenty-three incidents) were motivated by a gender bias.

Offenses by Bias Motivation within Incidents

Of the 6,837 single-bias hate crime offenses reported in the above incidents:

- 58.9 percent stemmed from a race/ethnicity/ancestry bias.
- 19.8 percent were motivated by religious bias.
- 17.8 percent resulted from sexual-orientation bias.
- 1.7 percent stemmed from gender-identity bias.
- 1.3 percent resulted from bias against disabilities.
- 0.4 percent (twenty-nine offenses) were prompted by gender bias.

Race/Ethnicity/Ancestry Bias

In 2015, law enforcement agencies reported that 4,029 single-bias hate crime offenses were motivated by race/ethnicity/ancestry. Of these offenses:

- 52.7 percent were motivated by anti-black or African American bias.
- 18.2 percent stemmed from anti-white bias.
- 9.4 percent were classified as anti-Hispanic or Latino bias.
- 3.4 percent were motivated by anti-American Indian or Alaska Native bias.
- 3.4 percent were a result of bias against groups of individuals consisting of more than one race (anti-multiple races, group).
- 3.3 percent resulted from anti-Asian bias.

- 1.2 percent were classified as anti-Arab bias.
- 0.1 percent (six offenses) were motivated by bias of anti-Native Hawaiian or other Pacific Islander.
- 8.2 percent were the result of an anti-other race/ethnicity/ancestry bias.

Religious Bias

Hate crimes motivated by religious bias accounted for 1,354 offenses reported by law enforcement. A breakdown of the bias motivation of religious-biased offenses showed:

- 51.3 percent were anti-Jewish.
- 22.2 percent were anti-Islamic (Muslim).
- 4.4 percent were anti-Catholic.
- 4.2 percent were anti-multiple religions, group.
- 3.7 percent were Anti-Eastern Orthodox (Russian, Greek, other).
- 3.5 percent were anti-Protestant.
- 1.3 percent were anti-other Christian.
- 0.6 percent were Anti-Mormon
- 0.4 percent (six offenses) were Anti-Sikh.
- 0.4 percent (five offenses) were Anti-Hindu.
- 0.1 percent (two offenses) were anti-Atheism/Agnosticism/etc.
- 0.1 percent (one offense) were Anti-Buddhist.
- 0.1 percent (one offense) were Anti-Jehovah's Witness.
- 7.7 percent were anti-other (unspecified) religion.

Sexual-orientation Bias

In 2015, law enforcement agencies reported 1,219 hate crime offenses based on sexual-orientation bias. Of these offenses:

- 62.2 percent were classified as anti-gay (male) bias.
- 19.3 percent were prompted by an anti-lesbian, gay, bisexual, or transgender (mixed group) bias.
- 13.8 percent were classified as anti-lesbian bias.
- 2.9 percent were classified as anti-bisexual bias.
- 1.9 percent were the result of an anti-heterosexual bias.

Gender-identity Bias

Of the single-bias incidents, 118 offenses were a result of gender-identity bias. Of these offenses:

- Seventy-five were anti-transgender.
- Forty-Three were anti-gender non-conforming.

Disability Bias

There were 88 reported hate crime offenses committed based on disability bias. Of these:

- Fifty-two offenses were reported as anti-physical disability.
- Thirty-six offenses were classified as anti-mental disability.

Gender Bias

There were twenty-nine offenses of gender bias reported in 2015. Of these:

- Twenty-one were anti-female.
- Eight were anti-male.

By Offense Types

Of the 6,885 reported hate crime offenses in 2015:

- 26.9 percent were intimidation.
- 24.7 percent were destruction/damage/vandalism.
- 24.6 percent were simple assault.
- 12.8 percent were aggravated assault.
- The remaining offenses included additional crimes against persons, property, and society.

Offenses by Crime Category

Among the 6,885 hate crime offenses reported:

- 65.1 percent were crimes against persons.
- 34.0 percent were crimes against property.
- The remaining offenses were crimes against society.

Crimes Against Persons

Law enforcement reported 4,482 hate crime offenses as crimes against persons. By offense type:

- 41.3 percent were intimidation.
- 37.8 percent were simple assault.
- 19.7 percent were aggravated assault.
- 0.7 percent consisted of eighteen murders and thirteen rapes (twelve rapes were submitted under the UCR Program's revised definition of rape).
- 0.4 percent involved the offense category other, which is collected only in NIBRS.

Crimes Against Property

- The majority of the 2,338 hate crime offenses that were crimes against property (72.6 percent) were acts of destruction/damage/vandalism.
- The remaining 27.4 percent of crimes against property consisted of robbery, burglary, larceny-theft, motor vehicle theft, arson, and other crimes.

Crimes Against Society

There were sixty-five offenses defined as crimes against society (e.g., drug or narcotic offenses or prostitution).

By Victim Type

When considering the 6,885 hate crime offenses and their targeted victims:

- 83.2 percent were directed at individuals.
- 4.5 percent were against businesses or financial institutions.
- 2.7 percent were against religious organizations.
- 2.1 percent were against government.
- 0.9 percent were against society/public.
- The remaining 6.6 percent were directed at other/unknown/multiple victim types.

An example of a state legislative response to hate crimes can be viewed in the New Jersey criminal code of Title 2C, we have listed the bias intimidation statutes below.

2C:16-1. Bias Intimidation.

a. Bias Intimidation. A person is guilty of the crime of bias intimidation if he commits, attempts to commit, conspires with another to commit, or threatens the immediate commission of an offense specified in chapters 11 through 18 of Title 2C of the New Jersey Statutes; N.J.S.2C:33-4; N.J.S.2C:39-3; N.J.S.2C:39-4 or N.J.S.2C:39-5,

   (1) with a purpose to intimidate an individual or group of individuals because of race, color, religion, gender, disability, sexual orientation, gender identity or expression, national origin, or ethnicity; or

   (2) knowing that the conduct constituting the offense would cause an individual or group of individuals to be intimidated because of race, color, religion, gender, disability, sexual orientation, gender identity or expression, national origin, or ethnicity; or

   (3) under circumstances that caused any victim of the underlying offense to be intimidated and the victim, considering the manner in which the offense was committed, reasonably believed either that (a) the offense was committed with a purpose to intimidate the victim or any person or entity in whose welfare the victim is interested because of race, color, religion, gender, disability, sexual orientation, gender identity or expression, national origin, or ethnicity, or (b) the victim or the victim's property was selected to be the target of the offense because of the victim's race, color, religion, gender, disability, sexual orientation, gender identity or expression, national origin, or ethnicity.

b. Permissive inference concerning selection of targeted person or property. Proof that the target of the underlying offense was selected by the defendant, or by another acting in concert with the defendant, because of race, color, religion, gender, disability, sexual orientation, gender identity or expression, national origin, or ethnicity shall give rise to a permissive inference by the trier of fact that the defendant acted with a purpose to intimidate an individual or group of individuals because of race, color, religion, gender, disability, sexual orientation, gender identity or expression, national origin, or ethnicity.

c. Grading. Bias intimidation is a crime of the fourth degree if the underlying offense referred to in subsection a. is a disorderly persons offense or petty disorderly persons offense. Otherwise, bias intimidation is a crime one degree higher than the most serious underlying crime referred to in subsection a., except that where the underlying crime is a crime of the first degree, bias intimidation is a first-degree crime and the defendant upon conviction thereof may, notwithstanding the provisions of paragraph (1) of subsection a. of N.J.S.2C:43-6, be sentenced to an ordinary term of imprisonment between fifteen years and thirty years, with a presumptive term of twenty years.

d. Gender exemption in sexual offense prosecutions. It shall not be a violation of subsection a. if the underlying criminal offense is a violation of chapter 14 of Title 2C of the New Jersey Statutes and the circumstance specified in paragraph (1), (2) or (3) of subsection a. of this section is based solely upon the gender of the victim.

e. Merger. Notwithstanding the provisions of N.J.S.2C:1-8 or any other provision of law, a conviction for bias intimidation shall not merge with a conviction of any of the underlying offenses referred to in subsection a. of this section, nor shall any conviction for such underlying offense merge with a conviction for bias intimidation. The court shall impose separate sentences upon a conviction for bias intimidation and a conviction of any underlying offense.

f. Additional Penalties. In addition to any fine imposed pursuant to N.J.S.2C:43-3 or any term of imprisonment imposed pursuant to N.J.S.2C:43-6, a court may order a person convicted of bias intimidation to one or more of the following:

(1) complete a class or program on sensitivity to diverse communities, or other similar training in the area of civil rights;

(2) complete a counseling program intended to reduce the tendency toward violent and antisocial behavior; and

(3) make payments or other compensation to a community-based program or local agency that provides services to victims of bias intimidation.

g. As used in this section "gender identity or expression" means having or being perceived as having a gender related identity or expression whether or not stereotypically associated with a person's assigned sex at birth.

h. It shall not be a defense to a prosecution for a crime under this section that the defendant was mistaken as to the race, color, religion, gender, disability, sexual orientation, gender identity or expression, national origin, or ethnicity of the victim.

L.2001, c.443, s.1; amended 2007, c.303, s.1.

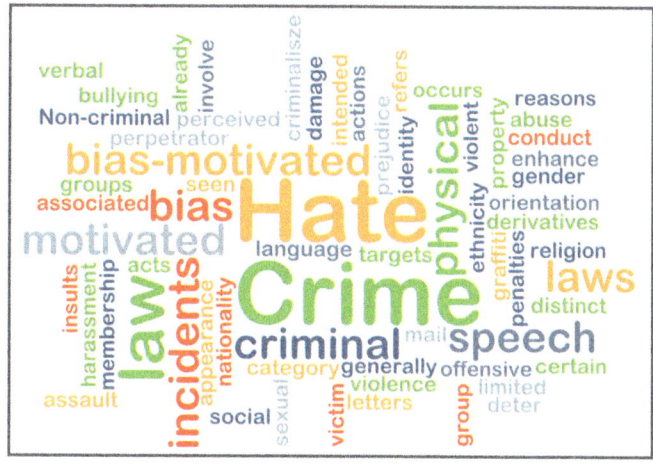

© Kheng Guan Toh/Shutterstock.com

HATE CRIMES TIMELINE

According to **http://www.hrc.org/resources/hate-crimes-timeline**

Here's a look at some of the bigger developments in the fight for passage of federal hate crimes legislation.

1989

February 22, 1989 | 101st Congress—The Hate Crimes Statistics Act is reintroduced in the U.S. House of Representatives. It was also introduced in the 99th and 100th congresses. It would require the Department of Justice to collect and publish data about crimes motivated by hatred based on race, religion, ethnicity ,and sexual orientation.

June 27, 1989 | House passes the Hate Crimes Statistics Act by a 368–47 vote.

1990

February 8, 1990 | The U.S. Senate passes the Hate Crimes Statistics Act by a 92–4 vote.

April 23, 1990 | President George H.W. Bush signs the bill into law.

1993

March 1, 1993 | 103rd Congress - The Hate Crimes Sentencing Enhancement Act is reintroduced in the House (it was also introduced in the 102nd Congress). It would allow judges to impose harsher penalties for hate crimes, including hate crimes based on gender, disability and sexual orientation that occur in national parks and on other federal property.

September 21, 1993 | House passes the Hate Crimes Sentencing Enhancement Act by a voice vote.

October 6, 1993 | The Hate Crimes Sentencing Enhancement Act is introduced in the Senate.

November 4, 1993 | The Hate Crimes Sentencing Enhancement Act is added as an amendment to the Violent Crime and Law Enforcement Act of 1994. It is later enacted.

"HATE CRIMES TIMELINE" FOUND: http://www.hrc.org/resources/hate-crimes-timeline

1997

June 7, 1997 | "Such hate crimes, committed solely because the victims have a different skin color or a different faith or are gays or lesbians, leave deep scars not only on the victims but on our larger community. They are acts of violence against America itself."—*President Bill Clinton in his weekly radio address*

June 7, 1997 | President Clinton devotes his weekly radio address to hate crimes, specifically citing bias crimes against LGBTQ people. He asks Attorney General Janet Reno to review the laws concerning hate crimes and help the federal government develop a plan of action.

November 13, 1997 | 105th Congress—The Hate Crimes Prevention Act is introduced in the House and the Senate. The bill would extend the protection of the current federal hate crimes law to include those who are victimized because of their sexual orientation, gender or disability. It would also strengthen current law regarding hate crimes based on race, religion, and national origin.

1998

June 7, 1998 | James Byrd Jr., forty-nine, of Jasper, Texas, accepts a ride from three white men. Instead of taking him home, the three men beat Byrd behind a convenience store, strip him naked, chain him by the ankles to their pickup truck and dragged him for three miles over rural roads outside Jasper. Forensic evidence suggests that Byrd had been attempting to keep his head up while being dragged, and an autopsy suggests that Byrd was alive during much of the dragging. Byrd dies after his right arm and head are severed after his body hit a culvert. His body had caught a sewage drain on the side of the road, resulting in his decapitation.

Officials quickly determined that the murderers were members of white supremacist groups, wore body tattoos from Aryan Pride, Nazi symbols and gang symbols of their affiliation with well known racist gangs. It was then documented as a hate crime.

October 6–7, 1998 | Matthew Shepard, twenty-one, of Laramie, Wyo., meets two men, Aaron McKinney and Russell Henderson, at a bar, and they drive him to a remote area east of Laramie, where they tie him to a split-rail fence, beat him and leave him to die in the cold of the night. Almost eighteen hours later, he is found by a cyclist, who initially mistakes him for a scarecrow.

October 12, 1998 | Matthew Shepard dies at a hospital in Fort Collins, Colo.

1999

May 1999 | "I know this measure is not a cure-all, and it won't stop all hate violence. But it will send the message that this senseless violence is unacceptable and un-American. My son Matthew was the victim of a brutal hate crime, and I believe this legislation is necessary to make sure no family again has to suffer like mine."—*Judy Shepard, speaking before a U.S. Senate panel to urge the passage of federal hate crimes legislation*

February 1999 | A Gallup poll indicates that 75 percent of Americans believe that "homosexuals" should be covered by hate crimes laws.

March 1999 | 106th Congress - The Hate Crimes Prevention Act is reintroduced in the House and the Senate.

April 5, 1999 | Russell Henderson pleads guilty to the murder of Matthew Shepard and agrees to testify against Aaron McKinney. In exchange for his testimony, Henderson receives two consecutive life sentences with no chance for parole.

May 1999 | Judy Shepard speaks before a U.S. Senate panel to urge the passage of hate crimes legislation.

July 22, 1999 | The Senate passes the Hate Crimes Prevention Act after it is incorporated as an amendment to the Commerce, Justice ,and State appropriations bill.

October 25, 1999 | Trial of Aaron McKinney begins. Defense lawyers plan to argue that McKinney snapped when Shepard supposedly made a pass at him at a bar, triggering memories of a childhood sexual assault. The judge rejects the so-called "gay panic" defense.

November 4, 1999 | Aaron McKinney is found guilty in the murder of Matthew Shepard. In a deal that is approved by the Shepard family, McKinney avoids the death penalty and is sentenced to two consecutive life sentences with no chance for parole.

2001

January 2001 | MTV airs a movie about the murder of Matthew Shepard and shuts down programming for seventeen hours to run a list of the names of hundreds of victims of hate crimes. More than 50,000 people send e-mails or signed petitions urging Congress and the Bush administration to support the hate crimes bill.

March 2001 | Judy Shepard joins the HRC Board of Directors.

Spring 2001 | 107th Congress—The Local Law Enforcement Hate Crimes Prevention Act is introduced in the House and the Local Law Enforcement Enhancement Act is introduced in the Senate. The legislation would provide federal assistance to states and local jurisdictions to prosecute hate crimes.

2003

April/May 2003 | 108th Congress—The Local Law Enforcement Hate Crimes Prevention Act is reintroduced in the House and the Local Law Enforcement Enhancement Act is reintroduced in the Senate.

2005

May 26, 2005 | 109th Congress—The Local Law Enforcement Hate Crimes Prevention Act is reintroduced in the House and the Local Law Enforcement Enhancement Act is reintroduced in the Senate.

2006 | Harris Interactive reports that 54 percent of LGBTQ people surveyed say they are concerned about being the victim of a hate crime.

2007

2007 | A Gallup poll shows that 68 percent of Americans favor including sexual orientation and gender identity in federal hate crimes law. More than half of conservatives (57 percent) and Republicans (60 percent) back inclusive legislation. Support is strongest among self-identified liberals (82 percent), Democrats (75 percent), those affiliated with non-Christian religious faiths (74 percent) and Catholics (72 percent).

March/April 2007 | 110th Congress—The Local Law Enforcement Hate Crimes Prevention Act is introduced in the House, and the Matthew Shepard Local Law Enforcement Enhancement Act is introduced in the Senate.

May 3, 2007 | The House passes the Local Law Enforcement Hate Crimes Prevention Act by a floor vote of 237–180.

Spring 2007 | Peter D. Hart Research Associates releases the results of a poll showing that support for protections against hate violence is strong—even across partisan and racial lines. The results show that three in four voters support including sexual orientation in federal hate crimes laws, including 85 percent of Democrats, 74 percent of Independents, 64 percent of Republicans, 74 percent of African-Americans, 74 percent of Latinos, and 74 percent of Caucasians.

September 27, 2007 | The Senate invokes cloture on the hate crimes legislation by a vote of 60-39. A voice vote adds the Matthew Shepard Local Law Enforcement Enhancement Act as an amendment to the Department of Defense Authorization Act. It is the first time that a transgender-inclusive piece of legislation passes both chambers of Congress.

2009

April 2009 | 111th Congress—The Local Law Enforcement Hate Crimes Prevention Act is introduced in the House, and the Matthew Shepard Hate Crimes Prevention Act is introduced in the Senate.

April 29, 2009 | The House passes the Local Law Enforcement Hate Crimes Prevention Act by a floor vote of 249–175.

July 16, 2009 | Senate cloture motion on the hate crimes bill passes by a 63–28 vote. The bill is added to the Defense Department Authorization bill.

July 23, 2009 | The Senate passes the Defense Department Authorization bill, on which the Matthew Shepard Hate Crimes Prevention Act is attached as an amendment. The bill goes to a conference committee to work out differences between the House and Senate versions of the legislation.

October 6, 2009 | The House fails to pass a motion, by a 178–234 vote, to instruct conferees to strip the hate crimes provision (now titled "Matthew Shepard and James Byrd, Jr. Hate Crimes Prevention Act") from the Defense Dept. authorization bill conference report.

October 8, 2009 | The House passes the conference report by a 281–146 vote.

October 10, 2009 | President Obama reiterates his support for hate crimes legislation at the thirteenth annual HRC National Dinner. Dennis and Judy Shepard are honored with the first annual Edward M. Kennedy National Leadership Award.

October 22, 2009 | October 22, 2009—The Senate votes 68–29 to pass the Defense Department authorization bill that includes a provision for inclusive federal hate crimes legislation.

October 28, 2009 | President Barack Obama signs the Matthew Shepard and James Byrd, Jr. Hate Crimes Prevention Act into law (as a provision of the National Defense Authorization Act).

The Underlying Causes of Bias and Hate Crimes

1. The continuing demographic change in the United States as the population becomes more diverse.
2. The continuing shift to a service economy and the economic uncertainties that provides a source of conflict between groups.
3. Prevalence of negative stereotypes in our culture, as well as an atmosphere of intolerance in politics and public debate.
4. Racial division among our youth and in schools, the persistence and continued vitality of hate groups, and continued violence by minorities against members of their own race.
5. Lack of hope among some ethnic groups. Note: www.nj.gov/oag/bias.

Who Are Often Victims?

1. The skin color black represents the group most frequently victimized by bias crimes.
2. The Jewish religion represents the religious group crimes.
3. The gay and lesbian community.
4. Immigrants and all other ethnic groups

Who Commits Bias and Hate Crimes?

1. Members of organized hate groups.
2. The majority of offenders are juveniles and young adults, between the ages of twelve–twenty-one.
3. Any individual if their actions fall within the elements of the crime.

Types of Bias / Hate Crimes

- Harassment
- Terroristic Threats
- Criminal Mischief
- Assault
- Arson
- Homicide

Information Needed When Reporting a Hate Crime

1. The name and address of the victim.
2. The time and place where the crime occurred.
3. The type of crime committed.
4. The description and license plate number of vehicle involved in crime.
5. A description of the perpetrator—i.e., race, sex, height, weight, scars, tattoos, hair color and style, clothing, and jewelry. Provide the name or street name if known.

Laws Protecting People Against Bias or Hate Crimes

Since 1979, nearly every state in the United States has enacted some form of bias crime statute. The most common statues are penalty enhancement and criminal civil rights statues. Other types of statues include institutional vandalism laws, cross-burning statutes, anti-masking laws, and laws prohibiting interference with religious worship.

Penalty Enhancements Statutes

These statutes increase the penalty for existing criminal offenses when a victim is targeted, based in whole or in part on the perception or beliefs of the actor, because of race, color, religion, gender, disability, sexual orientation, gender identity or expression, national origin, or ethnicity of that person, owner or occupant of that property, regardless of whether or not the perpetrator's belief was correct.

Civil Rights and Ethnic Intimidation Statutes

Unlike the penalty enhancements, these statutes do not require the charging of an underlying offense, such as an assault. However, prosecutors still have the option of charging additional offenses, such as assault, when applicable.

Institutional Vandalism Statutes

These statutes prohibit vandalism and other willful property damage to churches, synagogues and cemeteries. These laws have been enacted in approximately forty states.

Endnotes

1. Federal Bureau of Investigation. *Hate Crime Statistics, 2008*. Washington, DC: U.S. Department of Justice, Federal Bureau of Investigation, November 2007.
2. Harlow, C.W. Hate Crimes Reported by Victims and Police. *Special Report*. Washington, DC: U.S. Department of Justice, Bureau of Justice Statistics, 2005, NCJ 209911.
3. See "*Departments of Transportation and Housing and Urban Development, and Related Agencies Appropriations Act, 2010,*" House Report 111-366, December 8, 2009.
4. Strom, K.J. *Hate Crime Reported in NIBRS*, 1997–1999. Washington, DC: U.S. Department of Justice, Bureau of Justice Statistics, 2001, NCJ 186765.
5. McDevitt, J., J. Levin, and S. Bennett (2002). "Hate Crime Offenders: An Expanded Typology (abstract)." *Journal of Social Issues 58*(2): 303–317, NCJ 204396.

DISCUSSION QUESTIONS

1. What changes a criminal offense to make it into a hate crime?

2. Why are there enhanced penalties for criminal offenses that appear to be based upon bias or hate?

3. What are some motivating factors for hate offenders?

Name: _____   Date _____

You must use this form and turn in the original to the instructor. No other form will be accepted.

CHAPTER ASSIGNMENT

The text discusses the evolution of legislation for hate crimes in the United States. Provide examples and discuss why it took so long for such legislation to be enacted and mechanisms to enforce those laws?

_____
_____
_____
_____
_____
_____
_____
_____
_____
_____
_____
_____
_____
_____
_____
_____
_____
_____
_____
_____

Chapter Twelve

VICTIMS OF STALKING

LEARNING OBJECTIVES

After exploring Chapter Twelve (12), the student will be able to:

1. Define stalking.
2. Explain the anti-stalking federal law.
3. Describe how phones and email are used in stalking.
4. Discuss why all contact should stop with a stalker.

KEY TERMS

Stalking, Anti-stalking Law, Violence Against Women Act, Personal Safety Plan, National Center for Victims of Crime, Abusive relationship

According to—https://www.justice.gov/usao-ndga/victim-witness-assistance/interstate-stalking

INTERSTATE STALKING

In 1996 Congress passed an anti-stalking law as part of the Violence Against Women Act (VAWA). Under this law it is a federal felony to cross state lines to stalk or harass an individual if the conduct causes fear of serious bodily injury or death to the stalking victim or to the victim's immediate family members. It is a federal felony to stalk or harass on military or U.S. territorial lands, including Indian country (18 U.S.C.§ 2261A). It is also a federal crime to cross state lines or enter or leave Indian country in violation of a qualifying Protection Order (18 U.S.C. § 2262). There are also state laws dealing with the crime of stalking.

Just like the chapter on domestic violence/intimate partner violence, we are providing information in a first-person manner. The intent is to promote discussion and critical thinking. While reading, empathy needs to enter the process. Just as if you are a police officer, detective, prosecutor, lawyer, advocate, friend, relative, etc. Many people are affected by these traumas. A little understanding, no matter your role, will expand your tools and your thought process. To begin:

If You Are In Danger, Find A Safe Place To Go Such As

- Police/Fire Department
- Homes of friends or relatives preferably unknown to the stalker
- Family crisis shelters
- Crowded public buildings or places

After You Are Safe, Notify Appropriate Police Agencies

- Give an accurate description of the stalker, his or her vehicle, address (if known) and a recent photograph if you have one.
- Notify security personnel in apartments and/or appropriate personnel at your work place, or children's school, and other places that are a part of your normal routine. Ask law enforcement about security measures they can initiate. Some agencies have alarms available for stalking victims or "panic button" alarms can be rented from private security agencies.
- As well as helping to protect you, by reporting a crime of stalking, police can keep an independent record of the incidents, which can assist them in developing a threat assessment of the stalker.
- Police reports may also help you get a protection order from a court or demonstrate that an existing order has been violated.

Stop All Contact With A Stalker- Now And For Good

- Consult with a victim services provider about creating a personal safety plan ... and follow it.
- If you believe the stalker truly poses a threat, consider obtaining a restraining order, but be aware that service of the order to the stalker may provoke a response.

© notbad/Shutterstock.com

Document Stalking Behavior

- It is important to keep a record of incidents which may support a criminal prosecution. Record dates, times of day, and places of contact with the individual who is stalking you. Log any telephone calls and save answering machine messages.
- Save any correspondence from the stalker, including the envelope.
- Document threats in detail.
- Provide names and addresses of witnesses to any incidents to law enforcement or a prosecutor.

Other Unlawful Acts

If the stalker has assaulted you physically or sexually, has entered your home without permission, or has damaged or stolen your property, report it to police. They should also photograph injuries to your person or damage to your property. These are separate crimes which can be prosecuted.

Ways To Increase Your Home And Personal Safety

- Telling a stalker that you don't want to talk to him is still talking to him or her. Stop all contact.
- Treat any threat as legitimate and call police immediately. Install dead bolts. If you lose the key, change the locks.
- If possible, install outside lights activated by a motion detector.
- Maintain an unlisted phone number. If harassing calls persist, contact telephone company security and they can assist you with options to trace the origin of such calls.
- Use a telephone message machine to screen calls. This documents contact by a stalker, for police.
- Vary the routes you take and limit the time you spend walking.
- Keep children and pets indoors and always under supervision. If you have children in common, arrange through the court for the exchange of custody or visitation through a third party.
- Tell trusted relatives, friends, a landlord, and neighbors about the situation.
- Provide family, friends, neighbors, and your employer with a photo or description of the stalker and the car he or she drives.
- Advise your employer and co-workers of the problem and provide a picture of the stalker if available. If the stalker shows up at work, have someone contact the police, and avoid any personal contact.
- Don't park in secluded areas.

Help Is Available

If you are a victim of a stalking crime it is normal to sometimes feel frightened and vulnerable. The following agencies exist to help victims of crime. Seek their help.

National Assistance

- National Domestic Violence Hotline
  www.ndvh.org
  1-800-799-SAFE

© Vitezslav Valka/Shutterstock.com

© iQoncept/Shutterstock.com

- National Center for Victims of Crime
  www.ncvc.org
  1-800-FYI-CALL (1-800-394-2255)

- National Organization for Victim Assistance
  www.trynova.org
  1-800-TRY-NOVA (1-800-879-6682)

- National Coalition Against Domestic Violence
  303-839-1852

- If in crisis, call: 1-800-SUICIDE or 1-800-273-TALK

- Useful web links: Information Resources (**http://www.ojp.usdoj.gov/ovc/help/welcome.html**) and an online directory of crime victim services to assist you in locating non-emergency crime victim services (**http://ovc.ncjrs.gov/findvictimservices/**).

Local Assistance

- If you feel you are in danger, first contact your local Police or Sheriff Department. Dial 911.
- Domestic Violence Hotline in Georgia 1-800-33HAVEN (1-800-334-2836). Provides twenty-four hours statewide access to free and confidential help and information for victims and their family and friends.
- Contact your County Victim Assistance Program in Solicitor or District Attorney's Office.
- Federal Bureau of Investigation: To report interstate stalking crimes 404-679-9000
- 21.S. Attorney's Victim Witness Assistance Program 1-888-431-1918, 404-581-6102, or 404-581-6041. (For victims and witnesses of federal crime.)

https://victimsofcrime.org/our-programs/stalking-resource-center/help-for-victims

Things You Can Do

Stalking is unpredictable and dangerous. No two stalking situations are alike. There are no guarantees that what works for one person will work for another, yet you can take steps to increase your safety.

- If you are in immediate danger, call 911.
- Trust your instincts. Don't downplay the danger. If you feel you are unsafe, you probably are.
- Take threats seriously. Danger generally is higher when the stalker talks about suicide or murder, or when a victim tries to leave or end the relationship.
- Contact a crisis hotline, victim services agency, or a domestic violence or rape crisis program. They can help you devise a safety plan, give you information about local laws, weigh options such as seeking a protection order, and refer you to other services.
- Develop a safety plan, including things like changing your routine, arranging a place to stay, and having a friend or relative go places with you. Also, decide in advance what to do if the stalker shows up at your home, work, school, or somewhere else. Tell people how they can help you.
- Don't communicate with the stalker or respond to attempts to contact you.

- Keep evidence of the stalking. When the stalker follows you or contacts you, write down the time, date, and place. Keep emails, text messages, phone messages, letters, or notes. Photograph anything of yours the stalker damages and any injuries the stalker causes. Ask witnesses to write down what they saw.
- Contact the police. Every state has stalking laws. The stalker may also have broken other laws by doing things like assaulting you or stealing or destroying your property.
- Consider getting a court order that tells the stalker to stay away from you.
- Tell family, friends, roommates, and co-workers about the stalking and seek their support.
- Tell security staff at your job or school. Ask them to help watch out for your safety.

If Someone You Know Is Being Stalked

- Listen.
- Show support.
- Don't blame the victim for the crime.
- Remember that every situation is different, and allow the person being stalked to make choices about how to handle it.
- Find someone you can talk to about the situation.
- Take steps to ensure your own safety.

© Stuart Miles/Shutterstock.com

STALKING SAFETY PLANNING

Stalking Safety Planning Overview

Several murders of stalking victims have highlighted the fact that people who stalk can be very dangerous. Stalkers can threaten, attack, sexually assault, and even kill their victims. Unfortunately, there is no single psychological or behavioral profile that can predict what stalkers will do. Stalkers' behaviors can escalate, from more indirect ways of making contact (e.g., sending email or repeated phone calling) to more personal ways (delivering things to the victim's doorstep or showing up at their work).

Many victims struggle with how to respond to the stalker. Some victims try to reason with the stalker, try to "let them down easy" or "be nice" in hopes of getting the stalker to stop the behavior. Some victims tell themselves that the behavior "isn't that bad" or other sentiments that minimize the stalking behavior. Other victims may confront or threaten the stalker and/or try to "fight back." These methods rarely work because stalkers are actually encouraged by any contact with the victim, even negative interactions.

Victims of stalking cannot predict what stalkers will do but can determine their own responses to the stalking behavior. Personal safety and harm prevention is of the utmost importance for victims. While victims cannot control the stalking behavior, they can be empowered to take steps to keep themselves, family, and loved ones safe. The creation of a safety plan can assist victims in doing this.

Stalking Safety Plan—What is it?

A safety plan is a combination of suggestions, plans, and responses created to help victims reduce their risk of harm. It is a tool designed in response to the victim's specific situation that evaluates what the victim is currently experiencing, incorporates the pattern of previous behavior, and examines options that will positively impact the victim's safety. In a safety plan, the factors that are causing or contributing to the risk of harm to the victim and her/his loved ones are identified and interventions are developed.

Advocates and Stalking Safety Planning

While victims can make safety plans on their own, it is often helpful to enlist the assistance of trained professionals. These professionals, including advocates and law enforcement officers, can help a victim determine which options will best enhance their safety, and will work to devise a safety plan to address each unique situation and circumstance. Victim advocates can be found in local domestic violence and rape crisis programs, as well as, in victim assistance programs in local prosecutors' offices and in some law enforcement agencies.

Stalking Safety Plans—What To Include

When safety planning, victims can consider what is known about the stalker, the people who might help, how to improve safety in one's environment, and what to do in case of an emergency. The average stalking case lasts approximately two years; therefore, safety planning must begin when the victim first identifies the stalking behavior and continue throughout the duration of the case. Safety plans need to be re-evaluated and updated continuously as the stalker's behavior, the victim's routines, and access to services and support changes.

Below are suggestions to consider when developing a stalking safety plan. This is not an exhaustive list. In a safety plan, any recommended strategy must focus on what the victim feels will work in her best interest at any given point in time.

Documentation of Stalking and Reporting to Police

Victims are encouraged to keep a log of all stalking behaviors including e-mails and phone messages. The log, as well as any gifts or letters the stalker sends the victim, can be collected and used as evidence. The evidence will help prove what has been going on if the victim decides to report the stalking to the police or apply for a protective order.

Rely on Trusted People

Many victims have found simple ways to make the stalking affect them less. They may ask someone else to pick up and sort their mail, get a second phone number given only to trusted people, or have people at work or school screen phone calls or inform the police if the stalker shows up. Relying on trusted friends and family is important for victims of stalking to help keep victims safer and also reduce the isolation and feelings of desperation that stalking victims may experience.

Technology Safety Planning

Stalkers use technology to assist them in stalking their victims in various ways. It is important to consider how victims may be harmed by stalkers' use of technology. Stalkers use the Internet to contact or post things about the victim on message board or discussion forums. They may also verbally attack or threaten victims in chat rooms. Some stalkers will post threatening or personal information about the victim—including the victim's full name and address. Often stalkers will e-mail the victim, or fill their in-box with spam and have been known to send viruses or other harmful programs to victims' computers. These threatening messages should be saved, especially if the victim is considering contacting the police with the case.

If stalkers have access to a victim's computer, they can track them by looking at the history or websites visited on the computer. Also, stalkers have been known to install Spyware software on computers (sometimes sent through e-mail) that sends them a copy of every keystroke made, including passwords, websites visited, and e-mails sent. Spyware is very difficult to detect and a victim will likely not know she has it on her computer. If a victim believes s/he has a Spyware program on her/his computer, it is important the victim talk to a trained advocate.

Stalkers use cell phones enabled with Global Positioning System (GPS) to track victims. GPS technology can also be used to track or follow victims by placing them in the victim's car and will be able to tell everywhere the car travels. When safety planning with a victim about technology issues, ask a victim if her stalker has ever had access to her phone or computer. If so, it may be important to stop using the phone or computer, or only use it in a manner that will not give the stalker any information about the victim's location.

It is also important for victims of stalking to remain diligent about protecting their personal information that could be saved in databases. Businesses, for example, collect personal information about people, including addresses, phone numbers, last names, etc. This information can sometimes be accessed and exploited by stalkers. One stalking victim's ex-boyfriend learned of her new address by "innocently" inquiring at the local oil change station if she had recently brought in their car for an oil change. Because that business had her information stored, they gave the stalker the address the victim had wanted to keep unknown to the stalker. Victims are encouraged to consider who might have their personal information. They should instruct businesses to not give out any personal information. In many instances, victims can ask that their account be password protected. This password should be one only known to the victim and no information should be released or discussed until the password has been verified.

© Design Seed/Shutterstock.com

Although no safety plan guarantees safety, such plans are valuable and important tools to keep victims safer, document incidents that happen with the perpetrator, make surroundings more secure, and identify people who can help.

Stalking Safety Tips

Safety Anytime

- If possible, have a phone nearby at all times, preferably one to which the stalker has never had access. Memorize emergency numbers, and make sure that 911 and helpful family or friends are on speed dial.
- Treat all threats, direct and indirect, as legitimate and inform law enforcement immediately.
- Vary routines, including changing routes to work, school, the grocery store, and other places regularly frequented. Limit time spent alone and try to shop at different stores and visit different bank branches.
- When out of the house or work environment, try not to travel alone and try to stay in public areas.
- Get a new, unlisted phone number. Leave the old number active and connected to an answering machine or voicemail. Have a friend, advocate, or law enforcement screen the calls, and save any messages from the stalker. These messages, particularly those that are explicitly abusive or threatening, can be critical evidence for law enforcement to build a stalking case against the offender.
- Do not interact with the person stalking or harassing you. Responding to stalker's actions may reinforce their behavior.
- Consider obtaining a protective order against the stalker. Some states offer stalking protective orders and other victims may be eligible for protective orders under their state's domestic violence statutes.
- Trust your instincts. If you're somewhere that doesn't feel safe, either find ways to make it safer, or leave.

If in Imminent Danger, Locate a Safe Place. Consider Going to:

- Police Station
- Residences of family or friends (locations unknown to the perpetrators)
- Domestic violence shelters
- Place of worship
- Public areas (some stalkers may be less inclined toward violence or creating a disturbance in public places).

© trekandshoot/Shutterstock.com

Safety at Home:

- Identify escape routes out of your house. Teach them to your children.
- Install solid core doors with dead bolts. If all keys cannot be accounted for, change the locks and secure the spare keys. Fix any broken windows or doors.
- Have a code word you use with your children that tells them when they need to leave.
- Inform neighbors and, if residing in an apartment, any on-site managers about the situation, providing them with a photo or description of the stalker and any vehicles they may drive if known. Ask your neighbors to call the police if they see the stalker at your house. Agree on a signal you will use when you need them to call the police.

- Pack a bag with important items you'd need if you had to leave quickly. Put the bag in a safe place, or give it to a friend or relative you trust.
- Consider putting together a "stalking sack" that includes the stalking log, a camera, information about the offender, etc.

Safety at Work and School:

- Give a picture of the stalker to security and friends at work and school.
- Tell your supervisors. They have a responsibility to keep you safe at work.
- Ask a security guard to walk you to your car or to the bus.
- If the stalker contacts you, save any voicemails, text messages, and e-mails.
- Give the school or daycare center a copy of your protective order. Tell them not to release your children to anyone without talking to you first.
- Make sure your children know to tell a teacher or administrator at school if they see the stalker.
- Make sure that the school and work know not to give your address or phone number to anyone.
- Keep a copy of your protective order at work.

Stalking Fact Sheet

http://victimsofcrime.org/docs/default-source/src/stalking-fact-sheet-2015_eng.pdf?status=Temp&fvrsn=0.994206007104367

Stalking Victimization

- 7.5 million people are stalked in one year in the United States.
- 15 percent of women and 6 percent of men have experienced stalking victimization at some point during their lifetime in which they felt very fearful or believed that they or someone close to them would be harmed or killed.
- The majority of stalking victims are stalked by someone they know: 61 percent of female victims and 44 percent of male victims of stalking are stalked by a current or former intimate partner, 25 percent of female victims and 32 percent of male victims are stalked by an acquaintance.
- About half of all victims of stalking indicated that they were stalked before the age of twenty-five. About 14 percent of female victims and 16 percent of male victims experienced stalking between the ages of eleven and seventeen.
- Approaching the victim or showing up in places when the victim didn't want them to be there; making unwanted telephone calls; leaving the victim unwanted messages (text or voice); and watching or following the victim from a distance, or spying on the victim with a listening device, camera, or global positioning system were the most commonly reported stalker tactics by both female and male victims of stalking.
- 46 percent of stalking victims experience at least one unwanted contact per week.
- 11 percent of stalking victims have been stalked for five years or more.

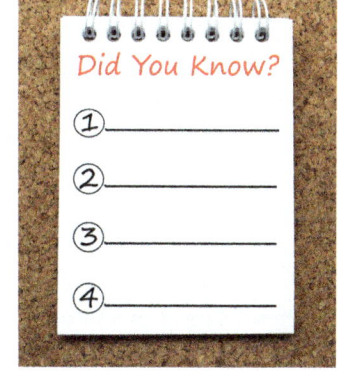

Stalking and Intimate Partner Femicide

- 76 percent of intimate partner femicide victims have been stalked by their intimate partner.
- 67 percent had been physically abused by their intimate partner.
- 89 percent of femicide victims who had been physically assaulted had also been stalked in the twelve months before their murder.
- 79 percent of abused femicide victims reported being stalked during the same period that they were abused.
- 54 percent of femicide victims reported stalking to police before they were killed by their stalkers.

Recon Study of Stalkers

- 2/3 of stalkers pursue their victims at least once per week, many daily, using more than one method.
- 78 percent of stalkers use more than one means of approach.
- Weapons are used to harm or threaten victims in one out of five cases.
- Almost one-third of stalkers have stalked before.
- Intimate partner stalkers frequently approach their targets, and their behaviors escalate quickly.

Impact of Stalking on Victims

- 46 percent of stalking victims fear not knowing what will happen next.
- 29 percent of stalking victims fear the stalking will never stop.
- One in eight employed stalking victims lose time from work as a result of their victimization and more than half lose five days of work or more.
- One in seven stalking victims move as a result of their victimization.
- The prevalence of anxiety, insomnia, social dysfunction, and severe depression is much higher among stalking victims than the general population, especially if the stalking involves being followed or having one's property destroyed

Stalking Laws

Stalking is a crime under the laws of fifty states, the District of Columbia, the U.S. Territories, and the federal government.

- Less than one-third of states classify stalking as a felony upon first offense.
- More than one-half of states classify stalking as a felony upon second or subsequent offense or when the crime involves aggravating factors.
- Aggravating factors may include: possession of a deadly weapon, violation of a court order or condition of probation/parole, victim under sixteen years, or same victim as prior occasions.

DISCUSSION QUESTIONS

1. What is stalking?

2. What are some common ways a stalker can use a phone to follow a person?

3. How can email be used to stalk someone?

Name: _____   Date _____

You must use this form and turn in the original to the instructor. No other form will be accepted.

CHAPTER ASSIGNMENT

The text defines stalking behavior, how to identify an abusive relationship, and how to end the likelihood for stalking to continue. List several ways how to stop stalking behavior, including phone and computer use. Why are these areas so important to include?

_____
_____
_____
_____
_____
_____
_____
_____
_____
_____
_____
_____
_____
_____
_____
_____
_____
_____

Chapter Thirteen

ELDER VICTIMS OF CRIME

LEARNING OBJECTIVES

After exploring Chapter Thirteen (13), the student will be able to:

1. Explain why the elderly population are vulnerable to victimization.
2. Identify crimes committed against the elderly.
3. Understand the different forms of elder abuse that exist in society.
4. Recognize the types of fraud committed against the elderly.

KEY TERMS

Elder abuse, Denial, Isolation, Telemarketing fraud, Identity theft, Fake check and Wire transactions, Fake charitable solicitation

INTRODUCTION

Who are the elderly? Rather than lumping everybody into a certain single age category, there are numerous groupings that have been presented. An examination of the crime statistics reveals that the elderly have the lowest odds of becoming crime victims. The average life expectancy has risen considerably which translates into older persons comprising a sizable segment of the population.

However, the entire population is becoming "grayer." The population data is showing that the baby boomers are now moving into their midlife. The elderly constitute a substantial amount of the very active political constituency. Moreover, they vote, lobby, and they participate in the legislative process. Despite greatly reduced chances of victimization, the elderly are extremely fearful of falling prey to criminals.

A growing social problem that has gained recognition in recent years is elder abuse and neglect. Caretakers maltreat the elderly. Economic pressure, role reversals, and other tensions sometimes make it difficult to provide appropriate extended care.

In addition to being subjected to neglect, the senior population is vulnerable to certain "scams" perpetuated by a criminal element through phone conversations and e-mail. There are various frauds and thefts designed to target the elderly. We will discuss these also in this chapter.

DEFINITION OF CONCEPTS

1. Elder Abuse: It's the mistreatment or neglect of an older person, usually by a relative or other caregiver.
2. Physical Abuse: Victims are kicked, punched, beaten, and even raped. Pain, injury, or death may result.
3. Neglect: Failure to provide medicine, food, or personal care.
4. Financial Exploitation: Abusers may steal or mismanage money, property, savings, or credit cards.
5. Psychological Abuse: Older people may be intentionally isolated or deprived companionship.
6. Other Abuse:
    a. Older people may be forced to live in unsanitary conditions, or in poorly heated or cooled rooms.
    b. Over/under medicating or withholding aids, eyeglasses, and dentures.

WHO ARE THE VICTIMS OF ELDER ABUSE?

The victims often live with family members and depend on them for daily care. The victims are more likely to be:

1. Age seventy-five or over
2. Women
3. Dependent on the abuser for basic needs
4. Suffering from a mental or physical illness

WHO ARE THE ABUSERS?

Many times they are family members who are acting as caregivers. Abusers often suffer from:

1. Stress.
2. Alcohol and other drug problems.
3. Dependency: The abuser may depend on the older person for basic needs or housing and money.

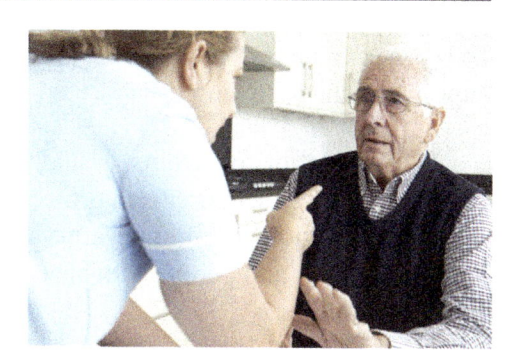

WHY DOES ELDER ABUSE HAPPEN?

© SpeedKingz/Shutterstock.com

The experts believe many factors may be involved:

1. Resentment: Caring for an elderly parent can be exhausting and resentment can build, which may lead to abuse.
2. Life crises: Living with the elderly parent can cause severe stress, especially of family members who are struggling with personal problems.
3. Lack of love and friendship: Often, a dependent parent returns to his or her family after being away for many years.
4. Attitudes towards violence: Violence is seen as an acceptable way to solve problems.
5. Retaliation: Some abusers may try to get back at their parents for post-mistreatment.
6. Lack of services: Without needed health and social services in the community, caregivers may be unable to handle the responsibility of caring for an elderly parent.
7. Money problems: Many families are on limited or fixed incomes. The relative or caregiver may be dependent on the older person for money.
8. Social problems: Unemployment, poor or crowded housing, or other living conditions may contribute to elder abuse.

WHY DOES THE PROBLEM CONTINUE?

The following represent the possible reasons:

1. Denial: Some older people simply refuse to accept the fact that they are being abused by their loved ones.
2. Physical/Mental illness: Older people must overcome the obstacles.
3. Lack of services: Temporary shelters and facilities are lacking for older persons.
4. Fear and shame: Older people are afraid of retaliation or too ashamed to take action.
5. Lack of involvement: Friends, relatives, or neighbors may tolerate abuse because they believe families should handle their own problems.
6. Dependence: Many feel that they have no one to turn to for help.
7. Lack of awareness: They may not be aware of the professional agencies available to help them.
8. Isolation: No contact with others outside the home.

PREVENTION

Everyone can help stop elder abuse. The society can help by supporting the following:

1. Prevention programs: Usually state agencies have elderly or senior citizen protective service programs.
2. Education: To fight negative attitudes toward older persons and people who have disabilities.
3. Resources:
   a. Home Health Aids
   b. Meal Delivery
   c. Day Care
   d. Transportation
   e. Counseling
   f. Assisted Living

© dizain/Shutterstock.com

The elder abuse poses a relatively new problem for the criminal justice system. While abuse may not be a new problem occurrence, it is a phenomenon that is just now gaining attention.

Victimologists are beginning to identify the intricacies of the problem, probe its causes, and offer some solutions. However, a great deal of additional work remains to be done at both the theoretical and practical levels.

As time marches on, we must develop more ways to detect and prevent the new symptoms and signs of the elder abuse.

Defrauding the Elderly

Some of senior population is vulnerable to certain types of crime (Dwan, 2004). Participants in the criminal element seek to exploit weaknesses for some type of gain. Frequently, the profit is financial (Carlson, 2006). These crimes against the elderly are born in deception, attacking people who are susceptible to various types of fraud (Slosarik, 2002). This could be due to the victim being of good nature and naïve; or it is attributed to certain mental deficiencies from general erosion of health due to age. In both circumstances, the perpetrator preys upon a perceived weakness to exploit the elderly for personal gain. There are several types of crimes devoted to manipulating the elderly. This section explores some of the common schemes used by criminals to steal from the elder population. Criminals tend to assertively seek out this population to commit their crimes. Telemarking fraud, identity theft, induced fake transactions (check and wire), and spurious charitable solicitations are just a select few of the strategies to pilfer funds from susceptible victims, commonly the elderly (Retrieved from **https://www.consumer.ftc.gov/**).

© SpeedKingz/Shutterstock.com

Telemarketing Fraud

Deceitful telemarketing scams have long been recognized. In addition, the elderly are documented has targets for this type of fraud (Lee & Geitsfeld, 1999). Telemarketing fraud is uncomplicated. First, the offender makes a phone call to the victim. This can be to an elder victim or not, but it is typically during daytime hours. The caller creates a deceitful scenario or promises something fictitious. Fundamentally, they lie. The caller distorts their message and presents a situation making the victim to turnover something of financial gain. Telemarking scams can encompass a range of set-ups of diverse details, left only to the creativity of the offender. For example, victims are advised they succeeded in winning a lottery in a foreign land, or are the recipient of a large endowment, however they must wire the cost of the taxes, fees, or shipping to a specific overseas address to be wired their money. This also can be achieved in conjunction with stealing bank account and identity information if the caller is skilled enough to swindle the victim, creating an avenue for the criminal to engage in a second criminal act, identity theft.

Unfortunately, there are numerous ploys used by con artists, more than can be detailed here. However, the scope extends from people claiming to be Internal Revenue Service (IRS) agents notifying the victim they are in arrears with their taxes and must send money to a certain location or risk being arrested. Another common ploy is the perpetrator claims to be a representative of a service provider (cable, gas, or electric company) advising the victim they are late on past bills threatening to discontinue service if money is not wired to a certain place. The plots are endless and people who are vulnerable tend to be the most inclined to become ensnared in the scheme.

Identity Theft

Identity theft stretches across all demographics, however the elderly are a particular mark due to several, general characteristics of seniors. The features of the elderly population, which enticing to the scammer, is the idea that the elder population is in financial stability (pension, savings, etc.) and funds are readily available (Mouallem, 2002). This is not always the case, but the thief is calculating the odds and betting the elderly is a viable target for the purposes of their scam.

Identity theft and other methods of fraud aimed towards the elderly are often compounded because it can be largely underreported. Often, when the elderly recognize they have been swindled out of funds or unintentionally provided personal identifying information to a criminal, they delay in reporting. Sometimes this may be from the general embarrassment of being tricked, or it can be that the victim doesn't have friends and family to know they are not as mentally aware as they once had been (Newman & McNally, 2005).

© frank_peters/Shutterstock.com

The elderly are considered prime targets due to them having some type of revenue stream (pensions, savings, government assistance, etc.) that can be easily diverted if the criminal has personal identifiers (name, date of birth, social security number, address, etc.) of the victim. In addition to the revenue stream, the elderly generally have good credit and will qualify for several types of loans or credit cards. Studies have been generated to understand the scope of identity theft and its effects on the elderly population (Allison, Schuck, & Lersch, 2005). This type of crime, regrettably, falls into similar categories of elder abuse by caregivers because invariably the criminal is a family member or caregiver. This is the case because these people have easy access to this information and also have the ability to hide the crime from the victim for limitless amounts of time, especially if they are the primary caregivers. This can occur in the private homes of the victim, and also in professional nursing homes, where a various amount of staff have access to the victims and their personal information.

Induced Fake Check and Wire Transactions

The elderly are typically targets of induced fake check and wire transactions (Mouallem, 2002). A common ploy for the criminal is to tell the senior that a family member (child, grandchild, bother, sister, etc.) is in trouble and money needs to be wired to help them. The skilled scammer has the name and some basic information of the person reported to be in "trouble." Using money orders or electronic cash transfers is an expedient method to wire someone money. Criminals prefer wire transfers because the funds are delivered quickly and the money will be gone in a short period of time, as the criminal will be, before the scam is detected. In addition to the speed of the transaction, criminals are aware that the transfer is very difficult to reverse, even if caught early in the process.

Criminals attempt to gain the assurance of their victims and commonly use what is termed "bait." While shading their own identities, the scammer will offer great deals on products or also use the lottery/prize scenario as discussed before in the telemarketing schemes. While over the phone or on-line, con artists can operate in anonymity and attempt with several different ruses to extract funds from the victim via wire transfer of checks (Retrieved from **https://www.fdic.gov/consumers/consumer/news/cnsum13/wire-transfer-scams.html**.)

© Waxen/Shutterstock.com

The fake check scam operates differently than the wire transfer fraud. Typically, a victim will be sent a check for a certain amount of money, let's say $50,000. The check looks credible and the victim believes they won a prize. The victim is instructed to deposit the $50,000 check in their bank account and send $2,000 to a location or wire transfer to cover taxes and fees. The victim completes the second transaction sending the $2,000 to the criminal. Meanwhile, the $50,000 check is waiting to clear. However, it never will because it is fake. The victim will have already sent $2,000 of his or her own "real" money to the scam artist, and is never going to receive their $50,000 prize. This is a common technique used by criminals to cipher money from unknowing victims, who often are the elderly.

Spurious Charitable Solicitation

Scammers go to many lengths to reach their desired goal: stealing the victim's money. Spurious charitable solicitations are callers attempting to pull at the heartstrings of the victim by trying to get them to donate money to a worthy cause (cancer research, bulletproof vests, homelessness, etc.) or for some type of disaster relief. Of course, in these scenarios the money is diverted to personal funds rather than getting directed to the legitimate source. The problem lies with the fact that after the money is "donated" is very difficult for the victim to know if the money went to its intended recipients. Essentially, the caller can misrepresent where the funds will actually be used (Mouallem, 2002).

In these scenarios, the caller will typically be vague about the organization, failing to give complete information about how and where the money will be specifically used. In addition, the organization will have a similar name to a reliable charity. Often, the caller is pushy and uses methods designed for an immediate donation (not taking no for an answer). The donation will typically be in the form of the electronic wire transfer as discussed previously in this chapter.

Additionally, the caller sometimes will guarantee a prize for donating, which it not legal. This method can also multiply the fraud by moving into the check fraud scenario or another duplicitous wire transfer.

CONCLUSION

Elder abuse is a serious issue. Protecting segments of the population who are the most vulnerable is critical for policy makers to understand. Additionally, as you can see, there are an assortment of means to defraud someone and the elderly are a clear target. Telemarketing fraud, identity theft, induced fake check and wire transactions, and spurious charitable donations are just some of the tactics used to steal from the elderly population. It is important to educate seniors, their caregivers, and the general population of the warning signs and tactics used by these criminals. Through this education, the community together can mitigate the effects and damage caused by these crimes against a vulnerable population.

REFERENCES

Allison, S. F., Schuck, A. M., & Lersch, K. M. (2005). Exploring the crime of identity theft: Prevalence, clearance rates, and victim/offender characteristics. *Journal of Criminal Justice, 33*(1), 19–29.

Carlson, E. L. (2006). Phishing for elderly victims: as the elderly migrate to the Internet fraudulent schemes targeting them follow. *Elder LJ, 14*, 423.

Dwan, B. (2004). Identity theft. *Computer Fraud & Security, 2004*(4), 14–17. Federal Trade Commission. Retrieved from https://www.consumer.ftc.gov/.

Federal Deposit Insurance Incorporation. Retrieved from https://www.fdic.gov/consumers/consumer/news/cnsum13/wire-transfer-scams.html.

Lee, J., & Geistfeld, L. V. (1999). Elderly consumers' receptiveness to telemarketing fraud. Journal of Public Policy & Marketing, 208–217.

Mouallem, L. (2001). Oh no, grandma has a computer: How Internet fraud will take the place of telemarketing fraud targeting the elderly. *Santa Clara L. Rev., 42*, 659.

Newman, G., & McNally, M. M. (2005). Identity theft literature review.

Slosarik, K. (2002). Identity theft: An overview of the problem. *The Justice Professional, 15*(4), 329–343.

DISCUSSION QUESTIONS

1. What are some precautions the elderly population can use to minimize their risks of becoming a victim of a crime?

2. Why are the elderly targets for particular financial crimes?

3. What are some of the reasons for elder abuse and why does the problem continue?

Name: Date

You must use this form and turn in the original to the instructor. No other form will be accepted.

CHAPTER ASSIGNMENT

Identity theft is a crime, permeating all age groups. What are some of the main reasons the elderly can fall to victimization by these crimes? Explain or devise a method for seniors to reduce their probability of becoming a target.

_____

_____

_____

_____

_____

_____

_____

_____

_____

_____

_____

_____

_____

_____

_____

_____

_____

_____

Chapter Fourteen

VICTIMS OF HUMAN TRAFFICKING

LEARNING OBJECTIVES

After exploring Chapter Fourteen (14), the student will be able to:

1. Define human trafficking.
2. Discuss the global impact of trafficking in persons.
3. Identify some of the resources available to persons in the United States who are victims of human trafficking.
4. Provide examples of legislation against human trafficking.
5. Explain some efforts to combat human trafficking.

KEY TERMS

Slavery, Human trafficking, Administration for Children and Families, Family and Youth Services Bureau, Polaris BeFree, Anti-Trafficking in Persons, Health and Human Services

INTRODUCTION

In January 2013, President Obama issued a Presidential Proclamation that declared January National Slavery and Human Trafficking Prevention Month to shed light on the exploitation of nearly 27 million women, men, and children worldwide;[1] these victims are often overlooked, and those who routinely interact with victims and survivors may lack awareness or tools to properly identify and assist them. Therefore, many victims go without help. The Federal Strategic Action Plan on Services for Victims of Human Trafficking in the United States (SAP) was developed in 2013 to support the ongoing battle against modern-day slavery to ensure that all victims of human trafficking in the United States have access to the tools and services they need to escape exploitation and rebuild their lives. The Family and Youth Services Bureau (FYSB) and all of its grantee partners are crucial to that effort.

STRATEGIC ACTION PLAN OBJECTIVES

In commemoration of the 150th anniversary of the Emancipation Proclamation, the Obama Administration asked federal agencies to develop a plan to strengthen services for victims of human trafficking. The SAP is a part of ongoing federal efforts to combat human trafficking at home and abroad. The plan strengthens collaboration across the federal government, increases coordination with other stakeholder partners, and builds capacity to empower survivors. The vision of the SAP is to produce coordinated efforts to ensure that every victim of human trafficking receives access to the services they need to recover and rebuild their lives through the creation of a responsive, sustainable, comprehensive, and trauma-informed victim services network that leverages public and private partners and resources effectively. The plan lays out four goals, each associated with action items for victim service improvements to achieve over the next five years. The four goals include: 1. Increase coordination and collaboration at the federal, regional, state, tribal and local levels; 2. Increase awareness of human trafficking among government and community leaders and the general public; 3. Expand access to services for victims of human trafficking; and 4. Improve outcomes related to health, safety, and well-being. FYSB grantees providing services to runaway and homeless youth and survivors of domestic violence and plays an important role in developing a coordinated, comprehensive victim services network for trafficking survivors.

Intersections with Runaway and Homeless Youth and Domestic Violence

Though trafficking can and does affect individuals from all walks of life—regardless of race, ethnicity, gender, sexual orientation, socioeconomic status, or citizenship status—traffickers frequently prey on individuals who are poor, lack stable social or familial support, or are in search of a better life[2]. The populations that FYSB serves are particularly at risk to exploitation by traffickers, who take advantage of these vulnerabilities.

It is not uncommon for a young person to be lured into trafficking by an older individual who builds their trust in the context of an intimate partner relationship. Individuals at risk for abuse and neglect, such as runaway and homeless youth, foster youth, LGBT youth, and Native American youth, are also at high risk of being trafficked. Like domestic violence, the trafficking of youth is an abuse of power; though victims come from a variety of backgrounds and circumstances, communities with lesser access to resources are the most vulnerable. Human trafficking intersects with domestic violence. It is not uncommon for victims of trafficking to be coerced into sex or labor by intimate partners who use threats of violence or intimidation. 1. 2012 Department of State Trafficking in Persons Report. 2. Risk Factors for and Consequences of Commercial Sexual Exploitation and Sex Trafficking of Minors in the United States.[3] Report by the Institute of Medicine and National Research Council.

Advocates across the fields of domestic violence, runaway and homeless youth, and human trafficking observe that survivors have endured multiple dimensions of abuse through emotional, verbal, physical and sexual violence, and economic exploitation. The partnerships strengthened by the Federal Strategic Action Plan enable advocates from each of these fields to leverage their collective expertise and resources to assist the millions of women, men, and children who are victims.

FYSB Resources

In addition to supporting the goals of the SAP, FYSB continued to support the work of grantees of the Family Violence Prevention and Services Program (FVPSA) and the Runaway and Homeless Youth Program (RHY). FVPSA supports training, services, and advocacy for both domestic and foreign victims of trafficking who come in contact with domestic violence programs through 1,600 shelters, 1,100 non-residential service sites, fifty-six state and territorial coalitions, and the National Domestic Violence Hotline. The RHY Program supports the work of more than 700 projects across the country that come into contact with trafficking victims almost every day. Listed below is a selection of resources for grantees:

- Trafficking: Considerations and Recommendations for Battered Women's Advocates and Health Issues Affecting Trafficked Individuals, published by the Asian Pacific Islander Institute on Domestic Violence, a FYSB grantee.
- Resources on Human Trafficking and Commercial Sexual Exploitation for Family and Youth Workers, published by the National Clearinghouse on Families & Youth.
- Special Collection on Human Trafficking on VAWnet.org, published by the National Resource Center on Domestic Violence, a FYSB grantee.

National Crisis Lines

- **FYSB** and the **Administration for Children and Families (ACF)** support several national crisis lines, serving victims twenty-four hours a day, seven days a week. Advocates answer the calls of thousands of individuals seeking support and safety each year, and are equipped to refer callers to local and national resources.
  1-888-373-7888
  Or text BeFree (233733)

- **National Domestic Violence Hotline**
  1-800-799-SAFE
  Or live chat online at: http://www.thehotline.org/what-is-live-chat/

- **National Runaway Safeline**
  1-800-RUNAWAY

- **The Federal Strategic Action Plant:**
  http://www.ovc.gov/pubs/FederalHumanTraffickingStrategicPlan.pdf

- For additional information on the **Federal Strategic Action Plan**, visit:
  http://www.acf.hhs.gov/programs/endtrafficking

- For additional information on the anti-trafficking resources in the Family and Youth Services Bureau:
  http://www.acf.hhs.gov/acf-response-to-human-trafficking

As public and government understanding of human trafficking has developed over the years, ACF helps ensure that victims of all forms of human trafficking—adults and children; foreign national, citizens, and legal residents; survivors of labor and commercial sexual exploitation—have access to the support they need to foster health and well-being.

The ACF-wide Anti-Human Trafficking Initiative is a step towards implementing the federal government's commitment to protecting victims by strengthening coordination across programs and federal departments.

The **Anti-Trafficking in Persons (ATIP) program** at ORR identifies and serves victims of human trafficking in the United States to become eligible for public benefits and services to the same extent as refugees. The program has initiated the Rescue & Restore Victims of Human Trafficking campaign to educate health care providers, social service organizations, and the law enforcement community about the issue of human trafficking. The purpose of the campaign is to encourage those individuals who are most likely to encounter victims on a daily basis to look beneath the surface, recognize clues, and ask the right questions to help victims.

© suns design/Shutterstock.com

The Philadelphia Region 3 office manages more than $4 billion in grant programs covering its five-state area of Delaware, Maryland, Pennsylvania, Virginia and West Virginia, and the District of Columbia.

ACF REGIONAL PROGRAMS

Grants Management Regional Unit

The Grants Management Regional Unit is headed by the regional grants management officer and supports the Chief Grants Officer/Deputy Assistant Secretary for Administration.

The unit's responsibilities include:

- Ensuring that business and financial responsibilities of grants administration are carried out.
- Managing ACF's discretionary, formula, entitlement and block grants in the region.
- Directing all grants and cooperative agreements.

- Ensuring compliance with applicable statutes, regulations, and policies.
- Performing audit resolutions.
- Providing leadership and technical guidance to ACF programs on grant operations and grants management issues.

Contact: Regional Grants Management Officer: Patty Fisher (215) 861-4004, e-mail: patricia.fisher@acf.hhs.gov

Children's Bureau Regional Program Unit

The Children's Bureau (CB) Regional Program Unit is headed by the regional program manager who reports to the associate commissioner of the Children's Bureau.

The unit is responsible for providing program and technical administration of CB formula, entitlement, block, and discretionary programs. These programs include:

- Child welfare, including child abuse and neglect
- Child protective services
- Family preservation and support
- Adoption
- Foster care
- Independent living

Contact: Regional Program Manager, Lisa Pearson (215) 861-4030, e-mail: lisa.pearson@acf.hhs.gov

OCSE Regional Program Unit

The Office of Child Support Enforcement (OCSE) Regional Program Unit is headed by the Regional Program Manager who reports to the Deputy Director/Commissioner, OCSE.

The unit is responsible for providing program and technical administration of OCSE entitlement and discretionary programs and for collaborating with ACF Central Office, states, tribes, and other grantees on all significant program and policy matters.

Contact: Regional Program Manager, Juanita DeVine (215) 861-4054, e-mail: juanita.devine@acf.hhs.gov

TANF Bureau Regional Program Unit

The Temporary Assistance for Needy Families (TANF) Regional Program Unit is headed by the Regional Program Manager who reports to the Associate Director, TANF, within the Office of Family Assistance.

The unit is responsible for providing centralized program and technical administration of the TANF block grant and for collaborating with ACF Central Office, states, and other grantees on all significant policy matters.

Contact: Regional Program Manager, Eileen Friedman (215) 861-4000, e-mail: eileen.friedman@acf.hhs.gov

Child Care Bureau Regional Program Unit

The Office of Child Care (OCC) Regional Program Unit is headed by a regional program manager who reports to the director of the Office of Child Care.

The unit is responsible for providing centralized program and technical administration of Child Care Development (CCDF) block grant and discretionary programs and for collaborating with ACF Central Office, states, and other grantees on all significant policy matters.

Contact: Regional Program Manager, Beverly Wellons (215) 861-4020, e-mail: beverly.wellons@acf.hhs.gov

Head Start Regional Program Unit

The Head Start Regional Program Unit is headed by the regional program manager who reports to the Program Operations Division in the Office of Head Start (OHS).

The unit is responsible for providing centralized program and technical administration of OHS discretionary programs and for collaborating with OHS State Collaboration Projects on all significant policy matters. The Regional Program Unit oversees the day-to-day management of Head Start grantees and the provision of technical assistance.

Contact: Regional Program Manager: Linda Savage (215) 861-4005, e-mail: linda.savage@acf.hhs.gov

States: Pennsylvania and West Virginia, Delaware, Maryland, Virginia, and the District of Columbia

Pennsylvania

Pennsylvania Child Care

Supports low-income working families through child care financial assistance and promotes children's learning by improving the quality of early care.

Pennsylvania Child Support

Assures that assistance in obtaining support (financial and medical) is available to children through locating parents and establishing paternity.

Pennsylvania Child Welfare

Provides for the safety, permanency, and well-being of children.

Pennsylvania Head Start and Early Head Start

Head Start programs promote school readiness by enhancing the social and cognitive development of children through the provision of educational, health, nutritional, social, and other services.

Pennsylvania Runaway and Homeless Youth

Family and Youth Services Bureau - Runaway and Homeless Youth

Assists youth who have run away from home or have become homeless for other reasons.

Pennsylvania Temporary Assistance for Needy Families (TANF)

Provides assistance and work opportunities to needy families. The assistance is time-limited and promotes work, responsibility, and self-sufficiency.

The Framework

The **Youth Framework** focuses on four **core outcomes** for youth:

- Housing stability
- Permanent connections
- Education and employment
- Well-being

The **Family Connection Framework** envisions that every family will have access to shelter when needed, the experience of homelessness is rare and brief, and families are connected to services that address their needs and support long-term stability.

Federal Partnerships

ACF works closely with:

- U.S. Interagency Council on Homelessness (USICH)
- Department of Health and Human Services (HHS)
- Department of Housing and Urban Development (HUD)
- Other federal agencies

Resources

- ACF Programs and Services for Homelessness
- U.S. Interagency Council on Homelessness

HUMAN TRAFFICKING

ACF Programs and Services for Human Trafficking

Office on Trafficking in Persons

ACF is committed to ensuring that victims of all forms for human trafficking—adults and children; foreign national, citizens, and legal residents; survivors of labor and sexual exploitation—have access to the support they need.

Look Beneath the Surface

Through the *Look Beneath the Surface* campaign, ACF works with grantees and stakeholders to raise awareness of human trafficking and the factors that make certain populations more at risk. You can download or order materials to spread the word and forge pathways to freedom for survivors and those at risk of human trafficking.

© Maria Maarbes/Shutterstock.com

National Human Trafficking Hotline: 1-888-373-7888

The National Human Trafficking Hotline is a national, toll-free hotline, available to answer calls and texts from anywhere in the country, twenty-four hours a day, seven days a week, every day of the year.

Call 1-888-373-7888 or Text HELP or INFO to BeFree (233733). Federal Services are Available for Survivors of Human Trafficking

Available services vary depending on many factors—age, status, income, residence, and others. Contact the local benefit-issuing agency directly to see if your client may receive services. You can also contact the National Human Trafficking Hotline for more information.

The National Human Trafficking Hotline is a 24/7, confidential, multilingual hotline for victims, survivors, and witnesses of human trafficking.

The hotline can be reached:

- By phone: 1-888-373-7888
- By email: help@humantraffickinghotline.org
- By text: Polaris's BeFree Textline: Text HELP to 233733 (BEFREE)
- Online: **www.humantraffickinghotline.org**

Hotline staff are trained to:

- Listen to survivors of all forms of human trafficking
- Provide immediate safety planning for people in crisis
- Field tips of suspected trafficking
- Help survivors understand their options for support without judgment

DOMESTIC VICTIMS

The Domestic Victims of Human Trafficking Program (DVHT) forges pathways to freedom by providing domestic survivors of human trafficking with comprehensive case management, direct services, and referrals to services, including:

- Short, and long-term housing options
- Substance abuse treatment
- Mental health counseling
- Educational opportunities
- Job training and skills development
- Legal advocacy
- Financial advocacy and counseling

The DVHT program empowers organizations and communities to deliver trauma-informed, strength-based, and victim-centered services for domestic survivors of trafficking. In addition, the program encourages innovative collaboration within communities to ensure long-term outcomes for domestic survivors of trafficking.

© life_in_a_pixel/Shutterstock.com

FOREIGN NATIONALS

The Trafficking Victim Assistance Program (TVAP) funds case management services for foreign national survivors and potential victims of trafficking that are pursuing HHS certification. The grantees assist survivors through a network of providers throughout the country.

Grantees can help with case management, referrals, and emergency assistance to survivors of human trafficking and assist certified survivors and certain family members with federal and state benefits and services. They also help them gain access to:

- Housing
- Employability services
- Mental health screening and therapy
- Medical care
- Legal services

FEDERAL ASSISTANCE

Contact the following federal resources for information about obtaining services for pre-certified victims of human trafficking.

HHS Services Grants

HHS Services Grants provide comprehensive case management services to foreign victims and potential victims of trafficking seeking HHS certification in any location in the United States. The grantees provide case management to assist a victim of trafficking to become certified, and other necessary services after certification, through a network of nongovernmental service organization sub-awardees in locations throughout the country.

These grants ensure the provision of efficient, high-quality services to victims of human trafficking. They also streamline support to help victims of human trafficking gain timely access to shelter, legal assistance, job training, and health care, enabling them to live free of violence and exploitation.

Please contact the grantees regarding services for a client or to obtain information on how to become a sub-awardee. Below is a list of the HHS Service Grantees, contact information, and the states for which it or its partners provide services:

- U.S. Committee for Refugees and Immigrants (USCRI)
  - Contact information: 1-800-307-4712 or traffickingvictims@uscridc.org. States: AK, AR, AZ, CA, CO, DC, DE, HI, IA, ID, KS, LA, MD, MO, MT, and the following territories: American Samoa, Commonwealth of Northern Mariana Islands, Federated States of Micronesia, Guam, Marshall Islands, and the Republic of Palau.

- Heartland Human Care Services Contact information: 1-800-837-5345
  - States: CT, IL, IN, MA, ME, MI, MN, NH, NJ, NY, OH, RI, VT, WI

- Tapestri, Inc.
  - Contact information: 404-299-2185. States: AL, FL, GA, KY, MS, NC, SC, TN

The National Human Trafficking Resource Center (NHTRC) is a national, toll-free hotline for the human trafficking field in the United States and is reached by calling 1-888-373-7888 or e-mailing NHTRC@PolarisProject.org. The NHTRC operates twenty-four hours a day, seven days a week, every day of the year. The NHTRC works to improve the national response to protect victims of human trafficking in the United States by providing callers with a range of comprehensive services, including crisis intervention, urgent and non-urgent referrals, tip reporting, and comprehensive anti-trafficking resources and technical assistance for the anti-trafficking field and those who wish to get involved.

The NHTRC is able to connect community members with additional tools to raise awareness and combat human trafficking in their local areas, as well as guide service providers and law enforcement personnel in their work with potential trafficking victims. To perform these functions, the NHTRC maintains a national database of organizations and individuals working in the anti-trafficking field, as well as a library of available anti-trafficking resources and materials. To view these materials, access online trainings or report tips online, go to the NHTRC website: **http://www.traffickingresourcecenter.org**.

Office for Victims of Crime

The U.S. Department of Justice's (USDOJ) Office of Victims of Crime (OVC) provides services for pre-certified trafficking victims (see USDOJ charts for more information). Services include housing or shelter; food; medical, mental health, and dental services; interpreter/translator services; criminal justice victim advocacy; legal services; social services advocacy; literacy education; and/or employment assistance.

See http://www.ojp.usdoj.gov/ovc/grants/traffickingmatrix.html for more information about these services. In addition, OVC's Online Directory of Crime Victim Services identifies local organizations providing services for crime victims: http://ovc.ncjrs.gov/findvictimservices/.

- Through TANF, States may only provide assistance to a financially needy family that consists of, at a minimum, a child living with his/her parent or other caretaker relative, or consists of a pregnant woman. Therefore, the adult individual must be the parent or other caretaker relative of a minor child or a pregnant woman. Conversely, the minor child must be living with his/her parent or other caretaker relative.
- All decisions regarding eligibility for these services and types of treatment are made at the local and state levels or by the benefit-granting agency.
- Includes persons who entered the United States without inspection or who overstayed their visas, and persons not in compliance with the terms of their visas or orders of the Immigration Court.
- Includes persons paroled for at least one year, persons whom the government has agreed not to remove from the United States for a temporary period, and some other categories. Also includes nonimmigrants who are persons admitted to the United States on a temporary basis, such as a person on a student visa, exchange visitor visa, or temporary worker visa.

Temporary Assistance for Needy Families (TANF), Office of Family Assistance (OFA), Administration for Children and Families (ACF), HHS: TANF funds state programs that provide assistance for families with children when the parents or other caretaker relatives are unable to provide for the family's basic needs. Each state and territory decides both the benefits it will provide and the eligibility criteria for receiving financial assistance payments or other types of TANF benefits and services. In order to be eligible for TANF, the client must be a member of an eligible family that also meets other TANF programmatic eligibility requirements, such as income, resources, and residency. If a certified adult victim (or eligible minor) is not eligible for TANF, he or she may be eligible for ORR Refugee Cash Assistance (RCA), as long as the victim meets RCA program eligibility requirements (see the following section on ORR benefits and services). Check with your local TANF office to obtain information on eligibility for TANF assistance or other TANF benefits and services. http://www.acf.hhs.gov/programs/ofa/

Medicaid, Centers for Medicare & Medicaid Services (CMS), HHS: Medicaid provides health coverage for low-income pregnant women, children, parents, adults, and those with disabilities who may have no insurance or inadequate medical insurance. Although the federal government establishes general guidelines for the program, each state establishes Medicaid program requirements. The local Medicaid office evaluates a certified adult victim for eligibility for Medicaid. If the Medicaid office determines the person is not eligible for Medicaid, then the victim may be eligible for ORR Refugee Medical Assistance (RMA), as long as the victim meets RMA program eligibility requirements. For specific information about enrollment in Medicaid, eligibility, coverage, and services for your state, please contact your local Medicaid office: http://www.govbenefits.gov/benefits/benefit-details/606. For additional information on Medicaid, go to: https://www.cms.hhs.gov/home/medicaid.asp.

Children's Health Insurance Program (CHIP), CMS, HHS: CHIP provides health coverage for children who do not qualify for Medicaid, yet do not have private insurance. Children who do not currently have health insurance may be eligible, even if parents are working. This insurance pays for doctor visits, prescription medicines, hospitalizations, and other services. The federal government and individual states jointly finance CHIP, and each state administers CHIP. Within broad Federal guidelines, each State determines the design of its program, eligibility groups, benefit packages, payment levels for coverage, and administrative and operating procedures. States have different eligibility rules, but in most states, uninsured children eighteen years old and younger, whose families earn up to $34,100 a year (for a family of four) are eligible. **https://www.cms.gov/home/chip.asp; www.insurekidsnow.gov, 1-877-KIDS-NOW**

Health Resources and Services Administration (HRSA), HHS: HRSA offers health care and support to uninsured, underserved, and special needs populations. HRSA issues grants to federally funded health centers that are available to anyone regardless of their ability to pay. The health centers charge patients using a sliding fee scale, based on their income. Health centers provide well-care checkups, treatment for sick patients, complete care for pregnant patients, immunizations and checkups for children, dental care, prescription drugs, as well as mental health and substance abuse care. Health centers are located in most cities and many rural areas. To find a health center, go to: **http://findahealthcenter.hrsa.gov/Search_HCC.aspx; http://www.hrsa.gov/index.html; 1-888-ASK-HRSA**

Medical Screenings, Office of Refugee Resettlement (ORR), Administration for Children and Families (ACF), HHS: Preventive health medical screenings and assessments are available to certified trafficked persons and eligible minors for early diagnosis and treatment of illnesses that are contagious or are barriers to self-sufficiency. This usually includes screening for tuberculosis (TB), parasites, and hepatitis B, as well as school vaccinations. Screenings are not available in every location. To arrange for a referral for a medical screening, contact your State Refugee Coordinator or Refugee Health Coordinator via the following website: **http://www.acf.hhs.gov/programs/orr/partners/state_partners.htm.**

Unaccompanied Refugee Minors Program (URM), ORR, ACF, HHS: ORR's URM program can provide care to an unaccompanied child victim of trafficking who has received an Eligibility Letter and met established criteria for reclassification or designation as an unaccompanied refugee minor. The URM program provides specialized, culturally appropriate foster care or other licensed care settings according to children's individual needs. Legal responsibility is established, under state law, to ensure that there is a legal authority to act in place of the child's unavailable parent(s). Unaccompanied child trafficking victims receive the full range of assistance, care, and services that are available to other foster children in the state. Depending on their individual needs, children are placed in foster homes, group care, independent living, or residential treatment settings. Services include: indirect financial support for housing, food, clothing, and medical care; intensive case management; family reunification; independent living skills training; educational supports; English-language training; career/college counseling; mental health services; assistance adjusting immigration status; cultural activities; recreational opportunities; support for social integration; and retention of ethnic and religious heritage. To access the URM program for a child victim of trafficking who has received an Eligibility Letter, contact the ORR Child Protection Specialist at 202-205-4582. For more information on ORR's URM program, visit the following website: **http://www.acf.hhs.gov/programs/orr/programs/unaccompanied_refugee_minors.htm.**

Services for Survivors of Torture Program, ORR, ACF, HHS: ORR's Services for Survivors of Torture provides rehabilitative services, including treatment for the psychological and physical effects of torture; social and legal services; and research and training for health care providers outside of treatment centers or programs. Individuals eligible for services are those who suffered torture in foreign countries and are now present in the United States regardless of their immigration status. Individuals who have suffered torture only as a result of trafficking experiences in the United States do not meet the eligibility standard for this program. http://www.acf.hhs.gov/programs/orr/programs/services_survivors_torture.htm

Child Nutrition Programs, Food and Nutrition Service, USDA: Child Nutrition programs offer nutritious meals and snacks for low-income children in schools, child care institutions, and after-school care programs. http://www.fns.usda.gov/cnd/

Supplemental Nutrition Assistance Program (formerly called the Food Stamp Program), Food and Nutrition Service, USDA: SNAP provides nutrition assistance to low-income individuals and families so they can buy the food needed for good health. Benefits are provided on an electronic card that is used like an ATM card at participating grocery stores. To apply for benefits, or for information about the SNAP, contact your local SNAP office at http://www.fns.usda.gov/snap/outreach/map.htm or call your state's SNAP hotline number at http://www.fns.usda.gov/snap/outreach/map.htm. An online Pre-Screening Tool is available at http://www.snap-step1.usda.gov/fns/ to find out if your client could be eligible prior to applying at your local office.

Special Supplemental Nutrition Program for Women, Infants, and Children (WIC), Food and Nutrition Service, USDA: WIC provides supplemental food packages for nutritionally at-risk, low-income pregnant, breastfeeding, and post-partum women; infants; and children up to five years of age. The following benefits are provided to WIC participants: supplemental nutritious foods; nutrition education and counseling at WIC clinics; and screening and referrals to other health, welfare, and social services. The following website has toll-free numbers for WIC state agencies: http://www.fns.usda.gov/wic/contacts/tollfreenumbers.htm.

- Child Welfare Information Gateway, Children's Bureau, Administration for Children and Families (ACF), HHS: This is a resource clearinghouse for child welfare professionals. See the following link (http://www.childwelfare.gov/organizations/index.cfm) for resources and services such as national hotlines and state child abuse reporting numbers; federal child services clearinghouses; organizations dealing with child protection/abuse, family and domestic violence, foster care, health, mental health, and substance abuse; state child welfare agency websites; and state foster care program managers. http://www.childwelfare.gov/aboutus.cfm
- Office for Victims of Crime, U.S. Department of Justice: Search OVC's online directory of crime victim services for public, nonprofit, and community agencies that provide assistance and services to victims. The directory includes local, national and international agencies; a directory of crime victim services (searchable by location, type of victimization, service needed); an interactive map to search for victim services and compensation programs for victims; links to national crime victim service organizations and hotline numbers for national victim-serving organizations, clearinghouses, and referral organizations. http://ovc.ncjrs.gov/findvictimservices/
- 2-1-1: This resource number connects individuals to local community services, including rent assistance, food banks, affordable housing, health resources, child care, after-school programs, elderly care, financial literacy, and job training programs. 2-1-1 systems operate in forty-one states, the District of Columbia, and Puerto Rico. The 24/7 number is accessible at no cost, and has multilingual capabilities. It is funded through local and state sources, including local United Ways and other nonprofits, foundations, businesses, and state and local government. http://www.211.org
- Child Protective Services (CPS): CPS programs operate in every state, providing services for children who have been abused or neglected, regardless of immigration status. The Childhelp National Child Abuse Hotline is 1-800-4-A-CHILD; http://www.childhelp.org/pages/hotline.

▶ For information on human trafficking and the HHS Anti-Trafficking in Persons Program, visit www.acf.hhs.gov/trafficking or contact the National Human Trafficking Resource Center at 1-888-373-7888.

Trafficking Victims Protection Act

In January 2013, the national UCR Program began collecting offense and arrest data regarding human trafficking as authorized by the *William Wilberforce Trafficking Victims Protection Reauthorization Act of 2008*. The act requires the FBI to collect human trafficking offense data and to make distinctions between prostitution, assisting or promoting prostitution, and purchasing prostitution.

The Wilberforce Act

The *Wilberforce Act* itself does not define human trafficking because it is a reauthorization of the *Trafficking Victims Protection Act (TVPA) of 2000*, which defines "severe forms of trafficking in persons" as:

(A) sex trafficking in which a commercial sex act is induced by force, fraud, or coercion, or in which the person induced to perform such an act has not attained eighteen years of age; or

(B) the recruitment, harboring, transportation, provision, or obtaining of a person for labor or services, through the use of force, fraud, or coercion for the purpose of subjection to involuntary servitude, peonage, debt bondage, or slavery. (See 22 U.S.C. §7102 (8)(2004).)

Addition of Human Trafficking to the UCR Program

To comply with the Wilberforce Act, the national UCR Program created two additional offenses in the Summary Reporting System and the National Incident-Based Reporting System for which the UCR Program has begun collecting both offense and arrest data. The definitions for these offenses are:

Human Trafficking/Commercial Sex Acts. Inducing a person by force, fraud, or coercion to participate in commercial sex acts, or in which the person induced to perform such act(s) has not attained eighteen years of age.

Human Trafficking/Involuntary Servitude. The obtaining of a person(s) through recruitment, harboring, transportation, or provision, and subjecting such persons by force, fraud, or coercion into involuntary servitude, peonage, debt bondage, or slavery (not to include commercial sex acts).

In addition to these changes, the national UCR Program staff has also updated the Supplementary Homicide Report form to incorporate a new circumstance code for human trafficking.

The addition of offense or arrest data to the UCR Program is a rarity. The last time the UCR Program added an offense to the list of Part I crimes was in 1982 when the collection of arson data was made permanent. However, given the dynamic nature of criminal justice issues, the UCR Program is being called on to make modifications to reflect the changing realities of law enforcement that were not present when the Program was established in the early part of the twentieth century. These changes are not without some impact to law enforcement agencies, and it often takes time for agencies to identify resources that make submission of the new data collections to the national UCR Program possible. As is the case in any new data collection, the first year of data is often sparse. However, the UCR Program anticipates that more data will be reported each year as participation in the new human trafficking data collection grows.

The data in the tables included in this report reflect the offenses and arrests recorded by state and local agencies that currently have the ability to report the data to the national UCR Program. As such, they should not be interpreted as a definitive statement of the level or characteristics of human trafficking as a whole.

In addition to the level of data reported to the UCR Program, it is important to note that this is only one view of a complex issue—the law enforcement perspective. The investigation of human trafficking by local, state, tribal, and federal agencies is one facet of this crime. However, due to the nature of human trafficking, many of these crimes are never reported to law enforcement. In addition to the law enforcement facet in fighting these crimes, there are victim service organizations whose mission it is to serve the needs of the victims of human trafficking. In order to have the complete picture of human trafficking, it would be necessary to gather information from all of these sources.

Specialized Services for Victims of Human Trafficking

https://ojp.gov/ovc/news/index.html#Roberts

Awards of up to $600,000 will be made to enhance the quality and quantity of specialized services available to assist all victims of human trafficking, including services for underserved or unserved populations such as men and boys, American Indians and Alaska Natives, African Americans, Asian Americans, Latinos, Native Hawaiians, Pacific Islanders, and individuals who identify as lesbian, gay, bisexual, transgender, queer, or questioning.

Funding will also support efforts to increase the capacity of communities to respond to human trafficking victims through the development of interagency partnerships, professional training, and public awareness activities.

Posted January 11th 2017

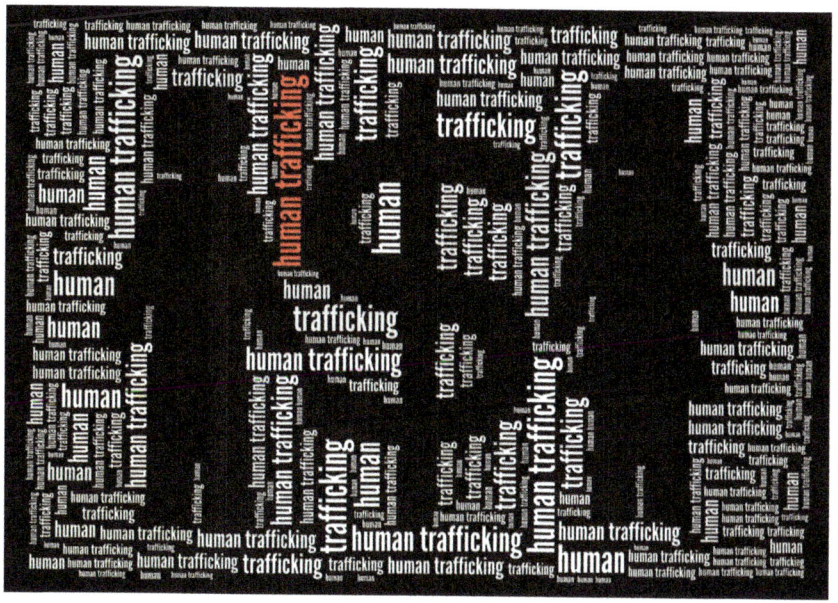

© mypokcik/Shutterstock.com

HUMAN TRAFFICKING INFORMATION

https://polarisproject.org/facts

Although slavery is commonly thought to be a thing of the past, human traffickers generate hundreds of billions of dollars in profits by trapping millions of people in horrific situations around the world, including here in the U.S. traffickers use violence, threats, deception, debt bondage, and other manipulative tactics to force people to engage in commercial sex or to provide labor or services against their will. While more research is needed on the scope of human trafficking, below are a few key statistics:

- The International Labour Organization estimates that there are 20.9 million victims of human trafficking globally.
- 68 percent of them are trapped in forced labor.
- 26 percent of them are children.
- 55 percent are women and girls.
- The International Labor Organization estimates that forced labor and human trafficking is a $150 billion industry worldwide.
- The U.S. Department of Labor has identified 139 goods from seventy-five countries made by forced and child labor.
- In 2015, an estimated one out of five endangered runaways reported to the National Center for Missing and Exploited Children were likely child sex trafficking victims.
- Of those, 74 percent were in the care of social services or foster care when they ran.
- There is no official estimate of the total number of human trafficking victims in the U.S. Polaris estimates that the total number of victims nationally reaches into the hundreds of thousands when estimates of both adults and minors and sex trafficking and labor trafficking are aggregated.
- More than 29,800 total cases of human trafficking have been reported to the Hotline in the last eight years.
- The Hotline annually receives multiple reports of human trafficking cases in each of the fifty states and D.C.
- The number of human trafficking cases that Polaris learns about in the U.S. increases every year.
- 23 percent of texting conversations on the Polaris BeFree Textline were from survivors of human trafficking compared to 11 percent of phone calls on the Hotline.
- The Hotline receives an average of 100 calls per day.

© oculo/Shutterstock.com

HUMAN TRAFFICKING ENACTMENTS 2005–2011

http://www.ncsl.org/research/civil-and-criminal-justice/human-trafficking-laws-in-the-states-updated-nov.aspx

Human trafficking is the control and exploitation of people for profit. As defined under U.S. federal law, victims of human trafficking include children involved in the sex trade, adults age eighteen or over who are coerced or deceived into commercial sex acts, and anyone compelled into forced labor.

Human trafficking has become an increased concern for many state legislators throughout the country. This has led to a proliferation of state laws; these laws attack the issue in varying ways. This document provides an abstract for each human trafficking law state by state. The laws are organized into the following six categories:

- Laws criminalizing human trafficking and increasing penalties
- Laws creating task forces on trafficking, state commissions or committees
- Laws providing services and protections to victims of human trafficking
- Laws that prohibit destruction, concealment, removal, or possession of any false passport, immigration or other government document
- Laws that establish extortion if threats to report immigration status

Miscellaneous Laws Criminalizing Human Trafficking and Increasing Penalties

Alabama H 432 (2010)

Relates to human trafficking; provides that it would be unlawful for a person, by coercion or deception, to cause another person to work or perform services having financial value or require that person to perform certain sexual activities; provides penalties; provides exemptions to a corporation if the corporation was not aware of the actions of its agents or employees.

Arizona HB 2405 (2011)

Relates to human smuggling organizations, provides offenses, penalties, and that a person so convicted shall not be eligible for suspension of sentence, probation or pardon until the sentence has been served, the person is eligible for release or the sentence is commuted; provides for temporary release under certain circumstances.

Arizona SB 1059 (2010)

Adds transport by deception, coercion, or force to current sex trafficking laws.

Arizona HB 2238 (2010)

Adds human trafficking to existing law.

Arizona SB 1281 (2009) (Also See Destruction of Government Document Section)

Expands the classification of sex trafficking by including a sexually-explicit performance and knowingly trafficking a minor with the knowledge that they will engage in any prostitution or sexually explicit performance. Expands the definition of forced labor or services to include the classification of trafficking of persons.

Arizona HB. 1372 (A.R.S. §13-306) (2005) (Also See Services to Victims Section)

Establishes human trafficking and human smuggling as felonies. Provides that sex trafficking, if committed against a person who is under fifteen years of age, is a dangerous crime against children.

Arizona SB 1338 nm (2005)

Adds "sex trafficking of a minor who is under 15 years of age" to those offenses which result in a presumptive sentence of thirty years of prison upon a subsequent offense of such qualifying crimes and to offenses requiring sex offender registration. Excluding certain offenders, prohibits approval of a registered sex offender's residence for probation unless the number of probationers who are required to register and who reside in the multi-family dwelling is less than 10 percent of the number of dwelling units that are contained in the multifamily dwelling in counties with a population of more 2,500,000 people. Includes the person's residence (where they live) and address (where they receive mail) among requirements for sex offender registration.

Arkansas S 222 (2010)

Affects probation and parole terms for human trafficking.

California AB 12 (2011)

Enacts the Abolition of Child Commerce, Exploitation and Sexual Slavery Act of 2011. Requires that anyone convicted of seeking to procure or procuring the sexual services of a prostitute, if the prostitute is under age eighteen, be ordered to pay an additional fine, not to exceed a specified amount, to fund programs and services for commercially exploited minors in the counties where the underlying offenses are committed.

California AB 22 (Cal Pen. Code §236.1) (2005) (Also See Services to Victims Section)

Establishes the crime of trafficking of a person for forced labor or services or for effecting or maintaining other specified felonies, and the crime of trafficking of a minor for those purposes, punishable by terms of imprisonment in the state prison for three, four, or five years, or four, six, or eight years, respectively.

Colorado SB 140 (2010)

Repeals and relocates, with amendments, provisions relating to trafficking in adults, trafficking in children, and coercion of involuntary servitude; requires proof of the use of force, fraud, or coercion to prove the crime of trafficking in adults or trafficking in children and proof of the use of force or fraud to prove the crime of coercion of involuntary servitude; adds trafficking in adults, trafficking in children, and coercion of involuntary servitude.

Colorado HB 1123 (2009)

Revises provisions concerning trafficking of children and coercion of involuntary servitude by providing that "child" means any person under eighteen years of age, rather than sixteen.

Specifies that the crime of trafficking in children is a Class 2 felony. Provides that a person commits "involuntary servitude" if he or she coerces another person to perform labor using threats of harm or a scheme to cause a person to believe that they will suffer harm.

Colorado SB 206 (2006)

Makes smuggling humans a Class 3 felony, unless the adult is an illegal immigrant, which makes the offense a Class 2 felony. Smuggling includes offering transportation to someone of illegal residency status to enter, pass through, or remain in either the United States or Colorado in exchange for money. A separate offense is brought against the smuggler for each person assisted.

Colorado SB 207 (2006)

Makes human trafficking a crime and increases penalties. Trafficking a human includes selling, exchanging, bartering or leasing an adult (sixteen years old or older) in exchange for money.

Trafficking also includes receiving the services of an adult in exchange for money (section 1). Trafficking of any child under the age of sixteen results in a Class 3 felony.

Connecticut SB 153 (2010)

Establishes penalties for prostitution and provides for the care of exploited children. Connecticut SB 153 (53-394 et seq.) (2006).

Enhances criminal and civil penalties for people who coerce others to perform labor or engage in human trafficking. Authorizes the state to prosecute traffickers under the racketeering statute when there is a pattern of such activity and to seize property related to the crime.

Delaware HB 116 (§787) (2007) (See Also Services Section)

Creates felony crime of trafficking of persons and involuntary servitude patterned after the federal Department of Justice's model legislation.

Florida SB 250 (2006) (See Also Services Section)

Makes human trafficking a crime. Trafficking includes threatening to destroy or destroying immigration documents for the purposes of forced employment.

Florida SB 1962 (Chapter 391) (2004)

Establishes the first degree felony of sex trafficking which provides up to thirty years in prison for anyone convicted for buying or selling minors for the purpose of prostitution or sex trafficking. Establishes two second degree felonies: obtaining forced labor; and, sex trafficking and human trafficking for anyone who knowingly participates in trafficking for purposes of forced labor or prostitution—this offense provides a criminal penalty of up to fifteen years in prison. Provides that any sex trafficking activity that results in death or is committed against a person who is under the age of fourteen be considered a first degree felony.

Idaho HB 235 (2011)

Relates to the Criminal Gang Enforcement Act; revises the definition of the term "pattern of criminal gang activity" to include reference to certain crimes, including possession of a weapon, bomb, or destructive device, and sexual exploitation or battery of a child; and establishes the maximum period of imprisonment that may be imposed for related crimes, including crimes committed on school grounds.

Idaho HB 536 (18-8501 et seq.) (2006) (See Also Services Section)

Increases the punishment for crimes if the human trafficking is involved. Requires reporting on human trafficking victim resources in Idaho and the relationship of these resources to federally-funded programs.

Illinois HB 1469 (Act No. 94-9) (2005) (See Also Services Section)

Creates the offenses of involuntary servitude, sexual servitude of a minor, and trafficking of persons for forced labor and services. Mandates restitution and provides that the Illinois Attorney General, in cooperation with the Administrative Office of the Illinois Courts, State's Attorneys, Circuit Court officials, the Dept. of Human Services, and the Dept. of Public Aid, must ensure that victims of trafficking or involuntary servitude are referred to appropriate social services, federal and state public benefits programs, victim protection services, and immigration assistance services.

Iowa SB 606 (2010)

This bill repeals the criminal offense of detention in a brothel. A similar criminal offense exists in Code chapter 710A (human trafficking)

Iowa SB 2219 (§710A.1 et seq.) (2006) (See Also Services and Task Force Sections)

Establishes human trafficking a felony under state laws. Orders training regarding the sensitive treatment of trafficking victims and encourages communication by law enforcement officials in the language of the victims. Institutes a Victim Compensation Fund for victims of trafficking. Calls for a study to examine the effects of trafficking on victims.

Kansas HB 2010 (2011)

Relates to civil procedure; relates to covered offenses and conduct giving rise to forfeiture to include theft, criminal discharge of a firearm, gambling, Medicaid fraud, dog and cock fighting or dog and cock fighting paraphernalia, prostitution, human trafficking, worthless checks, forgery, mistreatment of a dependent adult, identity theft or identity fraud, and criminal use of a financial card.

Kansas SB 37 (2011)

Amends the State Offender Registration Act regarding people who are required to register under out-of-state law and for offenses not otherwise required; relates to juvenile sex offenders, sexual exploitation of a child, sexually violent crimes, drug offenders, registration fees, registration violations, child care facility notification of registration, sex offender reporting, the registration time period for certain offenses, diversionary agreements or probation, Internet posting, and criminal records expungement.

Kansas SB 434 (2010)

Changes criminal procedures for a number of crimes; human trafficking is one of them.

Kansas SB 586 (2010)

Makes aggravated human trafficking a severity level 1, person felony.

Kansas SB 72 (K.S.A. §21-3707) (2005)

Creates the crime of trafficking as a severity level 2, person felony and aggravated trafficking as a severity level 1, person felony.

Kentucky SB 43 (§506.120 et seq.) (2007)

Creates felony crimes of human trafficking and promoting human trafficking. Adds human trafficking as an element to the crime of advancing prostitution.

Louisiana HB 49 (2011)

Relates to human trafficking; relates to the crimes of human trafficking and trafficking of children for sexual purposes; amends the elements of those crimes; provides for definitions; and provides for penalties.

Louisiana HB 531 (2010)

Amends the elements of the crime of human trafficking; provides for the crime of human trafficking and provides that it shall be unlawful for a person to knowingly recruit, harbor, transport, provide, solicit, or obtain another person through fraud, force, or coercion to provide services or labor.

Louisiana HB 825 (2010)

Adds the crimes of human trafficking and trafficking of children for sexual purposes to enumerated crimes of violence and sex offenses for purposes of sex offender registration and notification requirements.

Louisiana HB 564 (2009)

Creates the crime of trafficking of children for sexual purposes and establishes criminal penalties for such crime.

Louisiana HB 970 (15:541) (2007)

Adds human trafficking as a possible element to crime of sexual offense against a victim who is a minor.

Louisiana HB 56 (Act 187) (2005)

Creates the crime of human trafficking as a separate state crime, defined as intentionally recruiting, harboring, transporting, another person through fraud, force or coercion to provide services or labor. Provides the following penalties: (1) Human trafficking—a fine up to $10,000 and imprisonment for up to ten years. (2) Human trafficking when the purpose include certain forms of sexual activity—a fine of up to $15,000 and imprisonment for up to 20 years. (3) Human trafficking involving a person under the age of eighteen—a fine up to $25,000 and imprisonment for not less than five or more than twenty-five.

Maryland HB 345 (2011)

Adds specified human trafficking offenses to those crimes for which evidence may be gathered by, and a judge may grant an order authorizing, interception of oral, wire or electronic communications.

Maryland SB 299 (2011)

Adds human trafficking offenses to those crimes for which evidence may be gathered by interception of oral, wire, or electronic communications by investigative or law enforcement officers; provides that a judge may grant an order authorizing such wiretapping; and relates to murder, kidnapping, sexual offenses, child abuse, child pornography, gambling, robbery, bribery, extortion, controlled substances, fraudulent insurance acts, and destructive devices.

Maryland SB 517 (2010)

Adds and defines human trafficking in relation to gang laws.

Maryland HB 876 & SB 606 (11-303) (2007)

Provides felony penalties for human trafficking and human trafficking involving a minor. Massachusetts HB 3808 (2011).

The legislation establishes the state crime of human trafficking for sexual servitude. Defined as intentionally subjecting, enticing, harboring, transporting, or delivering another with the intent that the person engage in sexually explicit performance, production of pornography or sexual conduct for a fee or benefiting from sexual conduct of another, human trafficking for sexual servitude is now punishable by a mandatory-minimum term of five years, with a potential maximum sentence of up to twenty years, and a fine of up to $25,000. Human trafficking for sexual servitude involving a victim under eighteen carries a potential maximum sentence of life in prison. A business entity convicted of human trafficking for sexual servitude may be fined up to $1 million.

Michigan HB 5748 (§750.451 et seq.) (2006) (See Also Document Section)

Add human trafficking to the Michigan Penal Code as a felony. Stiffens penalties for human trafficking. The bill defines trafficking as compelling a person into forced labor by causing or threatening bodily harm. The penalty for this crime is a prison sentence varying from up to ten years to life, depending on the severity of the offense. The bill also forbids forced labor or services by threatening the destruction of immigration documents, and increases penalties for human trafficking. Makes the intention to traffic a human criminal. Finally, kidnapping, attempting to kill, murdering, or engaging in criminal sexual conduct with a trafficking victim is punishable by life imprisonment.

Minnesota HB 1505 (2009)

Increases the criminal penalties for certain promoting/sex trafficking offenses. Expands the sex trafficking and labor trafficking crimes; adds the promotion of prostitution/sex trafficking crime to the firearm law's definition of a crime of violence.

Mississippi HB 381 (§97-3-107) (2006)

Creates the Anti-Human Trafficking Act, prohibits trafficking of persons for forced labor or services, involuntary servitude, sexual servitude of a minor, and to provide for liability of an accomplice in those acts. Increases the penalties for a person found guilty of human trafficking of any kind to prison sentence of up to twenty years.

Missouri HB 214 (2011)

Revises human trafficking laws; expands the crimes of abuse of an individual through forced labor, slavery, involuntary servitude, peonage, sexual exploitation and sexual trafficking of a child; provides related criminal penalties; requires the court to order restitution; and provides an affirmative defense for prostitution.

Missouri HB 1487 (§168.071 R.S.Mo.) (2004) (See Also Services Section)

Establishes sexual trafficking of a child as a Class A felony. Also provides that abusing an individual through forced labor and of trafficking for either forced labor or sexual exploitation is a Class B felony. Establishes a Class D felony for contributing to human trafficking through the misuse of documentation. Provides that as part of the sentencing for a human trafficking offense, the court must order the perpetrator to pay restitution to the victim. Provides that victims of any trafficking crimes will also be afforded the rights and protections provided in the federal Trafficking Victims Protection Act of 2000.

Montana SB 385 (2007)

Creates crimes of involuntary servitude and trafficking of persons for involuntary servitude. Provides penalties ranging from 10-100 years imprisonment and up to $100,000 in fines.

Nebraska LB 771 (2010)

This bill changes provisions relating to criminal offenses against a pregnant woman; human trafficking is included. This bill also classifies persons convicted of human trafficking as dangerous sex offenders, thereby subjecting them to sex offender registration and probation laws.

Nevada AB 383 (§200) (2007)

Creates the felony crimes of trafficking in persons and trafficking for illegal purposes which involves engaging in certain acts concerning the transportation of an illegal alien into this state with the intent to subject the person to certain acts relating to involuntary servitude. Requires the Director of the Department of Business and Industry to include on its website a link to the Social Security Administration where an employer may verify the social security numbers of his employees to prevent unlawful hiring or employment.

New Hampshire HB 474 (2009)

Prohibits trafficking in persons. Provides penalties for forcing a trafficked person to engage in a commercial sex act or performance and provides for forfeiture of items used in connection with trafficking. Makes such offenses involving a person under eighteen years of age subject to an extended term of imprisonment.

New Jersey AB 2730 (Chapter 77) (2005)

Establishes human trafficking as a crime of the first degree, which is defined as "using a person for the purposes of engaging in unlawful sexual activity or providing unlawful labor or services." Provides a mandatory term of imprisonment where the defendant participates in the human trafficking scheme as an organizer, supervisor, financier, or manager. The mandatory term of imprisonment would be for a term of imprisonment of twenty years.

New Mexico SB 71 (2008)

Establishes human trafficking as a criminal offense and creates penalties.

New York SB 5902 (Penal Code §230.34, §135.35 et seq.) (2007)

Creates felony crimes and provides penalties related to human trafficking including sex trafficking and labor trafficking.

North Carolina HB 1896 (2006) (See Also Document Section)

Makes human trafficking a felony.

North Dakota SB 2209 (2009)

Makes human trafficking a felony and includes in the definition debt bondage, racketeering, and forced labor or services.

Ohio SB 162 (2010)

Revises state regulation of telephone companies; includes human trafficking as a type of unlawful behavior in relation to telephone companies.

Ohio SB 235 (2010)

Creates offenses for trafficking in persons and unlawful conduct with respect to documents. Revises the involuntary servitude-related elements of kidnapping, increases the penalty for the offense of abduction based on involuntary servitude and clarifies an element of compelling prostitution that relates to the compelling of another to engage in specified conduct. The bill also includes abduction and trafficking in persons within the offense of conspiracy.

Oklahoma SB 956 (2010)

Relates to crimes and punishments; prohibits human trafficking; modifies what constitutes unlawful human trafficking; increases the age of a related victim for punishment purposes; provides that a victim may bring a civil action for actual and punitive damages; allows reasonable attorneys fees in the civil action; sets a statute of limitations for recovery in the civil action; authorizes the forfeiture and seizure or property.

Oklahoma HB 2983 (2010)

Relates to crimes and punishments; prohibits a person from conducting any financial transaction using the proceeds of an act of terrorism with the intent to further the commission of such an act, conceal or disguise the source of the proceeds, or conceal or disguise the intent to avoid a financial transaction reporting requirement; makes changes relating to electronic funds transfers and violations of the Anti-terrorism Act and racketeer-influenced and corrupt organizations.

Organizations related to Human trafficking are included.

Oregon SB 578 (§131.602 et seq.) (2007)

Creates the felony crimes of trafficking in persons and subjecting another person to involuntary servitude.

Pennsylvania HB 1112 (§9720.2, §911) (2006)

Includes human trafficking as an element of racketeering and provides for a maximum sentence of life sentence when one commits trafficking while committing rape or kidnapping.

Rhode Island HB 5044 (2010)

This act would define the crime of prostitution to include any location, would create punishments for individuals who would attempt to procure the services of a prostitute, and would define the crime of permitting prostitution within a premise.

Rhode Island HB 5661 (2009)

Mandates a fine of no less than forty thousand dollars and imprisonment for up to life for anyone found guilty of sex trafficking of a minor.

Rhode Island SB 605 (2009)

This act would mandate a fine of no less than forty thousand dollars ($40,000) and imprisonment for up to life for anyone found guilty of sex trafficking of a minor.

Rhode Island SB 5881 & SB 692 (§11-67-1 et seq.) (2007)

Creates the felony crimes of involuntary servitude and trafficking of persons for forces labor or commercial sexual activity. Provides for penalties.

South Carolina HB 4202 (2010)

Adds human trafficking to a list of offenses and makes it a Class A felony.

South Dakota SB 176 (2011)

Provides for the crime of human trafficking, to establish the elements and degrees of the crime, and to provide penalties for the violation thereof; provides that no one may recruit, harbor, transport, provide or obtain, by any means, another person, knowing that force, fraud or coercion will be used to cause the person to engage in prostitution, forced labor or involuntary servitude; and provides for criminal penalties.

Tennessee HB 171 (2011)

As introduced, provides that real and personal property used in committing human trafficking offenses is subject to judicial forfeiture seizure and provides for disposition of funds from forfeited assets. Companion bill Tennessee SB 604 (2011).

Tennessee HB 1302 (2010)

This bill creates the new offenses of unlawful restraint, compelling prostitution, and compelling production of pornography and establishes a new civil cause of action against persons engaged in trafficking.

Tennessee SB 2724 (2010)

Under present law, the Tennessee Sexual Offender and Violent Sexual Offender Registration, Verification, and Tracking Act (the Act) requires a person who is convicted of a sexual offense or violent sexual offense to register and meet the other requirements of the Act. A sexual offense includes, among other offenses, kidnapping, except when committed by a parent of the minor.

This bill clarifies that kidnapping is a sexual offense under the Act only where the victim is a minor. This bill adds the offense of trafficking for sexual servitude to the list of offenses that are violent sexual offenses.

Texas HB 2096 (Tex. Penal Code §20A.02) (2003)

Establishes trafficking as a second-degree felony with a sentence of two to twenty years imprisonment. If the persons trafficked or transported are under the age of fourteen, or if the commission of the offense results in death, the offense is a first-degree felony with a sentence of five to ninety-nine years imprisonment.

Utah HB 230 (2010)

Modifies the Criminal Code regarding charging the offenses of human trafficking or human smuggling; provides that it is a separate offense regarding each person who is trafficked or smuggled in violation of current law.

Utah HB 339 (2008) (§76-5-308 et. seq.)

Provides for crimes of kidnapping, human trafficking, and smuggling.

Vermont HB 153 (2011)

Proposes to establish a comprehensive system of criminal penalties and prevention programs for human trafficking, and a program of services for human trafficking victims; and provides criminal punishments for child sex trafficking.

Vermont SB 125 (2009)

Create a new crime that addresses commercial sex trafficking by force, fraud or coercion.

Virginia HB 1898 (2011)

Amends existing law to make punishable as a Class 2 felony abduction of any child under age sixteen for the purpose of concubinage or prostitution, of any one for the purpose of prostitution, or of any minor for the purpose of manufacturing child pornography.

Virginia HB 2016 (2009) (See Also Document Section)

Expands "abduction" to include abducting a person with the intent to subject the person to forced labor or services.

Washington SB 5546 (2011)

Concerns changes to the crime of human trafficking.

Washington HB 1175 (A.R.C.W. §7.68.350) (2003)

Establishes first and second degree sex trafficking and labor trafficking as a Class A felony under Washington law. A first-degree offense carries a maximum sentence of fourteen years in prison and, trafficking in the second-degree hold a maximum of nine years. Provides that victims of trafficking may sue for damages and for the cost of bringing the suit.

Laws Creating Task Forces on Trafficking, State Commissions, or Committees

California AB 22 (Cal Pen. Code §236.1) (2005)

Establishes a task force to study various issues in connection with human trafficking and to advise the Legislature, as specified. The provisions relating to the task force would be repealed January 1, 2008.

California SB 180 (Cal Pen. Code § 13990) (2005)

Establishes the California Alliance to Combat Trafficking and Slavery (California ACTS) Task Force and require it to evaluate various programs available to victims of trafficking and various criminal statutes addressing human trafficking, and report to the Legislature, Governor, and Attorney General on or before July 1, 2007.

Colorado HB 1143 (C.R.S. §18-1.8-101) (2005)

Creates an interagency task force on human trafficking. Task force duties include: collecting and organizing data on the nature of trafficking in the state; investigating collaborative models for protecting the victims; measuring and evaluating progress of the state in preventing trafficking and prosecuting offenders; identifying available federal, state, and local programs that provide services to trafficking victims; evaluating approaches to increase public awareness of trafficking; and analyzing existing state criminal statutes for their adequacy in addressing trafficking.

Connecticut SB 398 (2007)

Establishes the Trafficking in Persons Council to develop recommendations to strengthen state and local efforts to prevent trafficking, protect and assist victims of trafficking, and prosecute traffickers.

Connecticut HB 5358 (Act No. 04-8) (2004)

Establishes an interagency task force on human trafficking to do the following: collect data on the nature of trafficking in the state and evaluate the state's progress on trafficking; identify available federal, state, and local programs that provide services to trafficking victims; evaluate approaches to increase public awareness of trafficking; analyze and make recommendations regarding existing state criminal statutes' ability to address trafficking; and, make recommendations on preventing trafficking, assisting victims, and prosecuting traffickers.

Florida SB 168 (2009)

Creates within the Executive Office of the Governor the Statewide Task Force on Human Trafficking to study the issues of human trafficking.

Hawaii HB 2051 (2006)

Establishes a task force to compile and review law and information from other states regarding support for victims of human trafficking and recommend changes to Hawaii law and programs on this topic.

Idaho HCR 18 (2005)

Authorizes the Legislative Council to appoint a committee to undertake and complete a study of human trafficking. The committee is charged with the following: data collection and findings on the nature and extent of human trafficking in Idaho; identification of available federal, state, and local programs that provide services to trafficking victims; analysis and recommendations regarding the ability of existing state criminal statutes to address trafficking; and recommendations regarding the prevention of trafficking, the prosecution of offenses, and victim assistance.

Iowa SB 2219 (§710A.1 et seq.) (2006) (See Also Services and Penalty Sections)

Calls for a study to examine the effects of trafficking on victims.

Louisiana SCR 58 (2011)

Requests various public agencies and private associations and stakeholders to collaborate through the Human Trafficking of Minors Study Group to study and make recommendations to the Legislature about methods that can be used to help eliminate human trafficking of minors in Louisiana.

Maine HB 893 (2006)

Creates the Human Trafficking Task Force to propose criminal statutes and develop methods for a coordinated approach to assisting victims of human trafficking.

Maryland HB 674 (2011)

Requires the State Department of Education, in collaboration with the Department of Health and Mental Hygiene, to provide awareness and training for student services directors in local education agencies on human trafficking, including strategies to prevent trafficking of children.

Minnesota HB 1505 (2009)

Authorizes the Commissioner of Public Safety to gather and compile data on human trafficking every two years.

New Hampshire SB 194 (2007)

Establishes a commission to study the trafficking of persons across borders for sexual and labor exploitation.

New York AB 6800 (2011)

Extends the Interagency Task Force on Human Trafficking until Sept. 1, 2013.

New York SB 5902 (Penal Code §230.34, §135.35 et seq.) (2007) (See Also Penalty and Services Sections)

Establishes an interagency task force on human trafficking.

Pennsylvania SR 253 (2010)

Directs the Joint State Government Commission to establish an advisory committee to study the problem of human trafficking and to make a report to the Senate on the issue of human trafficking. Includes a proposed state plan for the prevention of human trafficking and any recommendations for changes in state law, policies and procedures.

Rhode Island HB 8291 (2010)

(Resolution) Creates a House Commission whose purpose it would be to conduct a comprehensive study of human trafficking and the services that would be provided to the victims of human trafficking. This commission would be required to report its findings and results to the General Assembly on or before March 2, 2011, and said commission would expire on June 2, 2012.

Rhode Island HB 5661 (2009)

Creates an interagency human trafficking of persons task force.

Texas HCR 68 (2011)

Requests the Lieutenant Governor and the Speaker of the House of Representatives to create a joint interim committee to study human trafficking in Texas.

Texas HB 1930 (2011)

Relates to the membership and duties of the Human Trafficking Prevention Task Force. Examines the extent to which human trafficking is associated with the operation of sexually oriented businesses and the workplace or public health concerns that are created by the association of human trafficking and the operation of sexually oriented businesses.

Texas SB 379 (2009)

Requires the Texas Fusion Center provide an annual report by the Texas Fusion Center regarding criminal street gangs that includes law enforcement strategies that have been proven effective in deterring gang involvement in human trafficking of persons.

Utah HB 64 (2009)

Authorizes the Office of the Attorney General to administer and coordinate the operation of a multi-agency strike force to combat violent and other major felony crimes within the state associated with illegal immigration and human trafficking. Provides for voluntary participation in the strike force by officers of U.S. Immigration and Customs Enforcement and state and local law enforcement personnel.

Vermont SB 272 (2010)

Establishes the human trafficking task force; provides for a comprehensive system of criminal penalties, of prevention programs, and of services for human trafficking victims.

Vermont SB 125 (2010)

Expands sex registry laws to include human trafficking.

Virginia HB 2923 (§30-278) (2007)

Creates the Commission on the Prevention of Human Trafficking for the purpose of developing and implementing a state plan for the prevention of human trafficking.

Washington HB 2381 (RCW 7.68.350) (2003)

Establishes the Washington State Task Force Against the Trafficking of Persons to do the following: measure and evaluate the progress of the state in trafficking prevention activities; identify available federal, state, and local programs that provide services to victims of trafficking; and, make recommendations on methods to provide a coordinated system of support and assistance to victims of trafficking.

Laws Providing Services and Protections to Victims of Human Trafficking

Arizona HB 1372 (A.R.S. §13-306) (2005) (Also See Penalty Section)

Provides for restitution to victims of sex trafficking and persons who were trafficked for the purposes of forced labor or services.

California AB 90 (2011)

Includes within the definition of criminal profiteering activity any crime in which the perpetrator induces, encourages or persuades, or causes through force, fear, coercion, deceit, violence, duress, menace, or threat of unlawful injury to the victim or to another person, anyone under age eighteen to engage in a commercial sex act. Requires deposit of forfeiture proceeds from the above-referenced criminal activity into the Victim-Witness Assistance Fund for counseling and prevention programs.

California AB 764 (2011)

Allows taxpayers to designate on their tax returns that a specified amount in excess of the tax liability be transferred to the Child Victims of Human Trafficking Fund established in the State Treasury.

Provides that all money contributed to the fund, upon appropriation by the Legislature, be allocated to the Franchise Tax Board and the controller for reimbursement of costs, as provided, and to the California Emergency Management Agency, which would administer the funds granted to community-based organizations that serve minor victims of human trafficking, as provided.

California SB 1569 (Welfare & Inst. Code §13283 et seq.) (2006)

Extends eligibility for state and local public benefits, Medi-Cal health care and refugee cash assistance and employment services, to noncitizen victims of trafficking, domestic violence, and other serious crimes, to the same extent as available to individuals admitted to the United States as refugees.

California AB 22 (Cal Pen. Code §236.1) (2005) (Also See Penalty Section)

Permits a victim of trafficking to bring a civil action for actual damages, provide for restitution and punitive damages, and would establish a victim-caseworker privilege.

Colorado SB 85 (2011)

Concerns a diversion program (prostitution program courts) for those who commit prostitution-related offenses.

Colorado SB 225 (§24-33.5-211) (2006)

Requires the Chief of the Colorado State Patrol to create a division to address human smuggling and human trafficking on state highways. Requires the division to include at least twelve employees for the twelve-month period beginning July 1, 2006, and at least twenty-four employees for the twelve-month period beginning July 1, 2007.

Connecticut SB 1500A (§51-63) (2007)

Provides that the Office of Victim Services within the Judicial Department contract with nongovernmental organizations to develop a coordinated response system to assist victims of the offense of trafficking in persons.

Delaware HB 116 (§787) (2007) (See Also Penalty Section)

Provides for restitution and victim protection.

Florida HB 1127 (2011)

Relates to abortions; requires that an ultrasound be performed on all women obtaining an abortion; requires that the ultrasound be reviewed with the patient before the woman gives informed consent for an abortion; requires that the woman must certify in writing that she declined to review the ultrasound and did so of her own free will and without undue influence; and provides an exception for victims of rape, incest, domestic violence, human trafficking, or for women whose medical condition requires an abortion. Companion Bill FL SB 1744 (2011).

Florida HB 7181 (2007)

Requires the Department of Children and Family Services to provide services to immigrant survivors of human trafficking, domestic violence, and other serious crimes.

Florida SB 250 (2006) (See Also Penalty Section)

Provides that victims of trafficking can receive up to three times the monetary amount for their services as restitution.

Georgia HB 200 (2011)

Discourages trafficking of people for labor or sexual servitude and provides greater protections to those subject to such crimes. Provides for notification of federal assistance for certain people under the Crime Victims' Bill of Rights, and increases penalties for crimes involving youth.

Idaho HB 536 (18-8501 et seq.) (2006) (See Also Penalty Section)

Provides for restitution and rehabilitation costs for victims of human trafficking. Requires reporting on human trafficking victim resources in Idaho and the relationship of these resources to federally-funded programs.

Illinois SB 1037 (2011)

Amends the Criminal Code to allow motions to vacate a verdict of guilty in crimes that involve prostitution when the crime is later found to result from having been a victim of human trafficking. Includes involuntary sexual servitude of a minor.

Illinois HB 1469 (Act No. 94-9) (2005) (See Also Penalty Section)

Mandates restitution and provides that the Illinois Attorney General, in cooperation with the Administrative Office of the Illinois Courts, State's Attorneys, Circuit Court officials, the Dept. of Human Services, and the Dept. of Public Aid ensure that victims of trafficking or involuntary servitude are referred to appropriate social services, federal and state public benefits programs, victim protection services and immigration assistance services.

Iowa SB 2219 (§710A.1 et seq.) (2006) (See Also Penalty and Task Force Sections)

Orders training regarding the sensitive treatment of trafficking victims and encourages communication by law enforcement officials in the language of the victims. Institutes a Victim Compensation Fund for victims of trafficking.

Maryland SB 327 (2011)

Enacts the Human Trafficking Victim Protection Act; authorizes anyone convicted of prostitution to file a motion to vacate the judgment under certain circumstances; requires the court to hold a hearing on the motion under certain circumstances; authorizes the court to take certain actions in ruling on the motion; requires the court to state on the record the reasons for its ruling on the motion; and establishes that a defendant in a proceeding under this act has the burden of proof.

Missouri HB 353 (Section 566.200–566.223) (2005)

Addresses human trafficking by establishing requirements for international matchmaking organizations. Provides that intentionally providing false or incomplete information required by these provisions is a Class D felony.

Missouri HB 1487 (§168.071 R.S.Mo.) (2004) (See Also Penalty Section)

Provides that as part of the sentencing for a human trafficking offense, the court must order the perpetrator to pay restitution to the victim. Provides that victims of any trafficking crimes will also be afforded the rights and protections provided in the federal Trafficking Victims Protection Act of 2000.

New York SB 5902 (Penal Code §230.34, §135.35 et seq.) (2007) (See Also Penalty and Task Force Sections)

Provides services for victims of human trafficking.

Oklahoma SB 2258 (2010)

Creates the Greater Protecting Victims of Human Trafficking Act of 2010; relates to the transport of aliens; prohibits the destruction of documentation papers to extend an individual's legal status; relates to human trafficking victim guidelines; authorizes establishment of an emergency hotline for human trafficking victims; authorizes posting of rights of victims; adds the threat of reporting a person as illegally present in the country for something of value or to perform an action to blackmail crimes.

Oregon SB 839 (2009)

Includes a victim of human trafficking as a person eligible for Address Confidentiality Program.

Rhode Island HB 5350 (2009)

This act would provide services and protections to victims of human trafficking.

South Carolina SB 1079 (§14-43.11) (2007)

Provides that illegal residents of the state are eligible for public benefits if they are victims of human trafficking as defined.

Texas HB 4009 (2009)

Establishes a victim assistance program to provide services to domestic victims of sex trafficking.

Texas HB 1121 (Code of Crim. Pro. §42.0191 et seq) (2007)

Provides for services and protection for victims of human trafficking.

Texas HB 1751 (Govt. Code §420.008) (2007)

Provides that monies collected from a fee imposed on sexually oriented business be used for prosecution and victim services related to human trafficking.

Tennessee HB 172 (2011)

The National Human Trafficking Resource Center Hotline Act Creates an obligation for certain businesses to post the following sign. National Human Trafficking Resource Center Hotline at 1-888-373-7888. If you or someone you know is being forced to engage in any activity and cannot leave—whether it is commercial sex, housework, farm work, or any other activity—call the National Human Trafficking Hotline at 1-888-373-7888 to access help and services. Victims of human trafficking are protected under United States and Tennessee law.

Virginia HB 2190 (2011)

Requires the Department of Social Services to develop a plan to provide services to victims of human trafficking, which shall include provisions for identifying victims of human trafficking in the Commonwealth; helping human trafficking victims to apply for benefits and services to which they may be entitled; coordinating delivery of services for victims of human trafficking; preparing and disseminating educational and training programs and materials to increase awareness of human trafficking and services available to victims; developing and maintaining community-based services for victims of human trafficking; and helping victims to reunify with family reunification or return to their place of origin, if he or she so desires.

Washington SB 5482 (2011)

Authorizes existing funding to house victims of human trafficking and their families.

The Department of Commerce must use these funds to provide housing and shelter for extremely low-income households, including, but not limited to, housing for victims of human trafficking and their families and grants for building operation and maintenance costs of housing projects or units within housing projects that are affordable to extremely low-income households with incomes at or below 30 percent of the area median income, and that require a supplement to rent income to cover ongoing operating expenses.

Washington SB 5850 (2009)

Protects workers from human trafficking violations; requires domestic employers of foreign workers and international labor recruitment agencies to disclose certain information to foreign workers who have been referred to or hired by an employer in the state; requires persons licensed to practice medicine in this state to take a one-time course on human trafficking that teaches methods of recognizing victims of human trafficking.

Washington SB 6339 (2008)

Provides for address confidentiality of victims of trafficking.

Washington SB 5127 (Chapter 358) (2005)

Improves services to victims of human trafficking by requiring the Director of the Office of Community Development to convene a work group to develop written protocols for service delivery to victims of trafficking. The work group will include other state agencies and will develop protocols for policies and procedures for interagency coordinated operations. A database will be established which is available to all affected agencies, listing services to victims of human trafficking. This workgroup will submit the final written protocols with a report to the legislature and the Governor by January 1, 2006.

Laws that Prohibit Destruction, Concealment, Removal or Possession of Any False Passport, Immigration, or Other Government Document

Arizona SB 1281 (2009) (See Also Penalty Section)

Prohibits destruction of a person's identification, passport, government document, or immigration document.

Hawaii HB 1912 (2008)

Prohibit destruction, concealment, removal or possession of any false passport, immigration, or other government document.

Kansas SB 353 (2010)

Concerns trafficking; relates to coercing employment through force or fraud; concerns peonage, aggravated human trafficking of minors and involuntary servitude; provides for forfeiture; includes knowingly destroying, concealing, removing, confiscating or possessing any actual or purported government identification document of another person; provides for privacy of addresses.

Maryland HB 283 (2010)

This bill adds certain sexual coercive activity to existing human trafficking laws. Prohibits a person from knowingly engaging in a device, scheme, or continuing course of conduct intended to cause another to believe that if the other does not take part in a sexually explicit performance the other or a third person would suffer physical restraint or serious physical harm or from destroying, concealing, removing, confiscating, or possessing an actual or purported passport, immigration document, or government identification document of the other while doing so.

Maryland HB 65 (2010)

Requiring an international marriage broker to provide specified information to a recruit; requiring a client of an international marriage broker to provide specified information to the international marriage broker and to affirm that specified information is accurate and complete; requiring an international marriage broker to conduct a specified criminal history records check; prohibiting an international marriage broker from providing specified information to a specified client.

Maryland SB 542 (2010)

Requires the Department of Labor, Licensing, and Regulation to design a sign that contains specified information regarding the National Human Trafficking Resource Center Hotline; requiring the sign to meet specified requirements and be placed on the Department's website; requiring a lodging establishment to post a specified sign if the lodging establishment is located on property where arrests leading to conviction for prostitution, solicitation of a minor, or human trafficking have occurred.

Michigan HB 5748 (§750.451 et seq.) (2006) (See Also Penalty Section)

Forbids forced labor or services by threatening the destruction of immigration documents, and increases penalties for human trafficking.

North Carolina HB 1896 (2006) (See Also Penalty Section)

Includes in the definition of trafficking, threatening to destroy, conceal, remove, confiscate, or possess any actual or purported passport or other immigration document or any other actual or purported government identification document of another person.

Virginia HB 2016 (2009) (See Also Penalty Section)

Redefines intimidation to include withholding a person's passport or like documents.

Virginia SB 815 and SB 2212 (2007)

Provides that any person knowingly destroys, conceals, removes, confiscates, withholds, or threatens to withhold, or possesses any actual or purported passport or other immigration document, or any other actual or purported government identification document, of another person is guilty of a Class 5 felony.

Laws that Establish Extortion if Threats to Report Immigration Status

Colorado SB 004 and 005 (2006)

Makes threatening the destruction of immigration or work documents or threatening the notification of law enforcement officials of undocumented status in order to force a person into labor or services, with or without compensation, a Class 6 felony.

Virginia SB 291 (2006)

Makes the act of threatening an individual with reporting illegal status to officials for the purposes of extorting money a Class 5 felony.

Miscellaneous

California SB 657 (2010)

This bill would enact the California Transparency in Supply Chains Act of 2010, and would, beginning January 1, 2012, require retail sellers and manufacturers doing business in the state to disclose their efforts to eradicate slavery and human trafficking from their direct supply chains for tangible goods offered for sale, as specified. That provision would not apply to a retail seller or manufacturer having less than $100,000,000 in annual worldwide gross receipts. The bill would also make a specified statement of legislative intent regarding slavery and human trafficking. The bill would also require the Franchise Tax Board to make available to the Attorney General a list of retail sellers and manufacturers required to disclose efforts to eradicate slavery and human trafficking pursuant to that provision, as specified.

California ACR 6 (2011)

This resolution would recognize the month of January as National Slavery and Human Trafficking Prevention Month and Feb. 1, 2011, as California's Free from Slavery Day. The Legislature recognizes the vital role California can play in preventing, and one day ending, modern slavery.

Colorado HB 1326 (§16-22-108) (2007)

Requires those convicted of trafficking in children as defined to register their email address and any online identifier with the state.

Connecticut H 5030 (2010)

Concerns the forfeiture of money and property related to child sexual exploitation and human trafficking, the possession of child pornography and the siting of residential sexual offender treatment facilities.

Illinois HB 1299 (735 ILCS 5/13-225) (2006)

Creates the Predator Accountability Act which establishes a cause of action against a person who: (i) coerced an individual into prostitution; (ii) coerced an individual to remain in prostitution; (iii) used coercion to collect or receive any of an individual's earnings derived from prostitution; or (iv) advertised or published advertisements for purposes of recruitment into prostitution.

Indiana HB 1386 (§11-8-8-5 et seq.) (2007)

Allows those convicted of crimes related to human trafficking to be classified as a sex offender who may be required to register.

Iowa SF 120 (2011)

Adds grounds for which the Board of Educational Examiners is required to disqualify an applicant or to revoke a license; includes enticing a minor and human trafficking; includes crimes committed in another jurisdiction; and relates to any comparable offense that may be prosecuted in federal, military or foreign court.

Louisiana SB 56 (2010)

Provides for the seizure and impoundment of the personal property used in the commission of cyberstalking, human trafficking, trafficking of children for sexual purposes, felony carnal knowledge of a juvenile, indecent behavior with juveniles, pornography involving juveniles, molestation of a juvenile, computer-aided solicitation of a minor, and enticing persons into prostitution; provides for public sale of the property and for exemptions; provides penalty for falsifying information to exempt property.

Maryland HB 1322 (2010)

Requires the Department of Labor, Licensing, and Regulation to design a sign that contains information regarding the National Human Trafficking Resource Center Hotline that meets certain requirements and to be placed on the department's website; requires a lodging establishment to post a certain sign in certain places if certain conditions are met; provides a penalty for the violation of provisions of this act.

Missouri HB 353 (Section 566.200–566.223) (2005)

Addresses human trafficking by establishing requirements for international matchmaking organizations.

North Carolina HB 1403 (2010)

Requires that a DNA sample be taken from any person arrested for committing murder, manslaughter, kidnapping, abduction, human trafficking, burglary, and various sex and stalking offenses including cyberstalking; amends the statutes that provide for a DNA sample upon conviction; provides funding for the DNA database and databank.

Oregon HB 3623 a (2010)

Requires Oregon Liquor Control Commission to include informational materials regarding human trafficking with certain on-premises sales, off-premises sales or brewery-public house licensee renewal notices, if materials are supplied by nonprofit organization; applies to license renewal notices that commission sends before January 1, 2012; declares emergency, effective on passage.

Pennsylvania SR 12 (2011)

A resolution recognizing Jan. 11, 2011, as National Human Trafficking Awareness Day in Pennsylvania.

Rhode Island HB 7027 (2010)

(Resolution) Proclaims the month of January 2010 to be National Slavery and Human Trafficking Prevention Month" in the state of Rhode Island.

Tennessee SB 3267 (2010)

Requires reports of child abuse to include, to the extent known by the reporter, the name, address, telephone number, and age of the child and the person responsible for their care; relates to reports of alleged human trafficking or child pornography and investigation of severe child abuse; requires any school official, personnel, or member of a board of education who is aware of employee misconduct involving child abuse to immediately notify the Department of Children's Services or other specified entities. If the department receives information containing references to alleged human trafficking or child pornography which does or does not result in an investigation by the department, the department shall notify the appropriate law enforcement agency immediately upon receipt of such information.

Texas HR 1578 (2011)

Recognizes April 27, 2011, as Anti-Human Trafficking Day at the State Capitol.

Texas SR 826 (2011)

Recognizes April 27, 2011, as Anti-Human Trafficking Day at the State Capitol.

Texas HB 533 (2009)

Provides that it is not a defense to civil liability for trafficking of persons that a defendant has been acquitted or has not been prosecuted or convicted or has been convicted of a different offense.

Texas SB 11 & SCR 90 (Penal Code § 20A.01) (2007)

Provides additional language to the definition of human trafficking.

Virginia SB 1453 (2011)

Department of Criminal Justice Services; human trafficking. Requires the Department of Criminal Justice Services to, in conjunction with the Office of the Attorney General, advise law enforcement agencies and attorneys for the Commonwealth regarding identification, investigation, and prosecution of human trafficking offenses using the common law and existing Virginia criminal statutes.

Virginia HJR 561 (2010) (Adopted in 2011)

Designates Jan. 11 in 2011 and in each succeeding year as Global Human Trafficking Awareness Day in Virginia. The effort by individuals, businesses, organizations and governing bodies to promote the annual observance of the National Day of Human Trafficking Awareness on January 11 represents one of many examples of the ongoing commitment in the United States to raise awareness of and opposition to human trafficking.

Virginia HB 1113 (2010)

Requires that a vehicle knowingly used by the owner or another with the owner's knowledge during the commission of any felony abduction offense or pandering when the prostitute is a minor shall be seized by the arresting law-enforcement officer and forfeited to the Commonwealth.

Vermont HCR 26 (2011)

Creates National Human Trafficking Awareness Month in Vermont.

Washington HB 1874 (2011)

Permits law enforcement personnel to record a communication with one party's consent if there is probable cause to believe the communication involves commercial sexual abuse of a minor, promotes commercial sexual abuse of a minor, or promotes travel for commercial sexual abuse of a minor; and permits law enforcement personnel to employ a minor in investigating certain sex offenses when the minor's aid is limited to telephonic or electronic communication or when an investigation is authorized by the one-party consent laws. Companion bill Washington SB 5545 (2011).

Washington SR 8605 (2011)

Observes National Slavery and Human Trafficking Prevention month.

Washington SB 6330 (2010)

Permits the placement of human trafficking informational posters in rest areas; provides the posters may be in a variety of languages and include toll-free telephone numbers a person may call for assistance, including the number for national human trafficking resource center and the number for the state Office of Crime Victims Advocacy.

Washington SB 6332 (2010)

Modifies human trafficking provisions relating to the definition of foreign worker, furnishing disclosure statements and informational pamphlets, and liability of an international labor recruitment agency; requires the Department of Labor and Industries to integrate into existing posters and brochures, information on assisting victims of human trafficking.

DISCUSSION QUESTIONS

1. Why is Human Trafficking such a global problem?

2. How can Human Trafficking be a problem in the United States?

Name: Date

You must use this form and turn in the original to the instructor. No other form will be accepted.

CHAPTER ASSIGNMENT

The text discusses the global issue of trafficking in persons (Human Trafficking). Why is modern slavery such an issue. How can human servitude, forced labor, sexual slavery, child labor, exist in large scale in modern day?

Appendix A
GENERAL WEBSITES

Adam Walsh Resource Center (re: Missing and Exploited Children)

http://www.missingkids.org

"The National Center for Missing and Exploited Children® is a non-profit 501(c)(3) corporation whose mission is to help find missing children, reduce child sexual exploitation, and prevent child victimization."

American Bar Association, Center on Children and the Law and Criminal Justice Section, Victim-Witness Project

http://www.americanbar.org/groups/child_law.html

"The Center improves children's lives through advances in law, justice, knowledge, practice and public policy."

Bureau of Justice Statistics

https://www.bjs.gov

BJS's goal is "to collect, analyze, publish, and disseminate information on crime, criminal offenders, victims of crime, and the operation of justice systems at all levels of government."

Center for Disease Control and Prevention

https://www.cdc.gov

"The Centers for Disease Control and Prevention (CDC) serves as the national focus for developing and applying disease prevention and control, environmental health, and health promotion and health education activities designed to improve the health of the people of the United States."

Child Abuse Prevention Network

http://child.cornell.edu

Website for professionals in the field of child abuse and neglect. Provides "tools for all workers to support the identification, investigation, treatment, adjudication, and prevention of child abuse and neglect."

Child Help USA
https://www.childhelp.org

Provides a number of child abuse prevention, intervention, and treatment programs.

Child Welfare Information Gateway
https://www.childwelfare.gov

"Promotes the safety, permanency, and well-being of children, youth, and families by connecting child welfare, adoption, and related professionals as well as the public to information, resources, and tools covering topics on child welfare, child abuse and neglect, out-of-home care, adoption, and more."

Conflict Resource Education Network
http://www.creducation.org

Website for the promotion of conflict resolution education.

Federal Bureau of Investigation
https://www.fbi.gov

Federal law enforcement and investigation agency.

Kempe National Center for Prevention and Treatment of Child
http://www.ucdenver.edu/academics/colleges/medicalschool/departments/pediatrics/subs/can/Pages/ChildAbuse Neglect.aspx

Provides education and research into the treatment and prevention of child abuse and neglect.

Mothers Against Drunk Driving
http://www.madd.org

The "nation's largest nonprofit working to protect families from drunk driving, drugged driving and underage drinking. MADD also supports drunk and drugged driving victims and survivors at no charge."

National Association of Counsel for Children, NAC Child Law
http://www.nacchildlaw.org/

Provides news on child legal issues.

National Center on Elder Abuse
https://ncea.acl.gov

A "national resource center dedicated to the prevention of elder mistreatment."

National Center for Prosecution of Child Abuse
http://www.ndaa.org/ncpca.html

"NCPCA's mission is to reduce the number of children victimized and exploited by assisting prosecutors and allied professionals."

National Center for Victims of Crime

http://www.victimsofcrime.org

"A nonprofit organization that advocates for victims' rights, trains professionals who work with victims," and provides information on victims' issues.

National Coalition Against Domestic Violence

http://www.ncadv.org

Organization that affects public policy on domestic violence by providing programs and education.

National Committee for Prevention of Child Abuse

http://www.preventchildabuse.org

A national organization that provides services and education to prevent child abuse.

National Crime Prevention Council

http://www.ncpc.org

Organization designed to help "people keep themselves, their families, and their communities safe from crime. To achieve this, NCPC produces tools that communities can use to learn crime prevention strategies, engage community members, and coordinate with local agencies."

National Criminal Justice Reference Service Justice Information Center

https://www.ncjrs.org

A "federally funded resource offering justice and drug-related information to support research, policy, and program development worldwide."

National Crime Victim Bar Association

http://www.victimsofcrime.org/our-programs/national-crime-victim-bar-association/

"The nation's first professional association of attorneys and expert witnesses dedicated to helping victims seek justice through the civil system."

National Crime Victim Law Institute(NCVLI) Victim Resource Map

https://law.lclark.edu/centers/national_crime_victim_law_institute/for_victims/self_help/

Large, comprehensive database of victims' resources searchable by location, crime committed, and type of victim.

National Crime Victims Research and Treatment Center

http://academicdepartments.musc.edu/ncvc/

Provides research, education and training, evidence-based mental health treatment, prevention services, collaboration with victim service agencies, and consultation with public policy makers.

National Indian Justice Center

http://www.nijc.org

"Delivers legal education, research, and technical assistance programs which seek to improve the quality of life for Native communities and the administration of justice in Indian country."

National Institute of Mental Health

https://www.nimh.nih.gov/index.shtml

"The National Institute of Mental Health (NIMH) is the lead federal agency for research on mental disorders."

National Organization for Victim Assistance

http://www.trynova.org

Provides educational resources and programs to assist victims of crimes.

National Self-Help Clearinghouse

http://www.selfhelpweb.org

A non-profit that "facilitates access to self-help groups and increase the awareness of the importance of mutual support."

National Victim's Constitutional Amendment Network

http://www.nvcap.org

An organization that advocates for the passage of constitutional amendments for victims' rights.

Office for Victims of Crime (OVC) of the Office for Justice Programs

https://ojp.gov/ovc/

"OVC channels funding for victim compensation and assistance throughout the United States, raises awareness about victims' issues, promotes compliance with victims' rights laws, and provides training and technical assistance and publications and products to victim assistance professionals."

Office of Sex Offender Sentencing, Monitoring, Apprehending, Registering, and Tracking (SMART)

https://smart.gov

SMART "provides jurisdictions with guidance regarding the implementation of the Adam Walsh Act, and provides technical assistance to the states, territories, Indian tribes, local governments, and to public and private organizations. The SMART Office also tracks important legislative and legal developments related to sex offenders and administers grant programs related to the registration, notification, and management of sex offenders."

Parents of Murdered Children

http://www.pomc.com

Provides support and assistance to all the surviving family of homicide victims as well assisting criminal justice professionals who work with the grieving families.

Rape, Abuse, and Incest National Network (RAINN)

https://www.rainn.org

"RAINN is the nation's largest anti-sexual violence organization. RAINN created and operates the National Sexual Assault Hotline. RAINN also carries out programs to prevent sexual violence, help victims."

Sourcebook of Criminal Justice Statistics

http://www.albany.edu/sourcebook

Provides statistics on a wide variety of criminal justice topics.

The Stalking Victim's Sanctuary

http://www.stalkingvictims.com

Provides resources and education for victims of stalking.

Victim-Offender Reconciliation Program Information and Resource Center

http://www.vorp.com

Website providing education on victim-offender mediation programs.

World Society of Victimology

http://www.tilburguniversity.edu/research/institutes-and-research-groups/intervict/

Promotes international evidence-based research on victims and victimology.

Appendix B
VARIOUS VICTIM RESOURCES

Abused Deaf Women's Advocacy Services
http://www.adwas.org/

Information on domestic violence and sexual assault for the deaf community. Downloadable brochures for deaf children and adults on keeping safe and dealing with violence.

Administration for Children and Families, Trafficking Information
http://www.acf.hhs.gov/trafficking/about/factshe ets.html

Information about human trafficking, including services available to victims in English, Polish, Spanish, and Russian.

Boat People SOS, Victims of Exploitation and Trafficking Assistance (VETA)
http://www.bpsos.org

Information on the services offered by the Victims of Exploitation and Trafficking Assistance (VETA) program, including legal representation and case management.

Trafficking Information and Referral Hotline Number

Break the Cycle
http://www.breakthecycle.org/

Information on dating violence and how to get help, including Break the Cycle's program offering legal representation to teen victims.

Bureau of Justice Statistics, U.S. Department of Justice
https://bjs.gov/

Crime and victims statistics, including results from the National Crime Victimization Survey.

Child Welfare Information Gateway

http://www.childwelfare.gov/

Information on prevalence and impact of child maltreatment. Includes state laws relating to child abuse and neglect, child welfare, and adoption.

Childhelp

https://www.childhelp.org/

Information on child abuse, including types of child abuse and signs of abuse. Downloadable brochures and posters. Information for children who are being abused, including how to get help.

Coalition to Abolish Slavery and Trafficking

http://www.castla.org/homepage

Information on trafficking, including the services the coalition offers to victims such as representation in removal proceedings and securing release from detention.

Federal Trade Commission Identity Theft Site

https://www.consumer.ftc.gov/features/feature-0014-identity-theft

Information on preventing, detecting, and responding to identity theft. Downloadable brochures and online identity theft quiz.

Federal Victim Rights' Ombudsman

https://www.justice.gov/usao/resources/crime-victims-rights-ombudsman

Provides victims in federal cases with information on how to file a complaint against an employee of the Department of Justice (includes any attorney, investigator, or law enforcement officer within the department) if they feel their rights have been violated. Information about federal victims' rights. Downloadable complaint forms.

Gift from Within

http://www.giftfromwithin.org/

Information on Post-traumatic Stress Disorder (PTSD), including articles and video reviews. Q & A with PTSD expert. List of international trauma support groups.

Identity Theft Resource Center

http://www.idtheftcenter.org/

Resources for victims of identity theft, including a "Victim Guide 101." Information on how to get connected with a local support advocate.

Internet Crime Complaint Center (IC3)

https://www.ic3.gov/default.aspx

Online mechanism for victims to report Internet crime. IC3 refers complaints to appropriate law enforcement agencies. Frequently asked questions and crime prevention tips.

It Happened to Alexa

http://ithappenedtoalexa.org/

Information for survivors of sexual assault and their support persons. Frequently asked questions. Foundation offers financial assistance to support persons to defray costs of transportation and housing, so the victim's support person can attend criminal justice system proceedings.

List of Toll Free Helpline Numbers, Office of Justice Programs

https://www.ovc.gov/help/tollfree.html

List of toll-free helpline numbers for victims from the Office of Justice Programs, United States Department of Justice.

Love Is Not Abuse

https://www.breakthecycle.org/loveisnotabuse

Information on relationship violence. Downloadable handbooks for parents, women, girls, and boys. Materials available in Spanish. Information on the National Teen Dating Abuse Helpline.

Mothers Against Drunk Driving

http://www.madd.org

Information on the criminal justice system, victims' rights, and victim compensation. Online chats and message boards for victim support.

Search for local assistance by zip code or state. Contact information for MADD's victim assistance program.

National Center for State Courts, Tribal Courts Information

http://www.ncsc.org/Topics/Special-Jurisdiction/Tribal-Courts/Resource-Guide.aspx

Information about tribal courts, tribal court jurisdiction, the Major Crimes Act, judge selection for tribal courts, and tribal code construction. Online directory with links to tribal courts and tribal justice systems.

National Center for Victims of Crime

https://victimsofcrime.org/

Downloadable "GetHelp" bulletins on all types of crime and victimization, victims' rights, compensation, and civil justice, among many others. Toll-free helpline and email address for victims to receive information and referrals to services. Special information for teen victims of crime.

National Center on Elder Abuse

https://ncea.acl.gov/

Information on elder abuse. Frequently asked questions. List of elder abuse laws. Clickable map of resources across the country.

National Clearinghouse on Abuse in Later Life

http://www.ncall.us/

Online directory of services for victims of domestic abuse in later life and their advocates. Downloadable fact sheets. Frequently asked questions.

National Coalition Against Domestic Violence

http://www.ncadv.org/

Information for victims on safety planning, violence at the workplace, internet safety, and identity theft.

National Crime Victim Bar Association

https://victimsofcrime.org/our-programs/national-crime-victim-bar-association/about-us

Information on civil remedies for victims of crime, including how to select an attorney. Downloadable brochure about civil justice for victims. Toll-free number to obtain attorney referrals.

National Crime Victim Law Institute (NCVLI)

http://law.lclark.edu/centers/national_crime_victim_law_institute/

NCVLI assists attorneys who provide direct legal services to victims. Establishes clinics to represent crime victims in criminal courts. Files amicus briefs in trial and appellate courts on the rights of victims. Provides information, resources, and trainings on victims' rights to ensure these rights are enforced in courts.

National Criminal Justice Reference Service

https://www.ncjrs.gov/

Information on all types of crime and victimization. Downloadable publications for victims.

National Domestic Violence Hotline

http://www.thehotline.org/

Information on the services the hotline offers. Resources for victims about abuse, safety planning, and Internet safety. Information for immigrants, teens, family members, and other support persons.

National Organization for Victim Assistance

http://www.trynova.org/

Information on victimization, trauma, and how to find help. Specific information on crime victims with disabilities, elderly victims, and domestic violence. Criminal justice system glossary. Links to national and state victim resources.

National Sexual Violence Resource Center

http://www.nsvrc.org/

Articles and other materials about sexual violence. Links to other victim resources.

National Stalking Resource Center

http://victimsofcrime.org/our-programs/stalking-resource-center

Resources for stalking victims, including materials on safety planning, what to do if you are being stalked, and address confidentiality programs. Downloadable incident and behavior log. Stalking laws and court cases.

Office for Victims of Crime, United States Department of Justice

https://www.ovc.gov/

Online directory of victim services. Links to other resources and victim assistance programs by crime. Resources for international victims, victims of mass terrorism, and trafficking.

Office to Monitor and Combat Trafficking in Persons, United States Department of State

https://www.state.gov/j/tip/

Information on human trafficking, including slave labor and sexual servitude. Materials on identifying and helping trafficking victims.

Online Directory of Crime Victim Services, Office for Victims of Crime

https://ovc.ncjrs.gov/findvictimservices/

Searchable database of non-emergency crime victim services in the United States and abroad. Search by location, type of victimization, service needed, and agency type.

Parents of Murdered Children

http://www.pomc.org/

Resources for families and other survivors of homicide victims.

Information on grief, criminal justice system terminology, victim impact statements, and victim notification. Online support forums for victims.

Post-traumatic Stress Disorder (PTSD) Alliance

http://www.ptsdalliance.org/

Information on post-traumatic stress disorder (PTSD), including symptoms, diagnosis, and treatment options. Downloadable brochures.

Privacy Rights Clearinghouse

https://www.privacyrights.org/

Resources for victims of identity theft. Some fact sheets available in Spanish.

Rape, Abuse, and Incest National Network

https://www.rainn.org/

Online searchable directory of rape crisis centers. Statistics and other information on sexual assault, including post-traumatic stress disorder, depression, and incest.

Safe Horizon

https://www.safehorizon.org/

Information on all types of victimization and the services offered by Safe Horizon.

Social Security Administration Identity Theft Site

https://faq.ssa.gov/link/portal/34011/34019/Article/3792/What-should-I-do-if-I-think-someone-is-using-my-Social-Security-number

Information about what to do if you are a victim of identity theft.

Stalking Behavior Website

http://www.stalkingbehavior.com/

Information on stalking, including how to recognize stalking, cyber-stalking, safety planning, and types of stalkers.

Stalking Victims Sanctuary

http://stalkingvictims.com/

Information about stalking, including recognizing stalking, cyber-stalking, and safety planning. Online discussion boards for victim support.

The Compassionate Friends

https://www.compassionatefriends.org/

Resources for parents, grandparents, and siblings of a child who has died. Brochures for parents, grandparents, teachers, funeral directors, and many others. Local TCF chapter clickable map.

Victim Information and Notification Everyday (VINE)

https://www.vinelink.com/

Provides searchable information on offenders in many states who are currently in custody.

Allows victims to register to receive email notification about a change in an offender's status.

Victims of Crime With Disabilities Resource Guide

https://victimsofcrime.org/library/resource-directory-victims-with-disabilities

Searchable database of materials on victims of crime with disabilities. Online discussion forum.

Voices in Action

https://rvap.uiowa.edu/

Information for survivors of sexual trauma. Downloadable brochures, including a brochure for men. Information on how to pick a therapist.

WiredSafety

http://www.wiredsafety.com/

Information about online safety for parents, educators, librarians, law enforcement, and children and youth. Materials on cell phone safety. Online reporting mechanism for harassment, stalking via the Internet, and cyber-bullying.

Womenslaw.org

http://www.womenslaw.org/

State-by-state domestic violence legal information and resources. Includes information for immigrant victims and victims in the military. Resources for seeking protective orders, safety planning, and Internet safety. List of online chats and message boards for victim support.

Military

Department of Defense Victim and Witness Council
http://vwac.defense.gov/

Information about the victim and witness assistance program. Contact information for Victim and Witness Assistance Points of Contact for each military branch. Online forms for victim notification and compensation. PowerPoint overview of the military justice system.

Sexual Assault Prevention and Response Office (Department of Defense)
http://www.sapr.mil/

Information for victims on reporting options, the military's confidentiality policy, and the investigative process. Frequently asked questions.

Staff Judge Advocate, U.S. Marine Corps
http://www.hqmc.marines.mil/sja//

Fact sheets on the military justice system. Information on military jurisdiction, commander's disciplinary options, trial procedures, and a review of clemency, parole, and pardons, among many other topics.

The Family Advocacy Homepage on Interpersonal Abuse
http://www.militaryonesource.mil/

Information on domestic violence and the military response. How to recognize abuse. Downloadable directory of Family Advocacy Programs.

Alabama

Alabama Attorney General, Office of Victim Assistance
http://www.ago.state.al.us/Page-Victims-Assistance

General information on victims' rights, compensation, pardons and parole, victim notification, and more. Downloadable victim notification form. List of Alabama victim service officers by county. Victim assistance hotline number.

Alabama Board of Pardons and Parole
http://www.pardons.state.al.us/

Information on victims' rights in the pardons/parole process. List of scheduled parole hearings.

Alabama Crime Victim Compensation Program
https://acvcc.alabama.gov/

Victim compensation information. Downloadable victim compensation application form. Online form to check the status of a compensation claim. Information on victims' rights, the trial process, and the corrections process. Frequently asked questions.

Alaska

Alaska Attorney General, Victim Witness Assistance Program

http://www.law.alaska.gov/department/criminal/ victims_assist.html

Information on victims' rights and restitution collection. Links to other Alaskan victim services programs. Frequently asked questions. Includes a "Kids Go to Court" coloring book.

Alaska Crime Victim Compensation Program

http://doa.alaska.gov/vccb/

Victim compensation information.

Downloadable application form. How to appeal a denial of compensation application.

Alaska Department of Corrections, Victim Service Unit

http://www.correct.state.ak.us/probation-parole/victim-service-unit

Information about victim notification and the Victim Information and Notification Everyday (VINE) system. Downloadable notification form. Victim impact statements information and related forms. Links to other Alaskan and national vies. Toll-free number.

Alaska Judicial Council

http://www.ajc.state.ak.us/

Downloadable handbook, in English or Spanish, with information on the criminal justice process, definitions of commonly used terms, victims' rights, and safety planning. Directory of other Alaskan victim resources.

Alaska Office of Victims' Rights

https://ovr.akleg.gov/

Information about victims' rights and the victims' rights enforcement process. How to file a complaint for violation of rights. Downloadable information sheet, "How a typical case is prosecuted in Alaska."

American Samoa

American Samoa Crime Victim Compensation Program

http://dps.hawaii.gov/cvcc/

Contact information for the American Samoa victim compensation program.

Arizona

Arizona Attorney General, Office of Victim Services

https://www.azag.gov/victim-services

Information concerning duties of the office, including victims' rights enforcement and victims' rights training. Downloadable brochures on victims' rights to leave work, restitution, and the criminal appeals process, among others. Contact information for other Arizona victim service programs.

Arizona Crime Victim Compensation Program

http://www.azcjc.gov/ACJC.Web/victim/VictCo mp.aspx

Victim compensation information. Contact information for victim compensation programs by county. Downloadable compensation application.

Arizona Department of Corrections, Office of Victim Services

https://corrections.az.gov/victim-services

Online database to track inmates. Information about post-conviction notification, orders of protection, restitution, and restorative justice.

Arizona Supreme Court, Public Court Case Information

https://apps.supremecourt.az.gov/publicaccess/

Searchable database provides information about court cases from 142 of 180 Arizona courts (list of courts posted on website). Email notification for changes to cases in Maricopa County.

Arizona Victims' Rights Enforcement Officer

https://www.azag.gov/victim-services/victims-rights-enforcement-officer

Information about Arizona's Victims' Rights Enforcement Officer which receives and investigates complaints of crime victims concerning denial of victim's rights. Online complaint form.

Arizona Voice for Victims

http://www.voiceforvictims.org/

Victims' rights information and overview of the criminal justice system. Downloadable forms including Request for Notice of Conditions of Release and Motion To Allow Support Person for Victim During Trial Testimony. Contact information for other Arizona victim resources. Information on the Crime Victims' Legal Assistance Project.

Arkansas

Arkansas Attorney General, Crime Victim Information

http://arkansasag.gov/resources/victim-advocacy/

Victim compensation information. Downloadable application forms. Information about stalking, elder abuse, and missing children.

Arkansas Crime Information Center, Victim's Information

http://www.acic.org/

Downloadable guide to the justice system in Arkansas. Clemency and parole information. Contact information for other Arkansas and national victim resources.

Arkansas Crime Victim Compensation Program

http://arkansasag.gov/public-safety/resources/column-one/crime-victim-reparations/

Victim compensation information. Downloadable compensation claim form.

Arkansas Department of Corrections, Victim Notification Program

http://adc.arkansas.gov/victim-services

Information about the state's Victim Information and Notification Everyday (VINE) system, including how to register.

California

California Attorney General, Office of Victim Services

https://oag.ca.gov/victimservices

Overview of California's Office of Victim Services. Information on victims' rights. Downloadable form to request notification of criminal appeals. Frequently asked questions and informational brochures. Information about California and national victim resources.

California Crime Victim Compensation Program

http://vcgcb.ca.gov/victims/

Victim compensation information. Downloadable victim compensation form. Spanish forms. Brochure on victim restitution. Directory of victim witness assistance programs across the state.

California Department of Corrections, Office of Victim and Survivor Services

http://www.cdcr.ca.gov/victim_services/contact_ovsrs.html

Information about victims' rights and the correctional system, parole board hearings, and cases in which the offender is a juvenile. Downloadable victim notification form. Restitution information. Links to additional resources.

California Victims of Crime Resource Center

http://1800victims.org/

Overview of the Center and toll-free line for resources and referrals for victims. Links to California and national victim resources.

Colorado

Colorado Crime Victim Compensation Program

http://dcj.ovp.state.co.us/home/victims-compensation

Victim compensation information. Downloadable compensation claim form.

Colorado Department of Corrections, Victim Services

https://www.colorado.gov/pacific/cdoc/victim-services

Information on victim services available and victims' rights generally. Online victim notification request form. Online victim impact form. Information on other Colorado resources. Frequently asked questions.

Colorado Department of Public Safety, Crime Victim Services Advisory Board

https://sites.google.com/a/state.co.us/dcj-victim-program/home/additional-information/crime-victims-services-advisory-board

Information on Colorado's Victims' Rights Coordinating Committee which investigates victims' rights violations complaints. Downloadable complaint form.

Colorado Department of Public Safety, Office for Victims Programs

http://dcj.ovp.state.co.us/

Information on victims' rights in English and Spanish. Victim compensation information and downloadable compensation claim form. Links to other Colorado and national victim resources.

Colorado Organization for Victim Assistance

http://www.coloradocrimevictims.org/

Online directory of victim services in Colorado. Other information for victims and advocates.

Connecticut

Connecticut Crime Victim Compensation Program

https://www.jud.ct.gov/crimevictim/compensation.htm

Victim compensation information. Downloadable compensation application in English and Spanish.

Connecticut Department of Corrections, Victim Services Unit

http://www.ct.gov/doc/cwp/view.asp?a=1503& Q=483926&docNav

Downloadable request for victim notification. Victim Services contact information.

Connecticut Judicial Branch, Office of Victim Services

https://www.jud.ct.gov/crimevictim/

Victims' rights information in English and Spanish. Victim compensation and restitution information. Frequently asked questions Downloadable notification registration form. List of court-based advocates across the state. Links to other Connecticut and national victim resources.

Connecticut Office of the Victim Advocate

http://www.ct.gov/ova/site/default.asp

Information on the duties of the office, including monitoring the treatment of victims in the criminal justice system and receiving and investigating crime victim complaints of mistreatment by state agency or other entity providing services to victims. Summary of victims' rights. Contact information for other state and national victim resources.

Delaware

Delaware Attorney General, Victim Information

http://www.attorneygeneral.delaware.gov/VCAP/

Information about the criminal justice process and victims' rights. Telephone list for Delaware victim service agencies and related resources. Frequently asked questions.

Delaware Crime Victim Compensation Program

http://www.attorneygeneral.delaware.gov/vcap/compensation.shtml

Victim compensation information and contact numbers for staff of the program.

Delaware Department of Corrections, Victim Services Unit

http://www.doc.delaware.gov/victimServices.shtml

Information on the services offered by the Unit. Frequently asked questions.

Delaware State Police, Victim Services Section

http://dsp.delaware.gov/victim_services.shtml

Information about the Victim Services Section of the Delaware State Police and its 24-hour hotline. Contact numbers for other Delaware victim service resources.

District of Columbia

District of Columbia Crime Victim Compensation Program

http://www.dccourts.gov/internet/superior/crime victim/main.jsf

Victim compensation information and downloadable application form.

District of Columbia Mayor's Office, Office of Victim Services

http://ovsjg.dc.gov/

Victim compensation and notification information. Frequently asked questions. List of D.C. and national victim resources.

District of Columbia Metropolitan Police Department, Victim Assistance Unit

https://mpdc.dc.gov/page/victim-assistance

Information about victims' rights and compensation. Links and numbers for other D.C. and national resources for victims.

Florida

Florida Attorney General, Division of Victim Services

http://myfloridalegal.com/victims

Information on victims' rights. Victim compensation information and downloadable compensation application. Clickable map directory of Florida victim services.

Florida Crime Victim Compensation Information

http://myfloridalegal.com/pages.nsf/main/8DE75D8DEA1F3B2285256CFD00744575?OpenDocument

Downloadable victim compensation application form in English, Spanish, and Creole. Brochure on victim compensation.

Florida Department of Corrections, Victim Assistance Office

http://www.dc.state.fl.us/oth/victasst

Information for victims about what to expect after sentencing. Online victim notification request form. Online Inmate Information Search. Frequently asked questions. Additional Florida and national resources for victims.

Georgia

Georgia Attorney General, Crime Victim Information

http://law.ga.gov/crime-crime-victims

Information on victim notification. Downloadable victim notification form.

Georgia Board of Pardons and Parole, Office of Victim Services

https://pap.georgia.gov/georgia-office-victim-services

Information on victims' rights in the parole process. Downloadable victim notification form and online change of address form. Online victim impact form. Other Georgia victim services links.

Georgia Crime Victim Assistance Helpline

http://crimevictimcompensation.com/

The Helpline, available twenty-four hours a day, seven days a week, assists callers with finding resources as well as information about the Georgia Crime Victim Assistance Compensation Program.

Georgia Crime Victim Compensation Program

https://cjcc.georgia.gov/victims-compensation

Victim compensation information. Downloadable victim compensation application form.

Prosecuting Attorneys' Council of Georgia

http://www.pacga.org/site/area/32

Downloadable Georgia victim services directory as well as other victims' resources.

Guam

Guam Crime Victim Compensation Program

https://ovc.ncjrs.gov/ResourceByState.aspx?stat e=gu#tabs2

Contact information for Guam victim compensation program.

Guam Police Department, Victim Assistance Unit

http://guamservices.org/organizations_detail/?organizations_id=221

Information on family violence and the duties of a peace officer. Phone numbers for local victim resources. Frequently asked questions.

Hawaii

Hawaii Crime Victim Compensation Program

http://dps.hawaii.gov/cvcc/

Information about crime victim compensation. Downloadable compensation application form. Frequently asked questions. Phone numbers for numerous other Hawaii service providers.

Hawaii State Judiciary, First Judicial Circuit, Adult Client Services

http://www.courts.state.hi.us/general_information/contact/oahu

Information on victims' rights, including the right to restitution, notification, and compensation, and the right to give a victim impact statement. List of phone numbers for other Hawaii services for victims.

Hawaii United States Attorney, Victim Witness Assistance Program

https://www.justice.gov/usao-hi/victim-witness-assistance-program

Information on victims' rights, submitting a Crime Victims' Rights Act Complaint Form, victim notification, steps in a criminal prosecution, and preparing to testify. Links to Hawaiian and national victim resources.

Idaho

Idaho Attorney General, Manual on the Rights of Victims of Crime

http://www.ag.idaho.gov/publications/victims/VictimsRights.pdf

Manual describes the rights of crime victims in the state of Idaho.

Idaho Crime Victim Compensation Program

https://crimevictimcomp.idaho.gov/

Victim compensation information. Downloadable compensation application form and instructions.

Idaho Department of Corrections, Victim Services

https://www.idoc.idaho.gov/content/prisons/victim_services

Information about the Victim Information and Notification Everyday (VINE) system. Link to online registration for VINE.

Illinois

Illinois Attorney General, Crime Victim Services Division

http://ag.state.il.us/victims/index.html

Information on the services offered by the division. Downloadable brochure about registering for the state's Automated Victim Notification System. Toll-free number to provide victims with referrals for service. Numerous downloadable brochures on topics such as compensation for funeral providers and hospitals, post-traumatic stress disorder, and victim impact statements.

Illinois Crime Victim Compensation Program

http://www.ag.state.il.us/victims/cvc.html

Victim compensation information. Downloadable compensation application form.

Illinois Department of Corrections, Victims Services

https://www.illinois.gov/idoc/programs/pages/victimservices.aspx

Information on the services of the Victims Services Unit. Recent news relating to victim services in Illinois. Toll-free number.

Illinois Domestic Violence and Sexual Assault Directory

http://www.ag.state.il.us/women/dvsadir.html

Database of agencies and centers that provide assistance to victims of domestic violence and sexual assault. Can be downloaded or printed.

Indiana

Indiana Attorney General, Victim Assistance Division

http://www.in.gov/attorneygeneral/2340.htm

Information about victim notification, the appeals process and victims' rights, and the state's Address Confidentiality Program.

Indiana Crime Victim Compensation Program

http://www.in.gov/cji/2333.htm

Victim compensation information. Downloadable application form in English and Spanish.

Indiana Department of Corrections, Victim Witness Service Program

http://www.in.gov/idoc/2313.htm

Downloadable victim notification form. Information on Parole Board hearings. Information on "wrap-around services" for victim safety after offender release. Link to the Offender Public Information Search website.

Iowa

Iowa Attorney General, Crime Victim Assistance Division
https://www.iowaattorneygeneral.gov/for-crime-victims/victim-services-support-program/
Information on the services the division offers. Information on crime victim compensation.

Iowa Crime Victim Compensation Program
https://www.iowaattorneygeneral.gov/for-crime-victims/crime-victim-compensation-program/
Information on crime victim compensation. Downloadable compensation application.

Iowa Department of Corrections, Victim Programs
http://www.doc.state.ia.us/VictimPrograms
Information on the Victim and Restorative Justice Programs, restitution, victim notification, victim impact statements. List of common terms relating to the criminal justice system. Criminal justice system flowchart. Frequently asked questions. Offender information look-up. Links to more resources.

Kansas

Kansas Attorney General, Crime Victims' Rights Office
http://ag.ks.gov/victim-services
Information on the services provided by the office.

Kansas Crime Victim Compensation Program
https://ag.ks.gov/victim-services/victim-compensation
Victim compensation information. Downloadable compensation application form and eligibility requirements brochure.

Kansas Department of Corrections, Victim Witness Notification
https://www.doc.ks.gov/victim-services
Information on notification. Information on parole and public comment periods. Definition of commonly used terms in the correctional system. Link to secure web page for victims to obtain information specific to their case.

Kentucky

Kentucky Attorney General, Office of Victim Advocacy
http://ag.ky.gov/family/victims/Pages/default.as px
Information on the services offered. Brochures on victim impact statements and specific information about domestic violence. Link to information on the state victim notification system. Links to Kentucky and national victim service providers. Toll-free victim hotline.

Kentucky Crime Victim Compensation Program, Kentucky Claims Commission

http://cvcb.ky.gov/Pages/default.aspx

Victim compensation information. Frequently asked questions. Downloadable compensation application form.

Kentucky Department of Corrections, Office of Victim Services

http://corrections.ky.gov/victimservices/Pages/OfficeofVictimServices.aspx

Information on the services of the Office and the state's victim notification system (VINE).

Kentucky Victim Notification System

http://corrections.ky.gov/victimservices/Pages/VINE.aspx

Information on the state's victim notification system. Frequently asked questions, including how to register to receive notification.

Louisiana

Louisiana Attorney General, Victims' Rights Information

http://www.ag.state.la.us/Article.aspx?articleID=30&catID=0

Information on victims' rights under Louisiana law.

Louisiana Crime Victim Reparations Program

http://www.lcle.state.la.us/programs/cvr.asp

Crime victim reparations (compensation) information. Frequently asked questions. Downloadable application form. Downloadable statewide victim services directory.

Louisiana Department of Public Safety and Corrections, Crime Victims Services Bureau

http://www.doc.louisiana.gov/victim-services/

Information on the Bureau's services. Information on victim notification and downloadable registration form. Information on probation and parole and victim offender dialogue.

Louisiana Victims and Citizens Against Crime

http://louisiana.gov/

General information for victims of crime. Contact information for victim/witness coordinators across the state.

Maine

Maine Attorney General, Crime and Victims' Info

http://www.maine.gov/ag/crime/victims_compensation/detailed_program_description.shtml

Information on criminal justice system and frequently asked questions for homicide survivors and victims of sexual assault and domestic abuse. Information about victim compensation, including eligibility checklist and downloadable application forms. Links to Maine service providers and national resources.

Maine Crime Victim Compensation Program

http://www.maine.gov/ag/crime/victims_compensation/

Victim compensation information. Online eligibility checklist and downloadable application form.

Maine Department of Corrections, Victim Services

http://www.maine.gov/corrections/VictimServices/

Information on victims' rights, including restitution and notification. Online registration form for victim notification program.

Maryland

Maryland Attorney General, Victim Services Division

http://www.marylandattorneygeneral.gov/Pages/VictimServ/default.aspx

Information on the services provided by the office. Links to other victim services in the state.

Maryland Crime Victim Compensation Program

Information on victim compensation. Downloadable compensation application.

Maryland Crime Victims Resource Center

https://www.mdcrimevictims.org/

Information about victims' rights, including notification and restitution. Flowcharts describing the criminal and juvenile justice system process. Links to Maryland and national resources. Information on victims' rights compliance.

Maryland Crime Victims' Rights Compliance Initiative

http://goccp.maryland.gov/victims/rights-resources/compliance-initiative/

Information on Maryland's Compliance Initiative which works to ensure fair treatment of victims by the criminal justice system. Toll-free compliance line through which victims can make complaints and get referrals.

Maryland Department of Public Safety and Correctional Services, Victim Services

http://www.dpscs.state.md.us/victimservs/

Information on the services the DPSCS offers. Information on victims' rights and parole and probation. Downloadable flow chart describing victims' rights in the criminal justice system. Links to compensation division and other state and national resources. Link to victim notification program (VINELink), http://www.dpscs.state.md.us/victimservs/comm itment/main_pages/vs-vine.shtml.

Massachusetts

Massachusetts Crime Victim Compensation Program

http://www.mass.gov/ago/public-safety/resources-for-victims/victims-of-violent-crime/victim-compensation.html

Victim compensation information and downloadable application form in English and Spanish. Phone numbers for victim witness programs across the state and other victim resources.

Massachusetts Department of Corrections

http://www.mass.gov/eopss/agencies/doc/

Click on "Victim Services Unit" (no direct link exists). Frequently asked questions. Information about victim notification and certification to receive notification. Contact information for other Massachusetts and national resources.

Massachusetts Office for Victim Assistance

http://www.mass.gov/mova/

Information on local victim services for victims of all types of crimes. Safety planning information and court advocacy for domestic abuse survivors. Information on MOVAs victims' rights law project.

Victims' Rights Law Center

https://www.victimrights.org/

Information on the center's services, including free legal help for sexual assault victims in matters relating to privacy problems, education problems, immigration problems, or employment problems as a result of the crime. Resources for pro bono attorneys. Information on victim compensation.

Michigan

Michigan Department of Health and Human Services, Crime Victim Services

http://www.michigan.gov/mdhhs/0,5885,7-339-71548_54783_54853-14162--,00.html

Information on victims' rights, including victim notification. Compensation information and downloadable application.

Michigan Prosecuting Attorneys Council, Victims' Rights Information

https://www.michiganprosecutor.org/index.php? home=vr

Information on victims' rights. Summary of how a case progresses through the criminal justice system. Frequently asked questions. Commonly used terms defined. Information on victim compensation. Contact information for Victim Assistance Coordinators across the state. Links to Michigan and national resources.

Michigan Victim Alliance

https://law.lclark.edu/live/news/7461-michigan-victim-alliance

Information on the services the alliance offers. Links to helpful resources.

Minnesota

Minnesota Center for Crime Victim Services

https://dps.mn.gov/divisions/ojp/help-for-crime-victims/Pages/default.aspx

Information on various resources for crime victims with downloadable brochures.

Minnesota Crime Victim Reparations Program

https://dps.mn.gov/divisions/ojp/help-for-crime-victims/Pages/crime-victims-reparations.aspx

Victim reparations (compensation) information. Downloadable application form in English, Spanish, and Somali.

Minnesota Office of Justice Programs, Crime Victim Justice Unit

https://dps.mn.gov/divisions/ojp/help-for-crime-victims/Pages/default.aspx

Information on the Crime Victim Justice Unit's mission to ensure compliance with victims' rights laws. How to make a complaint for a victims' rights violation. Downloadable complaint forms.

Mississippi

Mississippi Attorney General, Victim Assistance

http://www.ago.state.ms.us/divisions/victim-assistance/

Information on victims' rights and the services offered by the office. Information on victim compensation and a "victim assistance fund" for crime scene cleanup and court-related travel. Downloadable request form for exercise of victims' rights. Checklist for victims' rights when working with the media.

Mississippi Crime Victim Compensation Program

http://www.ago.state.ms.us/divisions/victim-compensation/

Information on victim compensation. Frequently asked questions. Downloadable compensation application form.

Mississippi Department of Corrections, Division of Victim Services

http://www.mdoc.ms.gov/Victim-Services/Pages/Division-of-Victim-Services.aspx

Victim notification information and online request form. Criminal justice system handbook for victims.

Missouri

Missouri Attorney General, Victim Information

https://ago.mo.gov/divisions/public-safety/crime-victims

Information on crime victims' rights. Online request form for victim notification of criminal appellate proceedings. Links to state and national organizations that assist crime victims. List of victim service providers and victim witness advocates across the state. Downloadable information booklet on the criminal justice system process.

Missouri Crime Victim Compensation Program

http://dps.mo.gov/dir/programs/cvc/

Victim compensation information. Downloadable application form and online eligibility checklist in English and Spanish.

Missouri Department of Corrections, Office of Victim Services

http://doc.mo.gov/OD/DD/OVS.php

Downloadable victim notification form. Frequently asked questions. Information about parole hearings.

Missouri Department of Public Safety, Crime Victims Services Unit

https://dps.mo.gov/dir/programs/cvsu/

How to file a victims' rights violation complaint. Information on the Missouri Victim Automated Notification System. Clickable map of victim service providers by county.

Missouri Victim Assistance Network

http://www.movanet.org/

Glossary of criminal justice terms and information on the criminal justice process in Missouri. List of state and county prosecutor-based victim advocates. Victim services listed by county and by topic. State and national toll-free help numbers.

Montana

Montana Crime Victim Compensation Program

https://dojmt.gov/victims/crime-victim-compensation/

Victim compensation information, including eligibility requirements and how to file a claim.

Montana Department of Corrections, Victim Information

https://cor.mt.gov/Victims

Information on victim notification and downloadable forms to register. Contact information for victim information officers at each Montana correctional facility. Information on the victim offender dialogue program.

Montana Department of Justice, Office of Victim Services

https://dojmt.gov/victims/

Information on the services the office provides. Specific information on domestic violence, identity theft, rape exam payments, and restorative justice. List of crime victim services by city. Many downloadable resource documents, including booklets on victims' rights and the criminal justice system.

Nebraska

Nebraska Commission on Law Enforcement and Criminal Justice, Crime Victim Services

https://ncc.nebraska.gov/crime-victim-services

Information on the state victim notification system (Victim Information and Notification Everyday/ VINE). Information on victim compensation (reparations). Downloadable guide to the criminal justice system. Frequently asked questions.

Nebraska Crime Victim Reparations Program

https://ncc.nebraska.gov/crime-victims-reparations

Victim reparations information. Downloadable compensation claim form.

Nebraska Department of Corrections, Victim Assistance Program

http://www.corrections.nebraska.gov/victim.html

Links to each correctional facility's victim assistant representatives. Information on VINE and how to register. Links to other national resources. Frequently asked questions.

Nevada

Nevada Board of Parole Commissioners

http://parole.nv.gov/

Information on victims' rights and the parole process, including the right to notification of parole hearings. Downloadable notification registration form. Downloadable guide to parole hearings.

Nevada Crime Victim Compensation Program

http://voc.nv.gov/VOC/VOC_Home/

Victim compensation information, including frequently asked questions.

Nevada Department of Corrections, Victim Services Unit

http://doc.nv.gov/Victims/Contact/

Information on the services the unit offers. Downloadable victim notification registration forms. Information on the state's Confidential Address Program.

New Hampshire

New Hampshire Attorney General, State Office of Victim/Witness Assistance

http://www.doj.nh.gov/criminal/victim-assistance/

Office mainly provides information and support for homicide survivors. Web site contains downloadable guides on the New Hampshire criminal justice system and victims' right to give an impact statement. Contact information for victim witness assistance programs and domestic and sexual assault service providers across the state. Information on the state's Address Confidentiality Program.

New Hampshire Department of Corrections, Victim Services

https://www.nh.gov/nhdoc/divisions/victim/

Information on probation and parole, notification, protection from intimidation and harassment, and restitution, among others. List of victim services liaisons in the state's correctional facilities.

New Hampshire Joan Ellis Victim Assistance Network

http://www.victimsinc.org/

Information on the services of the network, including trauma intervention, court advocacy, and a program for kids and teens, "Grieving Assistance Program for Students."

New Hampshire Victim Compensation Program

http://www.doj.nh.gov/grants-management/victims-compensation-program/

Victim compensation information. Downloadable application form and compensation brochure.

New Hampshire Victim Services Directory

https://cola.unh.edu/sites/cola.unh.edu/files/departments/JusticeWorks/pdf/April20ll20Version.pdf

Listing of victim services and other related resources across the state of New Hampshire.

New Jersey

New Jersey Crime Victim Compensation Program

http://www.nj.gov/oag/njvictims/index.html

Information on victim compensation, including frequently asked questions. Downloadable compensation application form. Website also includes lists of rape crisis centers, domestic violence shelters, and victim witness offices across the state.

New Jersey Crime Victim Law Center

http://www.njcvlc.org/

Information on victims' rights and the services the NJCVLC offers, including pro bono legal assistance to victims.

New Jersey Department of Corrections, Office of Victim Services

http://www.nj.gov/corrections/pdf/OVS/ovs_brochure.PDF

Frequently asked questions. Information on other victim resources in the state. Offender status search web page.

New Jersey Office of the Attorney General, Office of Victim Witness Advocacy

http://www.njvw.org/

Information on the services the office offers, including court accompaniment and counseling and support services. Information on the state's victim notification system, including how to register. Downloadable guide to the criminal justice system. Links to other state victim services and resources. Lists of victim witness programs throughout the state.

New Jersey Parole Board

http://www.nj.gov/parole/

Information on the state victim notification system (VINELink). Online registration to receive notice of parole board hearings.

New Mexico

New Mexico Attorney General, Victims Services Advocate

http://www.nmag.gov/victim-services.aspx

Information on victims' rights and the services available through the Victim Services Advocate. Website also contains information on child sexual abuse and Internet exploitation of children.

New Mexico Crime Victim Reparations Program

http://www.cvrc.state.nm.us/

Victim reparations (compensation) information. Downloadable application in English and Spanish.

New Mexico Department of Corrections, Victim Services Program

http://cd.nm.gov/ocs/vs.html

Information on the services of the program, including a toll-free victim assistance number. Frequently asked questions.

New Mexico Victims' Rights Project

http://www.victimsrightsnm.org/

Information on victims' rights and pro bono services offered, including representation at court hearings, assistance with victim impact statements, filing for compensation, and victims' rights brochure. Contact information for other victim resources by county.

New York

New York Attorney General, Crime and Crime Victims

https://ovs.ny.gov/help-crime-victims

Website posts the state's toll-free victim helpline number and other helpful information.

New York Crime Victim Compensation Program

https://www.ovs.ny.gov/

Victim compensation information. Downloadable application in English and Spanish. Listing by county of victim witness programs across the state. Downloadable restitution brochure.

New York State Division of Parole, Victim Impact Unit

http://www.doccs.ny.gov/VictimSvc/victimimpa ct.html

Information on victim impact at parole proceedings and suggested topics for victim impact statements. Downloadable registration form, or online registration for the state victim notification system (VINE).

New York State Office of Victim Services

https://www.ovs.ny.gov/

Information on the state victim notification system (VINE). Offender status search available.

North Carolina

North Carolina Attorney General, Victims and Citizens Services

http://www.nc-van.org/directory/wake/VictimandCitizenServic esNCAttorneyGeneralsOffice.html

Information on victims' rights, the appeals process, and the state's Address Confidentiality Program. Frequently asked questions. Links to other victim resources across the state.

North Carolina Crime Victim Compensation Program

http://www.ncdps.gov/DPS-Services/Victim-Services/Crime-Victim-Compensation

Victim compensation information. Downloadable compensation application.

North Carolina Department of Corrections, Office of Victim Services

https://www.ncdps.gov/DPS-Services/Victim-Services

Information about victim notification, victim input into parole or post-release supervision. Downloadable victim notification request form. Online offender look-up.

North Carolina Statewide Automated Victim Assistance and Notification (SAVAN)

https://www.ncdps.gov/DPS-Services/Victim-Services/Statewide-Automated-Victim-Assistance-and-Notification-SAVAN

Information on the Statewide Automated Victim Assistance and Notification (SAVAN). Online registration.

North Carolina Victim Assistance Network

http://www.nc-van.org/

Clickable map of victim services across the state. Link to online offender search and victim compensation program website.

North Dakota

North Dakota Crime Victim Compensation Program

https://www.nd.gov/docr/programs/victims/vicc omp.html

Victim compensation information, including frequently asked questions.

North Dakota Crime Victim and Witness Assistance Association

http://ndvaa.org/about-us.html

Victims' rights and compensation information. Contact information for Victim and Witness Assistance programs across the state. Links to state and national victim resources.

North Dakota Department of Corrections, Victim Services Program

https://www.nd.gov/docr/programs/victims.html

Victims' rights after sentencing and victim notification information. Downloadable notification registration form.

Northern Mariana Islands

Northern Mariana Islands Crime Victim Compensation Program

https://victimsofcrime.org/our-programs/stalking-resource-center/help-for-victims/state-information/northern-mariana-islands

Contact information for the Northern Mariana victim compensation program.

Ohio

Ohio Attorney General, Victim Services Program

http://www.ohioattorneygeneral.gov/About-AG/Service-Divisions/Crime-Victim-Services

Information on victim notification and victim compensation. Online directory of victim services across the state. Materials on the Identity Theft Verification PASSPORT Program.

Ohio Crime Victim Compensation Program

http://www.ohioattorneygeneral.gov/VictimsCo mpensation.aspx

Victim compensation information. Online application and downloadable application form in English and Spanish. Online compensation claim status check.

Ohio Department of Rehabilitation and Correction, Office of Victim Services

http://www.drc.ohio.gov/victim-services

Information on the services the office provides. Downloadable registration form for victim notification. List of victim coordinators in each correctional facility. Information on parole.

Online offender status search.

Ohio Victim Witness Association

http://www.ovwa.org/

Victims' rights information, including downloadable brochure on Ohio's victims' rights laws.

Oklahoma

Oklahoma Attorney General, Victim Services Unit

https://www.oag.ok.gov/oagweb.nsf/vservices.ht ml

Information on the services the unit offers, including "Safeline," a toll free, V/TDD accessible 24-hour hotline for survivors of domestic violence, sexual assault, or stalking.

Oklahoma Crime Victim Compensation Program

https://www.ok.gov/dac/Victims/Victims_Compensation_Program/

Victim compensation information and downloadable application form in English and Spanish. Online compensation claim status lookup.

Oklahoma Department of Corrections, Victim Services

https://www.ok.gov/doc/Organization/Communications/Victim_Services/

Information on the services offered by the department, including victim notification. Downloadable notification form. Pardon and parole information.

Oregon Attorney General, Crime Victims' Assistance Section

http://www.doj.state.or.us/victims/Pages/index.aspx

Information on victim compensation and Victim Information and Notification Everyday (VINE). Victim services directory and directory of all the certified county and city victim/witness assistance programs located throughout Oregon.

Oregon Crime Victim Compensation Program

http://www.doj.state.or.us/victims/compensation.shtml

Information on victim compensation. Downloadable compensation application form.

Oregon Department of Corrections, VINE Information

http://www.doj.state.or.us/victims/pages/vine.aspx

Victim Information and Notification Everyday (VINE) information and link to register.

Pennsylvania

Pennsylvania Crime Victim Compensation Program

http://www.pccd.pa.gov/Victim-Services/Pages/Victims-Compensation-Assistance-Program-(VCAP).aspx

Information on victim compensation. Downloadable compensation claim form. Online claim status check. Downloadable handbook of victim service referrals arranged by county.

Pennsylvania Office of the Victim Advocate

http://www.ova.pa.gov/Pages/default.aspx

Information about victims' rights, including the right to notification, the right to restitution, and the right to give input. Map of victim services across the state. Information about the Address Confidentiality Program.

Puerto Rico

Puerto Rico Crime Victim Compensation Program
https://www.justice.gov/usao-pr/victim-witness-assistance
Information on Puerto Rico's victim compensation program in Spanish

Rhode Island

Rhode Island Attorney General, Victim Services Team
http://www.riag.ri.gov/CriminalUnit/VictimServicesUnit.php
Description of the services the Victim Services Team offers.

Rhode Island Crime Victim Compensation Program
http://www.treasury.ri.gov/treasury-divisions/crime-victim-compensation-program/
Victim compensation information. Downloadable compensation application in English and Spanish.

Rhode Island Department of Corrections, Office of Victim Services
http://www.doc.ri.gov/victims/index.php
Information about the state's notification system (Victim Information and Notification Everyday/VINE), including how to register.

Rhode Island Parole Board, Victim Information
http://www.paroleboard.ri.gov/parole/
Information on the parole process and victim input into parole hearings.

South Carolina

South Carolina Attorney General, Victim Assistance
http://www.scag.gov/victim-assistance
Information on the criminal justice process. List of other resources for victim assistance.

South Carolina Crime Victim Compensation Program
http://sova.sc.gov/sova.html
Information about victim compensation. Downloadable application. Frequently asked questions.

Crime Victim Ombudsman
http://cvo.sc.gov/
Information on South Carolina's Crime Victim Ombudsman which reviews and attempts to resolve victim complaints against the criminal or juvenile justice systems or victim assistance programs. Downloadable complaint form.

South Carolina Department of Probation, Parole and Pardons, Victim Services

https://www.dppps.sc.gov/Victim-Services

Online registration for victim notification of hearings. Information on probation, parole and pardons, restitution, and submitting a videotaped statement to the parole board. List of contact information for victim services coordinators in several counties. Online offender search.

South Carolina State Office of Victim Assistance

http://sova.sc.gov/

Information on victims' rights and victim compensation. Links to other state and national victim resources.

South Carolina Victim Assistance Network

http://www.scvan.org/

Information on the South Carolina Victim Assistance Network's crime victim legal network which provides free legal representation to victims in asserting their constitutional rights. Information on specific crimes and subjects such as restitution. Links to state, national, and other resources for victims.

South Dakota Crime Victim Compensation Program

https://dss.sd.gov/keyresources/victimservices/

Victim compensation information. Downloadable application form. Frequently asked questions.

South Dakota Department of Corrections, Victim Information

https://doc.sd.gov/about/victimserv/

Information about victims' rights. Downloadable victim notification request form.

South Dakota Division of Criminal Investigation, Crime Victim Services

http://atg.sd.gov/victim/crimevictimservices/default.aspx

Information on victims' rights and the impact of crime.

Tennessee

Tennessee Attorney General, Victim Information Services

https://www.tn.gov/attorneygeneral/section/victims

Information about victims' rights. Downloadable victim notification form. Links to state and national victim resources.

Tennessee Crime Victim Compensation Program

http://treasury.tn.gov/injury/

Information on victim compensation. Downloadable application forms. Frequently asked questions.

Tennessee Department of Correction, Victim Information and Services

https://www.tn.gov/correction/topic/tdoc-victim-services1

Information about the state's notification system, Victim Offender Information Caller Emissary, or VOICE hotline. Downloadable registration form. Felony Offender Information Lookup (FOIL) online. What to expect at a parole hearing brochure.

Tennessee District Attorneys General Conference, Victim Witness Handbook

https://www.justice.gov/usao-wdtn/victim-witness-program/handbook

Information about the criminal justice system, including "Misdemeanors & Felonies," "What Happens After The Trial," and "Length of Prison Terms in Tennessee."

Texas

Texas Attorney General, Crime Victim Services

https://www.texasattorneygeneral.gov/cvs/crime-victim-services-assisting-victims-of-violent-crime

Information on statewide victim notification system, protective orders, victims' rights, and victim compensation. Downloadable compensation forms. Links to sexual assault services programs.

Texas Crime Victim Compensation Program

https://texasattorneygeneral.gov/cvs/crime-victims-compensation

Victim compensation information, including relocation assistance for victims of family and sexual violence and travel reimbursement. Downloadable application form.

Texas Department of Criminal Justice, Victim Services Division

http://www.tdcj.state.tx.us/divisions/vs/

Information on the services of the division, including a toll-free victim referral line. Information on victim notification and how to register. Frequently asked questions. Statewide and national resource directory. Numerous brochures on victim-related topics.

Utah

Utah Attorney General, Victim Assistance

https://attorneygeneral.utah.gov/victim-advocacy

Information on the services the office provides.

Utah Crime Victim Compensation Program

https://justice.utah.gov/Crime/

Victim compensation information and downloadable application form.

Utah Department of Corrections, Office of Victim Services

https://corrections.utah.gov/index.php?option=com_content&view=article&id=1044&Itemid=104

Information on the services the office provides and the state's victim notification system, Victim Information and Notification Everyday (VINE).

Utah Statewide Victim Advocate Listing

http://udvc.org/media/PDF/linkline/linkline_adv ocates.pdf

Contact information for victim advocate programs across the state.

Vermont

Vermont Attorney General, Victim Assistance Program

http://www.ccvs.state.vt.us/victim-assistance-program

Information on victims' rights. List of other state and national victim resources.

Vermont Center for Crime Victim Services

http://www.ccvs.state.vt.us/victim-assistance-program

Information for victims on victim services and the criminal justice system. Vermont Victim Services Resource Directory and searchable directory by county. Links to other state victim resources.

Vermont Crime Victim Compensation Program

http://www.ccvs.state.vt.us/compensation

Victim compensation information and downloadable application form.

Vermont Department of Corrections, Victim Services

http://www.doc.state.vt.us/victim-services

Information about victims' rights and the corrections system. Victim notification information and downloadable registration form. Online offender status search.

Virgin Islands

Virgin Islands Crime Victim Compensation Program

http://www.dhs.gov.vi/commissioner/criminal_victims.html

Contact information for the Virgin Islands victim compensation program.

Virgin Islands, Women's Coalition of St. Croix

http://wcstx.org/about-us

Information on services the coalition offers. Links to national and local victim resources. Information for teens on dating violence, sexual assault, and healthy relationships.

Virginia

Virginia Attorney General, Victim Notification Information

http://www.oag.state.va.us/13-resource/507-about-the-victim-notification-program

Information on victim notification and downloadable registration form. Appeals process information.

Virginia Crime Victim Compensation Program Virginia Victims Fund

http://www.virginiavictimsfund.org/

Victim compensation information. Downloadable application form. Frequently asked questions.

Virginia Department of Corrections, Victim Services Unit

https://vadoc.virginia.gov/victim/

Information on the services the unit offers. Toll-free number for victims. Information on the state's victim notification system, Victim Information and Notification Everyday (VINE) and downloadable registration form.

Virginia Department of Criminal Justice, Victims Services Section

https://www.dcjs.virginia.gov/victims-services

Information on services the Victims Services Section offers, including the toll-free DCJS INFO-Line for victims.

Washington

Washington Coalition of Crime Victim Advocates

http://www.wccva.org/

Information on victims' rights. List of other Washington state resources for victims.

Washington Crime Victim Compensation Program

http://www.lni.wa.gov/ClaimsIns/CrimeVictims/

Victim compensation information and downloadable application form. Links to other state and national victim resources.

Washington Department of Corrections, Victim Services Program

http://www.doc.wa.gov/victims/

Information on the victim notification program and how to enroll. Frequently asked questions. Information on safety planning and the "victim wrap-around program."

Washington Department of Social and Health Services, Victim/Witness Notification Program

https://www.dshs.wa.gov/sesa/office-communications/victimwitness-notification-program

Information on the state Victim/Witness Notification Program and how to enroll.

Washington Indeterminate Sentence Review Board, Victim Information

http://doc.wa.gov/corrections/isrb/default.htm

Information about victims' rights at parole proceedings and how to request an opportunity to make a statement to the Indeterminate Sentence Review Board.

Washington Office of Crime Victim Advocacy (Department of Community, Trade & Economic Development)

http://www.commerce.wa.gov/serving-communities/crime-victims-public-safety/office-of-crime-victims-advocacy/

Information about the services of the Office of Crime Victim Advocacy, including advocacy for victims who have had trouble accessing services or whose rights have been denied. Directory of local, state, and national resources for victims, searchable by county. Downloadable brochures on topics such as restitution and post-traumatic stress disorder.

West Virginia

West Virgina Division of Corrections, Victim Services

http://www.wvdoc.com/wvdoc/VictimServices/t abid/38/Default.aspx

Information on the services provided. Information on the state victim notification system (Victim Information and Notification Everyday/VINE) and downloadable registration form.

West Virginia Crime Victim Compensation Program

http://www.legis.state.wv.us/Joint/Victims/crim e_victim_application.pdf

Information on victim compensation, including eligibility requirements and how to apply.

West Virginia Division of Criminal Justice Services, Service Provider Directory

http://www.wvdoc.com/wvdoc/Contact/tabid/41/Default.aspx

Downloadable directory of victim services providers by county.

Wisconsin

Wisconsin Attorney General, Office of Crime Victim Services

https://www.doj.state.wi.us/ocvs/office-crime-victim-services

Information on victims' rights and what to do if you believe your rights have been violated.

Information on victim compensation and downloadable application form. Victim service agencies listed by county and by crime.

Wisconsin Crime Victim Compensation Program

https://www.doj.state.wi.us/ocvs/compensation/crime-victim-compensation-program-compensation-your-financial-losses

Victim compensation information, including frequently asked questions. Downloadable compensation brochure and application. Main Office of Crime Victim Services site, **http://www.doj.state.wi.us/cvs/OCVS_pages/For_Victims.asp**.

Wisconsin Crime Victims' Rights Board

https://www.doj.state.wi.us/ocvs/victim-rights/crime-victims-rights-board

Information on the Wisconsin Crime Victims' Rights Board, which can review victim complaints of rights violations. Downloadable sample formal complaint form.

Wisconsin Department of Corrections, Victim Website

http://doc.wi.gov/victim-resources/victim-services

Information on the state's victim notification system and offender information search, Visual Offender Information Center/ Victim Information and Notification Everyday (VOICE/VINE).

Wyoming

Wyoming Crime Victim Compensation Program

http://ag.wyo.gov/victim-services-home-page/compensation

Victim compensation information, including frequently asked questions. Downloadable application form.

Wyoming Department of Corrections, Victim Notification Program

http://boardofparole.wyo.gov/victim-services/victimwitness-notification-program

Information on the state's victim notification program. Downloadable victim notification request form.

Appendix C
FEDERAL AGENCIES WEBSITES

Bureau of Justice Assistance
www.ojp.usdoj.gov/BJA

Bureau of Justice Statistics
www.ojp.usdoj.gov/bjs

Center for Substance Abuse Prevention
http://prevention.samhsa.gov

Center for Substance Abuse Treatment
http://csat.samhsa.gov

Centers for Disease Control and Prevention
www.cdc.gov

Federal Bureau of Investigation Uniform Crime Reports
www.fbi.gov/ucr/ucr.htm

National Archive of Criminal Justice Data
www.icpsr.umich.edu/NACJD/index.html

National Clearinghouse for Alcohol and Drug Information
www.ncadi.samhsa.gov/

National Criminal Justice Reference Service
www.ncjrs.org

National Highway Traffic Safety Administration
www.nhtsa.dot.gov

National Identity Theft Victim Assistance Network (NITVAN)
http://identitytheftnetwork.org/

National Institute of Justice
www.ojp.usdoj.gov/nij

National Institute on Alcohol Abuse and Alcoholism
www.niaaa.nih.gov

National Institute on Drug Abuse
www.drugabuse.gov

National Sex Offender Registry
www.nsopr.gov

Office for Victims of Crime (OVC)
www.ovc.gov

Office of Community Oriented Policing Services
www.cops.usdoj.gov

Office of Justice Programs
www.ojp.usdoj.gov

Office of Juvenile Justice and Delinquency Prevention
www.ojjdp.ncjrs.org

Office of National Drug Control Policy
www.whitehousedrugpolicy.gov

Office on Violence Against Women
www.usdoj.gov/ovw/

U.S. Department of Education:
www.edc.org/hec

Higher Education Center for Alcohol and Other Drug Prevention Office of Safe and Drug-Free Schools
www.ed.gov/about/offices/list/osdfs

U.S. Department of Health and Human Services: Grantsnet
www.hhs.gov/grantsnet

Grants Information
www.hrsa.gov/grants/default.htm

HRSA Funding Opportunities
www.hhs.gov/grants/index.shtml

U.S. Department of Justice
www.usdoj.gov

U.S. Department of Veterans Affairs National Center on PTSD
www.ncptsd.org

U.S. House of Representatives Victims' Rights Caucus
www.house.gov/poe/vrc/index.htm

Appendix D
STATE VICTIM COMPENSATION WEBSITES

STATE VICTIM COMPENSATION BOARDS

Alabama
www.acvcc.state.al.us

Alaska
www.state.ak.us/admin/vccb

Arizona
http://www.azdps.gov/Services/Crime_Victims/crimeVictim/

Arkansas
http://arkansasag.gov/programs/criminal-justice/crime-victim- reparations

California
http://vcgcb.ca.gov/victims/

Colorado
http://dcj.state.co.us/ovp/comp_english.htm

Connecticut
http://www.jud.ct.gov/crimevictim/

Delaware
http://attorneygeneral.delaware.gov/VCAP/

District of Columbia
http://www.dccourts.gov/internet/superior/crimevictim/main.jsf

Florida
www.myfloridalegal.com/victims

Georgia
http://cjcc.georgia.gov/victims-compensation

Hawaii
http://www.hawaii.gov/cvcc/

Idaho
http://crimevictimcomp.idaho.gov/

Illinois
http://illinoisattorneygeneral.gov/victims/cvc.html

Indiana
http://www.in.gov/cji/2348.htm

Iowa
http://www.iowa.gov/government/ag/helping_victims/ services/compensation_program.html

Kansas
http://ag.ks.gov/victim-services/victim-compensation

Kentucky
http://cvcb.ky.gov/Pages/default.aspx

Louisiana
http://www.lcle.la.gov/programs/cvr.asp

Maine
http://www.maine.gov/ag/crime/victims_compensation/

Maryland
http://www.dpscs.state.md.us/victimservs/commitment/ main_pages/vs-cicb.shtml

Massachusetts
http://www.mass.gov/ago/public-safety/resources-for- victims/victims-of-violent-crime/victim-compensation.html

Michigan

http://www.michigan.gov/mdch/0,1607,7-132-54783_54853---,00.html

Minnesota

www.ojp.state.mn.us/MCCVS/FinancialHelp

Mississippi

http://www.ago.state.ms.us/divisions/victim-compensation/

Missouri

www.dolir.state.mo.us/wc/cv_help.htm

Montana

www.doj.state.mt.us/victims/default.asp

Nebraska

http://www.ncc.state.ne.us/services_programs/ crime_victim_reparations.htm

Nevada

http://hearings.state.nv.us/Victims.htm

New Hampshire

http://doj.nh.gov/victim/compensation.html

New Jersey

www.state.nj.us/victims

New Mexico

www.state.nm.us/cvrc

New York

www.cvb.state.ny.us

North Carolina

www.nccrimecontrol.org/vjs

North Dakota

www.state.nd.us/docr/parole/victim_comp.htm

Ohio

http://www.ag.state.oh.us/web_applications/

Oklahoma

http://www.ok.gov/dac/Victims_Services/ Victims_Compensation_Program/index.html

Oregon
http://www.doj.state.or.us/crimev/comp.shtml

Pennsylvania
http://www.pccd.state.pa.us/

Rhode Island
http://www.treasury.state.ri.us/vcfund.htm

South Carolina
www.govoepp.state.sc.us/sova/vcfund.htm

South Dakota
www.state.sd.us/social/cvc/index.htm

Tennessee
www.treasury.state.tn.us/injury.htm

Texas
www.oag.state.tx.us/victims/cvc.shtml

Utah
www.crimevictim.utah.gov

Vermont
www.ccvs.state.vt.us/victcomp.html

Virginia
www.vwc.state.va.us/cicf/crime_intro.htm

Washington
www.lni.wa.gov/ClaimsInsurance/CrimeVictims

West Virginia
http://www.legis.state.wv.us/Joint/victims/main.cfm

Wisconsin
www.doj.state.wi.us/cvs

Wyoming
http://vssi.state.wy.us/cvcHome

Appendix E
RESOURCE PHONE NUMBERS

Appriss Inc. (Provider of the VINE Service)
800-816-0491

Battered Women's Justice Project
800-903-0111

Bureau of Indian Affairs Indian Country Child Abuse Hotline
800-633-5155

Childhelp USA National Hotline
800-4-A-CHILD

> **TDD**
> 800-2-A-CHILD

Federal Trade Commission Identity Theft Hotline
877-ID-THEFT

Justice Statistics Clearinghouse
800-851-3420

Juvenile Justice Clearinghouse
800-851-3420

Mothers Against Drunk Driving
800-GET-MADD

National Center for Missing and Exploited Children

800-843-5678

> **TDD**
>
> 800-826-7653

National Center for Victims of Crime

800-FYI-CALL

National Children's Alliance

800-239-9950

National Clearinghouse for Alcohol and Drug Information

800-729-6686

> **TDD Hotline**
>
> 800-487-4889
>
> **Hearing Impaired**
>
> 800-735-2258
>
> **Español**
>
> 877-767-8432

National Clearinghouse on Child Abuse and Neglect

800-394-3366

National Crime Prevention Council

800-NCPC-911

National Criminal Justice Reference Service

800-851-3420

National Domestic Violence Hotline

800-799-SAFE

> **TTY Hotline**
>
> 800-787-3224

National Fraud Information Hotline

800-876-7060

National Organization for Victim Assistance
800-TRY-NOVA

National Organization of Parents Of Murdered Children
888-818-POMC

National Resource Center on Domestic Violence
800-537-2238

TTY Hotline
800-553-2508

National Sexual Violence Resource Center
877-739-3895

Office for Victims of Crime Resource Center
800-851-3420

TTY
877-712-9279

Office for Victims of Crime Training and Technical Assistance Center
866-OVC-TTAC

TTY
866-682-8880

Rape, Abuse and Incest National Network
800-656-HOPE

Resource Center on Domestic Violence - Child Protection and Custody
800-527-3223

CPSIA information can be obtained
at www.ICGtesting.com
Printed in the USA
LVOW02s0114210617
538332LV00001B/1/P

9 781524 906177